Hypermedia Publishing
How to Build a Web Site

HYPERMEDIA PUBLISHING
HOW TO BUILD A WEB SITE

KATIE BLAKSTAD-COOKE

PRENTICE HALL
London New York Toronto Sydney Tokyo Singapore
Madrid Mexico City Munich

First published 1996 by
Prentice Hall Europe
Campus 400, Maylands Avenue
Hemel Hempstead
Hertfordshire, HP2 7EZ
A division of
Simon & Schuster International Group

Printed and bound in Great Britain by
T.J. Press (Padstow) Ltd

Library of Congress Cataloging-in-Publication Data

Blakstad-Cooke, Katie.
   Hypermedia publishing: how to build a Web site / Katie Blakstad
–Cooke.
      p. cm.
   Includes index.
   ISBN 0-13-237694-6
      1. Interactive multimedia. 2. HTML (Document markup
   language) 3. World Wide Web (Information retrieval system)
   4. Electronic publishing. I. Title.
   QA76.76.159B53 1996   96–9387
   025.04–dc20   CIP

British Library Cataloguing-in-Publication Data

A catalogue record for this book is available
from the British Library

ISBN 0-13-237694-6

1 2 3 4 5   00 99 98 97 96

Contents

SECTION 1: HYPERMEDIA PUBLISHING

SECTION 2: BASIC HTML

Introduction

The World Wide Web is a new medium with almost unlimited potential. How can we do it justice? Working in a new medium demands new ideas, new techniques and new models. Creating a Web site goes far beyond marking up a print document with a few tags.

This book gives you the tools you need to start developing rich, creative, well-structured hypermedia. This book goes beyond a simple "how to" manual of HTML. HTML is easy, but is only the starting point for building Web sites. This book covers the planning and production of Web sites, structuring and writing hypertext, and some of the possibilities of online interactivity and multimedia.

If you want to take an active role in the online revolution of publishing, you need to start with some knowledge of the building blocks of hypermedia. Building a Web site can be compared to building a house—you can probably build something serviceable with pre-fabricated parts and some patience, but if you want to build something special and something that will last you will need an architect, an engineer, a builder and an interior designer.

This book takes you through all these stages from planning to production, from the blueprints to the choice of wallpaper. The precise methods you use for each site will vary, but this book should provide you with the questions you need to ask when you are working with hypermedia. Although it is a highly practical guide to building Web sites, this book is an exploration rather that a set of instructions.

WHO SHOULD READ THIS BOOK?

If you want to publish on the web; if you believe in its potential as a medium; if you want to learn HTML—then this book is for you. If you're not sure what HTML is, but you want to put your voice on the Web, then this book is the place to start.

You may be a print publisher or author wishing to move into a new medium. You may have the responsibility for developing your company's Web site. You may be planning an art, education or personal project on the Web. Whatever you are doing, you want to go beyond just putting up a simple home page.

This book goes beyond the technology and mechanisms of the Web. If you are familiar with the Web, even if you know HTML already, this book is still highly relevant. You may want to skip some of the introductory chapters, although the discussions may be of interest even if the subject matter is familiar.

HOW TO READ THIS BOOK

I would like to think that you would start at the beginning and read all the way through, but I know that's unlikely. I don't read this sort of book in that way. *Hypermedia Publishing: How to build a Web site* is split into four main sections with each section covering a different area:

Hypermedia Publishing
- introduces the Web as a new medium;
- looks at the uses of Web sites;
- explores the nature of hypertext;
- covers planning, structuring and managing a Web site
- looks at the role of graphic design;
- considers the importance of interface and navigation

Basic HTML
- explains the need to know more about the mechanics of the medium;
- introduces the basic concepts of HTML;
- walks you through building a simple page;
- adds links and graphics to your page;
- expands your page to a small site;
- teaches you how to construct interactive forms;
- shows how to create image maps;
- looks at the most effective ways of adding audio and video to a site

Advanced HTML
- introduces more advanced tricks and techniques
- extends the use of graphics within a site
- gives designers more control over a web site
- explores the Netscape extensions to HTML
- looks at the proposals for HTML 3.0
- explains the construction of tables

Beyond HTML
- looks beyond HTML to see what else is being added to the Web
- looks at the Web as a means of distributing Acrobat documents
- explores interactivity
- introduces the use of scripting and programming
- examines the cross-over between different technologies
- introduces the possibilities of Java and Shockwave
- considers the role of virtual reality, QuickTime VR and VRML

In addition, the Appendices
- contain more information about Java, Shockwave and VR
- list sources for online information
- provide a good starting point for further reference

NOTES

All the screen shots in this book are of Web pages viewed with Netscape 2.0 or above on a Macintosh. The examples will look different if viewed with another browser.

I have used "she" as the third person singular throughout the book. No sexual bias should be assumed by this.

ABOUT THE AUTHOR

Katie Blakstad-Cooke is creative director of Question, a new media agency and Web production company based in London, and publisher of Ism Comics, a Web anthology of small press comics. In a former life, Katie managed Acme Comics Shop, and was involved in the destruction of way too many trees as a print designer.

Any comments, constructive or otherwise, can be emailed to katie@question.co.uk

THANKS AND ACKNOWLEDGEMENTS

I would like to thank my editors at Prentice Hall for their help and support during the writing of this book; Dave Raggett for permission to reprint his paper on Platform Independent VR; John Dowdell, Rachel Schindler and Harry Chesley at Macromedia for the help and information they gave me about Shockwave, including permission to reprint the paper on authoring Director movies for the Web; Jonni Kanerva and Kim Polese at Sun Microsystems for their help and for permission to reprint the Java Language White Paper; Douglass Turner at Apple for his assistance on QuickTime VR; Rick Brown at Adobe for information about Acrobat; Mike Bennett, William Julien and Paul Sonley from Sunbather for their help with the design of this book, and for their assistance with the design section; Phil Webster for all his work at Question, and for being such an all round good guy; and Jim Davies for his constant support and friendship.

Most of all I would like to thank Matthew for being deeply lovely.

This book is for my Father, who taught me that computers can be used to do really interesting things, and for my Mother who taught me that computers aren't everything.

TRADEMARKS AND COPYRIGHTS

Acrobat, PageMaker Postscript and Photoshop are registered trademarks of Adobe Systems Inc. Apple, Macintosh, Power Mac, QuickTime and QuickTime VR, LaserWriter, HyperTalk and HyperCard are registered trademarks of Apple Computer Inc. America Online is a service mark of America Online, Inc. NaviSoft, Inc. is an America Online, Inc. company and NaviPress is a trademark of America Online. Macromedia and Director are registered trademarks of Macromedia, Inc. Microsoft, Windows, Windows NT and other names of Microsoft products referenced herein are trademarks or registered trademarks of Microsoft Corporation. Netscape Communications, Netscape, Netscape Navigator and LiveWire are trademarks of Netscape Communications Corporation. SenseMedia is copyright Picosof. Silicon Graphics, SGI and WebSpace are trademarks of Silicon Graphics Inc. Java, HotJava, Sun, Sun Microsystems, and the Sun Logo are trademarks or registered trademarks of Sun Microsystems, Inc. in the U.S. and other countries. ColorHEX is copyright Unknown Species.

Hypermedia publishing

CHAPTER 1

Understanding the World Wide Web

The Web is not about computers.

You need a computer to publish on the Web; you need a computer to read the Web; but the Web is a medium, not a technology. The purpose of this book is to explore this new medium and how to work in it.

The World Wide Web will not bring about world peace, break down all the barriers of communication, or do your laundry. Ridiculous promises have been made for the Web and these have obscured the real potential of the medium. The Web is still in its infancy and the possibilities are just starting to emerge.

At the heart of the Web is *shared hypermedia.* The flexibility of hypermedia is its great strength and its biggest weakness. Hypermedia is created and experienced in new ways. The old methods will not always work. The rules are changing.

Hypermedia makes the Web a highly flexible, responsive, interactive medium. While facing challenges set by the current limitations of the medium, designers and developers are finding new methods and new forms as well as new ways to adapt established techniques and systems. The Web is a medium in its infancy that is having to fight against a great deal of hype, an awful lot of *?!*?! and masses of confusion. Groundbreaking work is being done that is pushing the boundaries of the possible.

The Web may be the exciting, user-friendly, graphical face of the Internet, but it's seen as a poor cousin of the CD-ROM. The implication is that it's rather slow, it's not very slick, and there's nothing of interest to look at. Most of this is changing by the minute.

Expectations have been so high that people used to all-singing all-dancing multi-media CD-ROMs, games and television may not have been over-impressed by the terrible wait for small still pictures to arrive via a modem.

This is not the first time we've seen this reaction. The first Macintosh computers were exciting, but terribly limited, and low on decent software. They were dismissed by many as toys, not to be used for serious work. The early adopters, the people who fell in love with the woefully under powered Mac, knew that they were on to something. In fact there was very little you could do with the original Mac, but there was a sense that there were great things to come. The Mac interface was designed to react in sensible ways. It responded to the user and you did not need strange arcane knowledge or programming skills to use it. If you wanted to program, you needed programming skills, but not if you just wanted to write a letter. There was a direct engagement with the machine. The Mac made pleasing noises. It smiled at you as it started working. It was a machine that encouraged an emotional attachment. But all of these were simply features of the machine itself, and had very little to do with the application of the Mac to the real world.

It was the second wave of development that gave the Mac real value and meaning outside itself. PageMaker and the LaserWriter were launched and the Mac became a powerful tool, putting the means of production directly into the hands of creative people.

The Web is probably at the start of the second wave. The first stage of development made it all possible. The first flush of enthusiasm amongst the early adopters brought millions into the medium, fascinated by its possibilities. Many see the Web as an interesting idea, but something they'll only take seriously when they see that it can perform in the ways that they have been led to expect. The second wave of people are more interested in what the Web can do in the real world than just what the Web can do.

Much of the current grumbling can be written off as the inevitable backlash against the wave of enthusiasm that began in 1994. Just about every magazine and paper ran articles that had the word "cyber" somewhere in the headline. There were way too many jokes about anoraks and trainspotting. Journalists all over the world wrote their piece about the Web, and there were queues of television companies waiting to film in every cybercafe. There was a sense of real excitement, a discovery of a new way of doing things.

By mid 1995, the backlash was in full swing, complete with the cries of boredom, of disappointment and of a chaotic mess of computer crime and child pornography. The main complaint was that although the Web may be fine in principle, there was nothing worth bothering with that couldn't be done better elsewhere. The other standard complaints were "There's nothing interesting out there"; "I wouldn't chat to these people if I met them in a bar, why should I be interested in talking to them online"; "You have to be a nerd to understand it, and I don't want to be a nerd" (cue some more anorak jokes); "It's too slow, and it's not as good as a CD-ROM".

But the growth in the Web continues faster than ever. Is it as hopeless as some of the press insist? The initial colonisation of the Web was by academia and computer companies, but it is the publishers, the film and music companies, the ad agencies, the designers and other creative individuals who are leading the second wave, in tandem with the developers who are providing the new technology. The content of the Web is shifting away from its initial bias towards computing. As the Web becomes used for more things than an examination of itself—which is an inevitable stage in its development—the balance will change to reflect the interests of the millions of people reading, viewing, listening and communicating there.

There is so much diversity on the Web that it's very easy to find something to illustrate how awful it is. By its very nature, backlash involves holding up the weakest, most obscure or offensive elements, and suggesting that the whole is as bad as the worst of its parts. The negative areas are used to damn the rest. We may as well damn all of film, fiction and art—because there are some lousy paintings, trite novels, and badly acted films with shaky camera work. In any medium the bad or the mediocre outweighs the excellent or the original. On the Web, the playing field is much flatter, and the weaker sites have a stronger chance of survival in the early years. A subject based search across the Web will bring back results based on content, not on quality, popularity or advertising expenditure.

Web sites can be advertised like any other product. Large companies are starting to spend time and money publicising their Web sites, just as they publicise all their other products. The Web site in question may be an advertising or marketing site, but it will probably be advertised. Web addresses, or *URLs*, appear in print and television advertising, on record sleeves, and on the sides of buses. The very existence of an associated Web site adds prestige or interest to the product. The site promotes the product. The product promotes the site. They both promote the company.

Web sites, however, live and die by their links. If a site is well liked, other people will build links to it. Advertising spaces with hyperlinks are for sale in popular, heavy traffic Web sites. The more routes there are to a site, the more it will thrive. There is something almost biological about the network of linked Web sites.

Once a medium grows large enough and wide enough to support any level of diversity, there will always be a range of content and quality. The Web is not a broadcast medium—if you have no interest in something, you need never see it. Nobody owns the Web, so there is no editorial policy or editorial approval to work around.

CHAPTER 2

Adjusting to a new medium

This chapter looks at why the Web is special, and what makes it different from other media. It introduces and explains the concept of hypermedia and the nature of hypertext. Looking at practical applications of the Web, it examines the potential of the Web as a commercial medium. There is a short history of the Web and a look at current problems and limitations.

The nature of the Web is being explored and played with. What can be done on the Web that can't be done elsewhere? Rather than repackaging material in uninteresting ways, forcing it into forms that don't work, content is now being developed specifically for the Web. Publishing on the Web is becoming a significant and a creative business.

New questions have to be asked along with the old. The decision to publish on the Web requires a reappraisal of intentions. Why put something on the Web in the first place? What will the focus of the Web site be? Who are the intended audience and what will the site offer them? These questions must be answered before the site is built. It is important that you do not assume that your Web site will be interesting just because it exists.

As the Web continues to develop, standards are being forced up. There are more and more excellent Web sites. There are sites of real value—whether in terms of the usefulness of their information, their entertainment or their beauty. In the initial stages of the World Wide Web *any* site was exciting—just because it was there. The "Ugly CEO Syndrome" was predominant. If you built it, they would come, even if the site was just an extract from the minutes of the AGM and a picture of the boss. The most boring sites on earth would get thousands of visits. A site that used design in a way that would be laughed at or ignored in print was praised on the Web as groundbreaking.

Some companies with sophisticated and successful marketing campaigns seemed to lose their focus when putting up a Web site. While some early sites had clear goals, and a strong sense of their own identity, too many were there just because they could be. The existence of the Web will cease to be exciting in its own right. It will be exciting in the way it is used. No audience makes a fuss about celluloid—they are interested in the *movie*. A novel is more interesting than a printed book.

There are many reasons for publishing on the Web. Publishing original content, in the way that books, music and art are published is one way to go, advertising or marketing a company, product or service is another. Direct selling and distribution is becoming more prevalent as secure, encrypted areas of the Web become more common. Providing, sharing and sorting information resources for love or for money is very common. Direct communication, collaborative art and shared social space, and personal projects are widespread. So much is possible within the World Wide Web, that it is often difficult to see how anybody could think of dismissing it as "glorified CB radio".

WHAT IS HYPERMEDIA?

Hypertext is a way of exploring linked ideas. No ideas are completely isolated. All memory is linked to other memories. Our lives are held together by a mesh of association. Hypertext is how we remember things. When we explain something new, we refer to something familiar. We use metaphors and similes to clarify our meanings. We quote, selectively, from relevant writings.

If you are having a conversation, and someone interrupts and asks you to explain what you said, you pause, branch off and elaborate on your meaning and then you may or may not return to the original subject. The new branch may have started you along a different thread of conversation.

Hypertext is a way of echoing our thought patterns in text. We rarely think in an entirely linear way. We think through options and alternatives, make choices constantly. Hypertext builds the cross references, the associations and the explanations into an integral part of the text itself. It is more than a system for adding footnotes. Hypertext allows for all the digressions, definitions, arguments and explanations to be rooted into the original text.

The World Wide Web is the first mass medium to be based on the idea of hypertext. *Hypertext Transfer Protocol* and *Hypertext Markup Language* are the underlying mechanisms of the Web. You use hypertext from the first Web page you visit. You choose which link to click on. When you visit a site you choose where you want to go. You can go back to places and retrace your path through a collection of links. As you begin to access information from different ends of the world, you begin to feel the strength of the links themselves—the connection between ideas—and a sense of navigable information space. Reading becomes an active process of exploration. A Web site can be more than a collection of pages, it can be a space to move within. Hypertext requires the involvement of the reader, as much as the author.

Hypertext is text with links, or cross references. *Hypermedia,* a term coined by Ted Nelson, is an expansion of the concept of hypertext, applying it to a mixture of media. But hypermedia is more than hypertext with video clips. Using a range of media allows demonstration as well as description. Hypermedia may employ multiple media, with video clips to demonstrate a chemical process, sound clips to illustrate a chord progression and text to explain them. Hypermedia is more concerned with the richness of experience than it is with the particular media used.

All hypermedia is interactive. The reader must find her own way through a mass of information, in the way that best suits her. This does not mean that hypermedia needs to be without structure—if anything it needs more structure and control than linear media. The structure needs to pre-empt a reader's questions and provide strong routes to the answers. Writing hypermedia requires additional thought and planning to allow for sensible sequences that do not make assumptions about a preset path of reading. Hypermedia is not a linear process—it can't be. A Web page that has nothing but a "next page" link on it is not really hypermedia. It may use the same technical set-up as hypermedia, but then a blank CD-ROM used as a drinks mat is not multimedia.

The choices made by the reader, following associative links through multiple media, are at the root of hypermedia.

IS THERE ANY DIFFERENCE BETWEEN HYPERMEDIA AND MULTIMEDIA?

The term "multimedia" has become synonymous with CD-ROM technology. More specifically, multimedia usually means something authored in Macromedia Director.

What exactly do you mean by multimedia? A CD with sound and video, some text and some interactive choices?

A presentation with an introductory fanfare, a slide show and printed notes is multimedia.

If there's a question and answer session, it's interactive.

Multimedia is not necessarily interactive. Although some multimedia products are designed to involve the participation of the audience, others are *presentations* aimed at a more passive audience. Hypermedia, on the other hand, *requires* the involvement of its viewers. The viewers become readers, even editors.

What is the connection between the two? Is hypermedia a sub-set of multimedia, or vice versa? I believe that both are true. Multimedia is a sub-set of hypermedia and hypermedia is a sub-set of multimedia. Hypermedia offers the reader multiple media, and multimedia typically involves hypermedia linking and interactivity.

The Web has been criticised for not being able to cope with "real" multimedia. It's true. A CD-ROM is a high bandwidth fast access format. It can hold over an hour of full screen video or thousands of pages of text, and any of the content can be accessed in moments. But CD-ROMs are finite. Despite the large storage capacity of a silver disk there is a physical limit to the amount of information that can be held. The compression and storage technologies will continue to improve, but even an increased limit is a limit. A CD-ROM, as a physical thing, is frozen in time. Once a completed product is distributed on disk, it cannot be changed.

The Web, in contrast, has no such limits. Any Web site can be linked to any other, and can be updated at any time. The whole content of the World Wide Web can be accessed from your home computer. Anything that has been published onto the Web is available. But the Web is not yet an ideal vehicle for fully integrated multimedia. Mostly that's down to bandwidth. X pages of text, or x minutes of sound, or x seconds of video—the storage sizes are the same on CD-ROM or on a Web site. Accessing a video clip on the Web means that you have to transfer it from the remote site, to your computer over phone lines. The time it will take varies wildly depending on your type of connection to the Net, but video takes longer than text just because video is so much bigger.

Currently it is not possible to play video live through a Web page. There is a long delay while the information is downloaded and the video is then played in a separate window, with an external *helper application*. There have been recent developments that mean that sound can be delivered in real time. The incorporation of "traditional multimedia" elements with *Shockwave* and *Java* directly into Web pages is leading to some interesting developments. These allow fluid animations, sound and direct response to be an integral part of a Web site. There's more information about these new directions and technologies in "Section 4: Beyond HTML".

THE WEB AS A COMMERCIAL MEDIUM

It would be difficult to deny that the Web is a commercial medium. Whether it is profitable or not is another matter. Unlike other parts of the Internet, the Web is full of commercial activity. These activities may be frowned upon in some areas of the Internet, but the Web is a powerful tool for communication and as such it is inevitable that it will be used for business. This is not necessarily a bad thing, because commercial organisations now have a vested interest in supporting and expanding the infrastructure of the Internet. If commerce uses the Web well, it will benefit the vast majority of users who will have easy access to the information, services and products that they want.

Companies are buying and selling their goods over the Web. They are advertising and marketing their products and services. They are establishing Web sites as a means of communicating with existing and potential customers. It is, however, unreasonable to expect that the Web will behave as any other media or that it should be approached in the same way. Advertising in particular is a very different creature on the Web. The often purely sensual appeal of broadcast adverts needs to be rethought for the Web. It is important not to lose the high production values and craft of good television and print advertising, but they need to be backed up with useful content and information. Do broadcast adverts encourage immediate product sales, or are they more concerned with brand reinforcement? At the moment, the percentage of Web readers who buy products directly over the Net may be rather low, but how many gather the information on the Web and go on to buy in "real life"?

If a visitor to a Web site reads through your product information, you know that they are more interested than someone who has flicked past it in a magazine. You know that an advert has appeared in all 30,000 copies of the magazine in which you have bought space but do you know how many people stopped to read it? A company can get more complete information about the success of their advertising from the Web than from any other medium. They will know exactly how many people have been exposed to the brand, how many have read their material, and which pages are most popular, they will have a clear indication of how long people have spent reading each page, and where the readers are. They know that each visitor has chosen to read through the site.

The potential for customer support and customer relations is very high, but not if the Web site is left to fend for itself or used to replace traditional support mechanisms. The Web may be the first point of contact that a company has with a client, but it should not be the only one. Visitors to the site may be encouraged to respond to the company immediately, and the company should respond with a similar level of immediacy. There should be people within the company who are able to respond to any questions or leads that the Web site generates. They need to be able to respond fast, and with the ability to speak for the company.

The Web is another medium to add to all the others that a company can use. It should not be seen as a replacement.

There are some companies who are uncomfortable with the open nature of the Web. They have heard the phrase about information wanting to be free, and they hate it. They spend thousands, maybe millions a year on print and broadcast advertising. They understand the need for this, and see that it gives them a real benefit. They are now planning to set up a Web site, full of marketing and advertising information, and they resent the idea that it will be free. They will have considerable outlay setting up a site, paying for the hardware and time needed to publish onto the Web, and they expect that visitors should pay to read their material even if it duplicates their free leaflets and catalogues. The data they will gather may be unbelievably valuable, but they still wish they could charge for access.

You can charge for access to your site, but only if the site contains something that people want to pay for. Why should anyone pay to read an advert? Why should anybody pay for something they can get more easily, for nothing, elsewhere? What are you offering? There is a huge difference between the information offered by advertising and marketing, and the information offered as content provision. Original content—fiction, reportage, comment, analysis—can be sold in a way that product information can not. If the material or service is useful, entertaining or informative, people may pay. If you are offering convenience—all the relevant information collected together and accessible from a single point—it might be feasible to charge money to use your Web site.

A magazine may seem like an obvious candidate for a Web site, but if the content is free to read, how can it make any money? The money raised by the retail price of a print magazine rarely goes to the writers, editors and photographers who create the content. It covers the paper costs, the print costs and the distribution costs involved in producing each copy of the magazine and shipping it to every newsagent around the country. The bulk of a magazine's money is raised by selling advertising space. If you remove the costs involved in print, the costs that remain are generated by the content and the production. Can these costs be covered by advertising or sponsorship? Can they be covered by a subscription or pay-per-view scheme? The cost per copy is removed. The readership or circulation of the magazine can be increased dramatically because there are almost no limits on print run or distribution. This may be very attractive to advertisers, who may be prepared to buy advertising space, or links, from key pages of the online publication.

There are problems to be faced when producing an online magazine. The quality of images will be far lower than they could be in print. Typesetting and design cannot be controlled in the same ways as it can be in print. Readers have to bear the download time and cost to read the magazine, and reading on screen is far less comfortable and convenient than reading print.

As the Web expands, organisational skills and research services will become more useful. Services aimed at a more specialised knowledge and interest base—doctors, lawyers, mechanics, kindergarten teachers—will command a premium. Anything that helps locate the signal amongst all the noise will become more valuable. Some very popular sites are subscription based, and online services like CompuServe and America OnLine continue to thrive because they are offering something valuable. They can offer ease of use, organisation of material, original content, and convenience for an hourly charge, even when the vast majority of the Internet is free.

WHY USE THE WEB?

Because it's there.

If you are interested in publishing in a rich and fluid medium, use the Web. It may not always be the correct medium for a project that you have in mind—some are more suited to print, or video, or radio—but it's another medium to add to the options. Working in hypermedia can be a reason in itself. Hypermedia is a young medium. It's early enough to produce work that will have a major impact on the future development of the Web. The rules have not been carved in stone, and the freedom for experimentation and invention is immense.

The World Wide Web is nothing to do with computing. Decisions should be based around using the medium as a whole, not just the newness and the technological concerns. You need to work with computers to publish on the Web, but it isn't computing.

What can you do with the Web? You can do far more than you probably imagine. The scope for new uses for the Web is enormous. The Web is a publishing medium, an art medium, a social medium, a learning and teaching medium, a commercial medium. If it's not been done yet, somebody is probably working on it. You can publish into a huge inter-connected society of information. You can push the boundaries forwards.

There *are* limitations and constraints imposed by the nature of the Web. There are things that you cannot do in the way that you first expect. The constraints and frustrations can lead to the most creative solutions. The major frustration for many is that HTML was never intended to be a tool for designers. Hypermedia, however, cries out for good design, and a great deal can be achieved within the current constraints.

WHAT ARE THE STRENGTHS OF PUBLISHING ON THE WEB?

Beyond the strengths of the medium itself, a major decision making factor is the mechanism for delivery of the material. Once you have made something accessible on the Web, once it lives on a Web server, there are very few distribution problems. There is no trouble getting the product to the audience. There are no trucks, no warehouses, no physical storefronts. The Internet can be used for secure financial transactions, and for the eventual delivery of an information product. (An information product is something made of bits rather than atoms.) Why deliver your product as a physical unit in a box if you can deliver it directly as data?

There are many millions of people using the Web already. Once you publish onto the Web, they can visit your site. There are no barriers of distance.

The fluidity of the Web can be used to great advantage. If you want to change your content, it can be done immediately. There is no printing or manufacturing process to delay the implementation of change.

The Web provides high levels of feedback. Users are often happy to let you know what they think, and you have a clear picture of just how many readers you have.

WHAT'S INVOLVED IN PUBLISHING ON THE WEB?

The production and planning process is really not that different from any other medium. There still needs to be an appraisal of the intentions of the project, and of the intended audience. An unfocused site will not necessarily appeal to the millions of Web users, any more than a poorly targeted magazine will be bought by the millions of potential magazine buyers.

The development process will go through the general stages of proposal, planning, design, prototype, production, testing, editing and maintenance. Some developers may have additional stages, but this seems to be the broad outline of the process. This process is covered in detail in chapter 4 "Planning a Web site".

Once you have decided to publish onto the Web, you need to produce your material in a suitable form. Whether you are producing something specifically for the Web, or repurposing an existing project, the material has to be in the appropriate form and format.

A self-contained file to download is not a Web site. Existing material can be reused, but not without some changes. Every element of your site needs to be in a format that can be displayed by browsers and used by your readers' machines. Every page needs to be marked up with HTML. Graphics need to be produced in a format that browsers can read.

One of the ideas at the heart of the Web is that it is totally cross-platform, but this can cause problems with platform-specific elements. Specific formats are covered in "Section 2: Basic HTML".

Is the Web the right medium for your project? Hypermedia is a powerful medium that has a direct effect on readers. It has advantages that no other medium can offer—the openness and the range, and the essential interactivity—but there are limitations to consider. What are you trying to achieve? Can your aims be met by a Web site? Would you be better served by producing the project in a different medium—as a CD-ROM, or as a book? The Web is another medium, but it won't always be the right one.

As you become more familiar with the possibilities and constraints of web publishing, the decision will become easier to make. The decision has to be project specific.

A SHORT HISTORY OF THE WEB

The World Wide Web has several histories—some starting as recently as 1989, others going back to 1945, or even back to the *Talmud,* the *Mahabarata* and *Tristram Shandy.*

The term hypertext was defined in 1965 by Ted Nelson. Nelson's book, *Literary Machines,* explains "By hypertext I mean nonsequential writing—text that branches and allows choice to the reader, best read at an interactive screen."

Branching choices in reading and writing have been central to all ideas about hypertext, including Vannevar Bush's Memex proposals. This was the first conceptualisation of an electronic system of storing and linking documents. "The summation of human experience is being expanded at a prodigious rate [but] the means we use for threading through the consequent maze to the momentarily important item is the same as was used in the days of square-rigged ships." Bush's 1945 article, *As We May Think* suggested a method of storing a vast library of documents on microfilm and building methods of sorting and annotating ideas in such a way that there was always a trail of association between related text and illustrations.

The Memex system was never built, but inspired Ted Nelson's Xanadu project. If this chapter was part of the Xanadu system, you would be able to reach *Literary Machines* from the quote above, and read any other relevant material by following links directly to them. Xanadu is still under development, but the World Wide Web embodies many of the ideals of hypermedia.

Nelson's ideas caused a great deal of excitement during the visionary early years of the personal computer. Between the writing of *Literary Machines,* and the introduction of the Web, several hypertext and hypermedia systems were developed. Possibly the most influential of these was Bill Atkinson's *HyperCard.*

"HyperCard was meant to occupy a central place in the world of Macintosh, a node from which would tumble all the wierd facts, semiremembered appointments, and quickly jotted phone numbers that all too often had previously gotten lost in the shuffle of information clutter. It would be a virtual cockpit; by pushing its buttons and tweaking its instruments one could retrieve the aggregate wisdom of cyberspace—the equivalent of the libraries of Alexandria, all accessible from a familiar home card that automatically appeared when you opened the program." (Steven Levy, *Insanely Great,* 1994)

A major similarity between HyperCard and the Web is the ease of creating rich hypermedia. HyperCard did not require programming skills, any more than HTML does.

Tim Berners Lee, the father of the Web as we know it, was influenced by Nelson and Bush's ideas, but had himself already experimented with a hypertext system known as *Enquire Within.* Enquire Within, developed in 1984 at the CERN Laboratory in Geneva, was a system for writing documents which automatically asked the writer to provide relationships with other topics and documents. By 1989 this idea had grown as Berners Lee, together with Robert Cailliau, brought hypertext and the Internet together with their specification of the World Wide Web. Their conception was of a viral growth of hyperlinked documents based around a completely open system of reading and writing. Although the original purpose of the Web was to share research information, its incredible popularity launched it into a far wider audience. Berners Lee openly invited the expansion of the Web, encouraging others to develop browsers and Web sites.

While an undergraduate at the University of Illinois, and at the National Centre for Supercomputing Applications, Marc Andreessen developed the browser that has been described as the "killer app" of the Internet. *Mosaic* opened the Web up to normal users. By *normal users*, I mean those people who want their technology to be as transparent as possible. At the other end of the spectrum are the hobbyists who take as much pleasure in setting up a system, battling with strange configurations and finally cowing their PCs into submission as they do from using their computers to do non-computer things. Some people want to use a computer to do things, and some people just want to use computers.

Once you got online, Mosaic made the Web a piece of cake to use, and it looked great. You could point and click your way around the world, which was suddenly full of graphics. You no longer had to deal with a heavy duty UNIX command line interface. There was a surge of interest and involvement and some really exciting things began to appear on the Web. Major companies moved onto the Web to promote themselves and their products. The potential for self-publishing into a mass audience was leapt upon by artists, writers and musicians, along with individuals who wanted to share their interests with the world.

The arrival of the Netscape Navigator, developed by Andreessen and the Mosaic development team, who had recently broken away from NCSA, shook things up even more. With a greater emphasis on the appearance of Web pages, Netscape has been seen as both the bright and shining new hope of the Web, and the badly behaved upstart child who is insisting on getting its own way. There have been heated words flying around in mailing lists and news groups about the alleged crimes against HTML perpetrated by Netscape, and about the design potential that the Netscape "extensions" offer. Whatever the rights and wrongs of the situation, Netscape has become very much the browser of choice for the majority of people using the Web.

The Web is now a significant part of the fabric of international communication, and is expanding rapidly. Moving beyond its academic and computing roots, the Web has become a medium in its own right. We can hardly begin to guess what may happen in the future of the Web.

Bandwidth Blues and the Problems with the Web

The biggest limiting factor of the Web is the delivery of material over the networks. Regular users of the Web have developed a form of patience that makes little sense to newcomers. The long wait for high bandwidth elements—like graphics, sound or video—seems unbearable when you begin to explore the Web. Why does anybody wait? Slow access times seem to write off the Web as a viable medium. CD-ROM speeds were never as slow as the Web. There has been a considerable advance over the last few years. Speeds will improve. Anybody who has used both a slow modem and then tried a fast, direct line can see the potential.

This slowness removes a level of immediacy. The exploration of Web space is a fluid one, and increased speeds would enhance the feeling that all the material, and all the information, was connected as part of a whole. The long wait for a web page, the slow movement along the progress bar, makes the Web feel anything but seamless, even as you point and click around the world.

Waiting for a page to fill encourages a new way of reading, or using a page. As the words and pictures drop in, you begin to scan the page to see whether it is worth the wait. The mouse hovers over the "back" button. With a slow connection the reader has to judge whether a page is worth the time, or whether they should keep on moving. A reader wants something worthwhile for their time investment—whether it's information, entertainment or a jumping off point to somewhere that can deliver what they want. The standards of judgement are much higher when a reader's patience is tried. Designing a page to entice an impatient reader is an intriguing challenge.

The technology behind the Web has not reached a dead end. A more complete network of high bandwidth cable is growing daily, and the way in which information can be delivered along those cables is improving. If the information can be moved faster along the cables, even the existing network of phone lines and fibre should manage fine. Compression techniques are growing more sophisticated and more effective. Moving information around the Internet as fast as possible has become something of a priority. It is inevitable that the technology will get the boost that it needs.

HOW THE WEB DIFFERS FROM OTHER MEDIA

The Web is not print. Printed material has many advantages over a medium that depends upon computers. You can take a book on a train, you can read it in the bath, or on the beach. It's relatively cheap—a reader does not need to invest in expensive hardware. Computers are far less portable and far more expensive. But these are limitations of current technology. A connection to the Internet will become simpler, and less of a novelty. It is inevitable that reading devices will grow cheaper and more portable. Laptop computers are a great step forward—much of this book was written whilst sitting on a rock in the Outer Hebrides. New reading habits will develop as technology spreads deeper into our lives.

Typesetting is not a real option on the Web. Unlike working with print, a designer does not have complete control over the look of a page. Different browsers display Web pages in very different ways—there is no standard. The reader can choose a typeface, a colour, even the size of the page. The reader can choose not to display the images. The Web was not designed as a page layout device, but as a means of sharing information. HTML was designed as a way of structuring information in a logical way, rather than displaying it as an item of beauty. This is not to say that good design is impossible, even within the strict confines of "correct" HTML. Design considerations must not be sacrificed or ignored.

The Web is not linear, or finite in the way that print is. Printed material, in almost all cases, is designed to be read in clearly defined sequences, and the choice of sequence is made by the author, rather than the reader. Associative reading is at the heart of the Web. Hyperlinking encourages non-linear reading and thinking.

The Web is not a multimedia presentation. A slide show has a predetermined order of fixed elements that are presented to an audience, but the Web is based around exploration rather than presentation. Presentation expects a passive audience, but hypermedia relies on an active reader. Elements within a Web site can be based around the format of a slide show, but using this as a model for a site is essentially limiting.

A CD-ROM is finite. The storage capability of a silver disk is large, but limited. The access times for a CD-ROM are considerably faster than for a Web site—anybody using the Web at the moment needs to develop patience. Speeds will change, but physical proximity will have the speed advantage for quite a while.

A CD-ROM is a completed product. Once it is manufactured and distributed, it cannot be changed. Web sites can be updated continually.

The potential for combining the benefits of CD-ROMs and Web sites, however, is very exciting. "Section 4: Beyond HTML" explores some of the possibilities.

The Web is not a broadcast medium. When a reader visits a Web site, they are making a direct connection with the content. They make the choices about which areas they visit, which links they follow, how long they stay. When you watch television, you choose which programmes to watch, but they are broadcast in a fixed order, often with commercial breaks. The broadcasting network decides what you are able to watch, and at what times of day. The broadcast is available only in certain geographical areas— even satellite channels are available in limited areas. On the Web, however, you can access sites from anywhere in the world, read newspapers you will never see in print, and listen to radio shows way beyond the range of their broadcast. More importantly, readers access sites when they want to. The content of a site need not be restricted to a single appearance, but can be made available on an ongoing basis.

Advertising is broadcast to a mostly unwilling audience—it interrupts the sitcom or the music. More people may see each advert on the television than those who see each advert on the Web, but there is no sure way of knowing whether someone was making a cup of tea at the time your ad was aired. If you have set up a site on the Web, and people visit it, they have made a conscious decision to do so. They are not passive receivers. Being able to count every willing visitor to an advertisement is a powerful ability. A well focused Web site allows advertisers to reach very specific target groups. The Web is a request medium, not a broadcast one.

CHAPTER 3

Moving beyond the printed page

This chapter looks at how the Web differs from the printed page, and how this affects your site. The Web makes different demands on the reader as well as the writer and designer, and this chapter will help you address those needs. The structure of a Web site can be as important as the content, and this chapter will help explain how to make your site welcoming and accessible for readers.

It is very easy to complain about how difficult it is to make a Web page look really good, but HTML was never intended to be a page layout language, or a means of type-setting. HTML is meant to instruct the reader's machine how to use the text, not how to display it. Hypertext Markup Language could not be more different from PostScript, Adobe Inc.'s "page description" language. PostScript describes the complete appearance of a document, to give a consistent result on any display device or printer. It gives a very complete description of not just what is in the page, but how it should look on the page.

With HTML you can mark text so that it is used as a top level heading, a sub heading, or a citation, or body text. You cannot mark a heading so that it is displayed in 14 point Garamond with an extra two points of leading. How the different elements are displayed is controlled by the browser, although it can be configured to a certain extent by the person using the browser.

The browser interprets HTML in a way that differentiates between the code and the text. The HTML tags are instructions to the Web browser and the marked up text is displayed in different ways according to the particular browser being used. The tags are descriptions of what the elements of the page are, not how they should look.

As different browsers interpret the same Web page, the underlying structure of the page will stay the same, but the display will vary. A list will be treated as a list, a second level subheading as a second level subheading. One browser may vary the point size of different levels of heading, another may indent them, or embolden them. One browser may add bullet points to the items of a list, whilst another may use dashes. The ways in which the elements are displayed are encoded within the browser, not the HTML.

Some browsers allow the user to configure the display to their liking, letting the user choose which fonts are used, and at what size, and whether quotes are indented or displayed in italics. This cannot be decided by the designer of the Web pages. The designer may have a particular hatred of Helvetica, but if the user chooses to view a page in Helvetica, then there's nothing the designer can do about it.

BUT I WANT TO SPECIFY A FONT!

There is no way a designer can specify the font that is used for the text of a web page. There are some designers who are wary of the looseness of the Web and they may feel uncomfortable with the high levels of control the reader has over the look of "their" pages. You can suggest that the viewer uses a particular font to view a page, but you cannot enforce it. The reader may not have a copy of that typeface, and not all typefaces are available on all platforms.

It is possible to lay out some text, with the leading and kerning and typeface and colour that you want, and use it on a Web page as a graphic, but it will then be treated as a graphic rather than as text. It will take far longer to transfer to the reader's machine, and it will not behave in quite the same way as hypertext. You can convert it to a page element called an image map, which allows for hyperlinks within the graphic, but it is still heavier on the bandwidth than text.

If a reader comes to graphics only pages without the ability to view graphics, they will see nothing. If your information depends upon graphics, use all the graphics you need. If, however, the graphics are unnecessary, you may be alienating readers who are struggling with low bandwidth connections. Turning some text into graphical elements can be a highly effective way of using type on a page, but may be avoiding the real nature of the medium. It is not a question of *acceptable use* but of opening the medium up.

Some Web users and Web developers are against any use of graphics, seeing them as an obfuscation of the original purpose of the Web. But the Web is changing, and Web users are changing. It is no longer the exclusive province of the inventors and developers of the medium. Now that the Web is open to a far wider general audience, expectations are changing. As the Web is becoming less exciting just for existing, and more important as a medium, good use of design is becoming significant.

Designing with the Web can be far more effective than fighting against it. A strong understanding of the nature of the medium, its limitations and its strengths can help a designer make the most of a potentially difficult job. The process and considerations of designing for the Web are covered in more detail in the chapter "Design for the Web".

If you want total control of the look of a page, the Web is not the right medium to work with. There are ways of transmitting complete typeset and designed pages across the Internet, using Adobe Acrobat's Portable Document Format (PDF) for example, but you may be sacrificing the immediacy of the Web.

Web pages are live, and interconnected with the rest of the World Wide Web, and that can be an incredible strength. The advantages of immediacy and flexibility can outweigh the satisfaction of perfect type. The combination of speed and design would be, and will be, the best solution.

WHAT IS A WEB PAGE?

A Web page is a contained entity, with a top and a bottom. It is called a page, but could just as easily be called a *place*. Web *page* is a very misleading name.

Unlike a paper page, there is no limit to the size of a Web page. The question "how many words to a page?" is meaningless—a Web page can contain one word, or a million, and has nothing to do with paper size.

Choosing to put more or less on a page will affect the way that it is read. The freedom to link to other pages that contain other information adds significance to the amount of information you choose to put on a single page. Because there are no real limits to the amount of content you can put on a page, choosing to put everything on one page may imply that it should be read as a single piece, from top to bottom. Taking the same information, and splitting it up over several interlinked pages means that it is likely to be read in a less linear fashion. Readers of the printed page are accustomed to starting at the first page, reading top to bottom, then reading the second page, and so on. Writers are more familiar with writing for linear reading. If there is no single string to lead the reader through the information in a predetermined way, how will the information be understood?

There are questions about whether it is better to have one long page, which takes a long time to download initially, or many smaller pages, each of which must be loaded separately. There is no single right answer to a question like this, and there need not be. The decision needs to be based on meaning and content, rather than on physical boundaries of paper size, and type size. The flexibility of the page makes decisions like this a case by case matter.

The limit of a page lies not so much in how much can be put on one page, but how much can be seen through a window at once. Bounded only by the size of the monitor that it is being viewed on, a page becomes a much looser concept.

THE DIFFERENCES BETWEEN THE PAGE AND THE SCREEN

The differences between a screen and a page have more to do with the viewing technology than the contents. Reading on a computer screen allows the reader less control of their environment, and sustained reading on-screen is more tiring on the eyes. Sitting in front of a computer to read can be less conducive to a sustained attention span than sitting on a comfortable chair with a more traditional book. Consider the implications of on-screen reading when you are building your site. Make your pages more legible and less dense than you would for the same material on paper.

The printed page is a fixed item, with a predetermined set of contents, whereas the screen can be used as a viewing device for any page on the Web. The screen is just a window onto a Web page, a tool for reading the page. The browser window, with its buttons and scroll bars, has very little to do with the page itself. It is something to look beyond. Some browsers enforce their own design onto a Web page to a greater extent than others, but even this will change.

On a very basic level, readers are used to the page being *portrait,* and the screen being *landscape.* The current default setting for most Web browsers is a portrait display window. Forcing an A4 paper standard onto a Web page is very limiting. Transferring the contents and design of something that has been designed for an A4 magazine, or for a broadsheet newspaper to the Web can be problematic. Most readers will not have a 21 inch monitor, and will not be able to view the whole page at once. How are you expecting readers to read your Web pages? If your design depends upon the whole page being seen as a single entity, you will need to work to the current lowest common denominator. Your page designs will have greater impact if you remain aware of page and screen size and work with it. Remember that if readers have to scroll up and down a page to see everything, the page will not be seen all at once. If you feel that it is necessary for a reader to see everything at once, you must make sure that it can be displayed in its entirety on a small monitor.

You cannot control the size of the screen, the window onto your page. The size is more to do with the reader's monitor than it is to do with your design. You can encourage or suggest a width or a height, but if their monitor is narrower than a graphic you've used, they will not be able to see it without scrolling backwards and forwards.

If you have more than a single screen of information on your page, you do not know exactly how the reader will position their viewing window over your page. Will this affect the impact of your design? You can break your content up into self-contained, but interlinked chunks, but you cannot insist that they go to every page. Is it essential that a visitor reads every word to get your message across? Will a reader bother to scroll down to the bottom of a page? Think about your own reading patterns and what you do when you are faced with a Web page that is several screens long. The right length or size of a page will vary according to the content and purpose of a page. When you are thinking about how much to put on a Web page, it is not about how much you can fit on a page, but how much makes sense for this page.

FLEXIBILITY OF PAGE SHAPE

The amount you choose to put onto a Web page depends on how you want the information to be seen and used, rather than on paper size. If you want short, punchy nuggets of information to be read in a glance, there is no need to expand your content to fill an arbitrary page size.

The way that you break information up, using larger or smaller pages, depends upon the content and the structure of your Web site. The only limits are the current standards of technology—the size of computer monitors, the transmission of large amounts of information over the Internet and the amount of memory required to handle very large pages. The choice of page length should be based on the subject matter, the complexity of the topic and the intended audience. Your page can be as long or as short as it needs to be. It is possible to build links that jump not to the top of a new page, but to a specific point on a page. This internal linking can make a yard long stream of text more useful than it could possibly be on paper. A poorly designed yard long stream of text, however, will be hard to read, difficult to digest and problematic to navigate. Paper has a predetermined top and bottom—if a reader is scrolling up and down a very long and poorly signposted Web page she can become confused and disorientated. With the complete freedom of size, strong information design and clear navigational aids become very important.

CONTENT, STRUCTURE AND DESIGN

An awareness of the freedom of movement around the World Wide Web can help you build a clear structure into your own Web site. As a reader, you become frustrated by dead ends, and illogical jumps to other pages. As a Web designer, or Web builder, it is important to remember the process of Web reading. If you are looking for information about a product, you do not want to be led down the side track of a company report. If you want to look at some pictures, you might not want to read about how the paints were made. On the other hand, knowing that the information is available if you want it can encourage you to explore areas that you might not previously have considered.

Knowing that you can always hit the browser's Back button, or type in a new URL gives you the freedom to leave at any moment. The waiting involved for a page makes you decide very quickly whether you want to stay. If you are forced to hunt through layers and layers of non-relevant information, you will probably choose to look elsewhere. If you are frustrated by a site you will leave.

Because you have more control over the structure of your Web pages than over the precise finished appearance of them, the structure requires the greatest amount of design. Each page must be carefully thought out, and the structure of the whole site, and the movement around it must be given careful consideration. The pieces of the Web site need a logical structure that even a casual reader can grasp. On a simple level, chapters and sections can be broken up as they would be in a non-linear reference book, such as an encyclopaedia. You can then consult an index, and skip to the required section of the text. This may cross-refer to a related topic, which itself refers on to another. The pattern of reading and using an encyclopaedia is the closest text equivalent to hypermedia. Although many Web sites are very different from reference works, a site will have links within its own content, or to the content of any other accessible material.

On a more complex level, the information can be broken up to suit readers with different interests and needs, or to encourage the experience of an explorable space, and the sense of unfolding and uncovering ideas. You can build in progress along a site, or deeper into a site, and suggest a passage through time as well as pages.

Most media have a clear progress through time, a passage from start to finish. Even as they play with the idea of time, they move through them in a single flow. A novel may skip backwards and forwards in described time, but the reader follows the novel's structure from beginning to end. The storytelling moves through its own time space, but the story moves through from the opening words to the final sentence.

Hypermedia, however, has a presence in space as well as time. The movement through a Web space follows the readers' and the writers' association of ideas rather than a single constructed path. It is important to indicate the range of paths through your site, and signpost them clearly, without overloading your readers with options. If your information is poorly signposted, nobody will find it. They won't just "turn the page" to discover the next chapter, because there is no single *next* page.

DESIGNING INFORMATION

Whether your site is a game, a display of water-colour paintings or a thesis on Wittgenstein, it contains information. *Information* is a very broad concept and is not a synonym for *facts* or *data*.

Suppose someone was given too large a dose of a truth drug. The person administering the drug would have done so in the quest for useful information. The resulting babble of words, the unstoppable flow of facts would be almost useless. There would be so much raw data, the information could be lost. The secret combination of the safe would be buried under the weight of descriptions of summer holidays and a recital of telephone numbers.

Information is data that has been sifted and structured, the signal within the noise. If the dialogue of your favourite film was presented to you on paper as a stream of text without any punctuation, stage directions, or mention of who was speaking, it's unlikely you would recognise it as drama. Sorting and labelling data, and breaking it down into manageable pieces can turn it into useful information.

If a visitor to your site cannot work out how to play the game, or how to find the paintings, it is the information that has been poorly designed. The game is there, but is useless if it cannot be played. Some Web sites are full of data and contain no information at all.

If a reader cannot find her way through the data, the mass of content, there is no reason for it to be there. Some time spent on information design can make all the difference.

Just as graphic design is concerned with shaping the visual elements of a page so that they take a form that has the necessary impact, so information design is concerned with structuring the content in a way that conveys the necessary information. The order of the content, and the clear labelling of parts helps the reader to make sense of a large body of data.

The mechanics of navigating information, and the provision of clear paths through it, are very much part of the remit of the information designer. Information design and graphic design can work together to enhance the reader's experience of the information. At times, however, they will be in opposition. Clarity may not be the main focus of the graphic designer, whereas it is of utmost importance to the information designer, whose main role must be to assist the reader through the content. Information designers will never be comfortable with the idea of illegible, though beautiful, typesetting.

Working with Web pages, an information designer should be aware of the multiple routes through a Web site—building a single track path is avoiding the richness of the medium.

Readers should be encouraged to explore, but never to feel lost. There should be a sense of what else is in the site, and whether they are by the edges of the content, or deep within the heart of it. This should not need an overload of possibly irrelevant detail. Too many signs can be as confusing as too few. Good information design is not about endless lists and indices, but about making clear sense of the content.

Structuring a Web site, so that related information is accessible without having to follow a circuitous route, is fairly straightforward with the judicious use of hyperlinks. Descriptive links give the reader a good idea of what is on the other end of a link. Clear labelling of information and links helps the reader decide their most effective route.

Providing clues is very important. Self explanatory titles of pages are more helpful than those that contain no hints of their contents. *A brief history of the Eilean Glas Lighthouse* is far more useful than *Page 45*, especially as the linear numbering of Web pages rarely makes sense. (Descriptive titles are also more useful when you're considering subject indices and search engines, particularly those that are compiled by software agents rather than humans.)

WRITING HYPERTEXT

Reading badly written hypertext is difficult. Readers start to feel lost and confused and any valuable information can be lost in a flurry of meaningless links. Hypertext is not automatically meaningful.

Writing for the Web requires some understanding of how different people read hypertext. There are many different ways of reading the Web, and a great deal depends on how the text is written, and how the site is structured. The writing of a Web site can provide useful clues and directions for a reader who is unsure of what information is available or how she is meant to find her way through. Associative links are very powerful, allowing readers to follow their own trains of thought through the content, but they are not always the most appropriate or useful forms of linking. Providing guidance and recommended routes is not incompatible with free exploration of the information space of hypermedia. The main aim is to provide a reader with all the navigational and explanatory material she needs.

Completely free-form association can reduce the impact of the information that you are providing. Linking absolutely everything together can confuse and disorient readers. On a very simple level, a page that is filled with hyperlinks can overload the reader. Links are brightly coloured and jump out from the main body of the text. Whilst this can be very useful because the links are simple to find, they can overshadow the main text. Overloading a page with multiple links can give the impression that the page has no content of its own but is merely a jumping point for other pages. If there are too many links, a reader may be unable to find the right link for her purpose. This can encourage *surfing.*

Web surfing is as insidious as channel surfing. The pauses between stops on the Web are often just long enough to find the next link that grabs the eye and activates the mouse finger. Scanning endlessly for the next interesting link provides the user with the feeling that they have covered vast tracts of information, when all they have done is flicked through the pages of a book, or hopped between television channels. It is as easy to click from link to link on the Web as it is to buzz between multiple channels on the television. Surfing the Web can be a useless activity. It may lead you down routes that you might normally not have found, into areas that might be of interest, but it is too easy to keep skimming the surface without engaging with any of the content. If readers connect with your information only on a very superficial level, you may not be able to achieve the levels of communication that you desire. The routes out of the page can be more visible than the content of the page.

There are ways of helping a reader *into* rather than over or out of your site. The ways into the information need to be accessible and clearly signposted. The information needs to be presented attractively and legibly to make it easy to read. The structure needs to be planned in such a way that it supports the reading paths that are most suitable for you and for your readers. A loose web site with poorly thought out links can obscure the best information and defeat the most interested of readers. Whilst the ideal of the Web—with all the information in the world available at the click of the mouse—is very exciting, it is less useful if you cannot find your way through it. Self-chosen routes and individual paths of enquiry can be extremely rewarding but if the routes are obscured by poor planning, the enquiries can be left unanswered.

Writing hypertext is not always easy. You cannot assume that the reader has taken a single, predictable route through a Web site. You cannot assume that she has read the introductory or explanatory material first. You cannot use phrases like *we have previously seen that* because there is no guarantee that the previous material has been seen. You can, however, make such material accessible without constant repetition. Hypertext allows you to refer to other material as and when it is needed. Readers who are familiar with the subject matter need not follow the references, but new readers should be able to find all the back up and explanation that they need.

Information can be structured so that it is useful for novices as well as experienced readers. There is no need to put everything on a single page. Branching text is a very useful way of splitting up levels of information and explanation. Let the structure follow the content. If the information requires a step by step guide to a process, it is important to provide a sequential route through the information. This does not, however, rule out sideways links to more detailed information, explanation or expansion of the sequence. Footnotes and sidebars can be linked in without destroying the step by step sequence. It is important to distinguish the different reading routes—there should be clear indications whether a link is part of the sequence, or a diversion from the main flow. If there are sideways links from a linear sequence, you should build links back into the main sequence.

Think about the position of links within the text. Do they occur at meaningful points? Links can interrupt the flow of reading, simply because they are more visible than the body text, so their position needs to be taken into consideration. Building a link out of a page in the middle of the flow of an argument or explanation may not be always be a good idea. Links should provide a path to more useful information rather than destroying the usefulness of existing information. If you are breaking the flow of text with a hyperlink, it should be a link to information that is necessary or relevant at that point. Building links to material that has only a passing connection with the link material can distract the reader.

It is important to avoid repetition of explanatory material. Repetition can confuse more than it can elucidate. If a reader comes across the same information or the same material on different Web pages within the same site, it is very easy for her to assume that she has doubled back on herself, that she has been there before. There is no need for this. If there is some information that is relevant in multiple areas of a site, clear signposts from multiple pages are more efficient than repeating the information on all the pages where it is relevant. If your site contains technical or specialised terminology, you should provide a glossary, and make it accessible from every page, rather than explaining each term every time that it is used. Key terms should be explained in context at some points, but it is inefficient and distracting to repeat them endlessly.

If you allow more than one route through your Web site, you need to plan for every possible route. Every page has an URL, and each page can be accessed as a separate entity. You need to allow for each page to be the first page that a reader encounters. Each page needs to contain a main topic, and cover that topic fully, on whatever level. Self-contained topics are the most useful way of breaking up information for a Web site. This does not mean that all possible information about the topic needs to be contained on a single page, but any questions raised by the topic should be recognised and answered. The page can refer and link to another page that contains a greater depth of information about these topics, but there needs to be some level of closure within the page itself. Provide links to related topics, or to any introductory material necessary. The relationships between different topics are important, and you will need to make the key associations more prominent than any secondary relationships. There is no need to cover everything in one place. Repeat the links to the information rather than the information itself.

Providing short summaries at the top of pages can assist the readers. A good introduction to the page can put it in context. Make it clear what subject is covered on each page—both on the page itself and on pages that link to it. When moving around a Web site, it helps to know if you have arrived in the right place. The title of the page is one useful indication of the content of the page, but only if the title is descriptive and does not depend on prior knowledge or reading within the site. A summary can help the reader on several counts. Firstly, it gives a clear indication of what they have found, and whether it is what they are looking for. Secondly, a summary can be very reassuring to a reader who is partly familiar with the information as it helps her recognise which knowledge she already has, and which is new. Rather than having to read through an entire page to find that it covers material that is already known to her, she can see that this information is familiar and she can then move on to more detailed levels.

A strong understanding of the general questions that readers ask can help you structure your site to provide the answers. There is no need to overwhelm readers with all levels of information about your subject matter. Clear introductory levels can lead to more detailed reserves of information deeper within the site. A reader can then choose her own level of reading. It is important to signal where more information is available and where it can be found.

The way that links are presented and explained is key to the reading process. Links should be self-explanatory. Well-worded link text allows the reader to make a more informed choice about her sequence of reading. The link should give a clear indication of its destination.

It is very important to have as clear a picture of your target audience as possible. If the information is intended as entertainment for young children it needs to be written and structured very differently from a site intended to provide an on-line help system for users of your engineering software. This may sound very obvious, but it cannot be ignored. Different age groups and different interest groups read hypertext in different ways. Children who are very familiar with technology may be more comfortable reading on-screen than some older readers may be.

To return to the question of the length of pages, the amount of guidance and explanation will vary from site to site depending upon its purpose. Some sites need short, punchy nuggets of information whilst others suit long involved arguments in a linear form. The size of the page should be based on the content. Some chunks of information need to be longer than others. Self-contained topics should be kept together where possible—too much division can make the reading process unnatural and broken up. On the other hand, unconnected information should not be combined on a single page to bring a page up to the "normal" length. A web page can be as long or as short as its content demands. Keeping the size of individual pages down can encourage readers to read the entire contents of the pages. Most readers are uncomfortable with reading long streams of text on a computer screen. It can be hard on the eyes, and disorienting if the reader needs to scroll up and down a long page. A page usually needs to be read in a linear fashion even if the site is not. Many people print out longer pages to read later, or they skip over them altogether. In some situations, long pages can be appropriate but in general shorter chunks are more digestible on-line.

The style of the writing and the style of the links need to be suitable for your intended audience. Novice readers will need more guidance than experienced readers of hypertext. Novice readers may find guided or suggested routes through the site more useful than completely freeform links. Helping your readers though a site does not mean you need to remove their choices. You can lead readers towards a preferred route without removing independent travel.

However your site is written and structured, you will need to provide some indication of the scale and the scope of the information within it. Because of the nature of the Web, you can see what's on a Web page only when you have downloaded it. Unless you tell your readers what is in your site, and how big your site is, they will not know until they have been all over it. Picking up a book, you can see how long it is. There are no such obvious clues about a Web site. If the information is there within your Web site, readers will find it only if you let them. A graphical representation of how the site fits together can be useful if it shows the structure of the information and content rather than the structure of the directory. A map can also act as a navigational device to help a reader find the best paths of reading.

READING AND EXPLORING HYPERTEXT

Hypermedia requires activity on the part of the reader. The reader needs to choose a direction, which link to click, which chain of association to follow. Reading hypertext is a form of exploration, but it should not leave the reader lost in a mass of pages that have no obvious connection to each other.

Well-designed hypermedia is structured in a sensible way. The links are placed where they are needed, and the content is broken up into meaningful chunks. Although a page need have no limit to its length, and all related content could be on a single page, it can be helpful to break the whole down into its component pieces. The pieces need not be read one after the other, and can be interlinked to provide a more useful ordering of the information for different readers.

Reading a page of hypertext that has no link but one to the *next page* can leave you wondering why it is on the Web, rather than on paper. Although the ease of distribution persuades some people to publish on the Web, if you're going to make the leap online you should take advantage of the strengths of hypertext. Handing over control to the reader can be unnerving, but no choice but "next page" is no choice at all. Open the site up a little. Recommended reading routes can be provided in association with an open approach to the reader's movement. Provide alternative routes, even if it is simply a way back to the *home page* without having to hit the back button repeatedly. Web sites should not need to depend on the navigational devices of the browser to help the reader move around the information.

TAKING A CRITICAL LOOK AT SOME WEB SITES

If you've read through this far, it might be a good idea to take a break. Fire up your browser and have a look at some Web sites. Go back to a site you've visited before, and re-read it. Try a couple of random sites, places you've never been before.

Fast connections may make you a little more forgiving of over-large graphics and dead end links. If you are on a fast link, it's worth trying this on a slower connection than one to which you are accustomed—if your patience is stretched, you will be far less tolerant of a poorly designed site.

Move around the site, thinking about the demands that it makes upon you. As you explore, try asking some of the following questions. Compare the success and failure of different sites. Be critical, because other people will be when they look at your sites.

- Do you know where you are within the site? Does the site give you any suggestion of its own scope? Can you find your way around?

- Are there any links that land you in places radically different from what you were expecting? Are there any links that are labelled "back" that take you to a place that you haven't previously visited?

- How are the graphics used—do they add to the overall impact of the site? Are they an integral part of the design, or are they tacked on for decoration? Are they worth the wait? Does the site look good?

- Try looking at the site again, without viewing the graphics at all. Does the site make any sense? Does the structure of a page hold without any images?

- As you move through a Web site, think about the flow of connections that you make. How did you choose the links that you followed? Did you find what you expected on the other side? Did you follow your original plans, or find a new chain of thought that seemed more interesting?

- Did you end up on any pages where you had to hit the back button to escape? How often did you have to pass through the home page? Were the links written into the text, or in the form of a menu or a list?

- Who had more control—you as the reader, or the designer of the Web site? How did that feel? Were you encouraged to follow certain paths and if so, did the sequence make sense?

Returning to the role of the reader can be quite enlightening when you've been working to build and design Web sites. The assumptions that you make about reading patterns should be based on reading, not on writing. Think about who your site is meant to reach, and make sure that you are addressing them in the right way because it goes far beyond the choice of words and the choice of images.

Now that you have applied a critical eye to existing sites, we move on in the next chapter to the processes involved in planning your own site.

Chapter 4

Planning a Web site

Planning is an essential part of building a Web site. Before you start to build your site, you need a very clear idea of what you want to do, whom you are trying to reach and how you are going to do so. You need to plan the structure, content and treatment of the site, as well as the production process itself. Following the look at reading patterns and hypertext in the previous chapter, this chapter covers the planning process.

In the rush onto the Web, too many people are putting anything up, just so that they have a Web presence. There are sites that have so little focus, you can only wonder at whom they were aimed. The mixture of information, in itself, is not a bad thing, but the organisation of it is terrible. Do you want to see a picture of the CEO's grandmother when you're buying a bottle of wine? Do you want to read the annual report when you go into a record shop?

The backwaters of specialist interest are given as much emphasis as the key content. Imagine if all the extras and spear carriers on stage were to start talking very loudly, all at once, and with the same amplification as the leading players. Being able to pick out the information you need would be almost impossible—you wouldn't have a clue what was going on.

The process of sifting information and structuring content so that it is suitable for the Web requires careful planning. Converting existing literature for a good Web site requires more than some quick scanning and a bit of HTML.

Thorough planning and strong information design can turn a jumble of information into an effective Web site. Time spent on the structure and the navigational systems can help readers find their way through the Web to the information they might be looking for. Poor design might mean that a reader is completely unaware of the range of content in your site.

A Web site can grow over time—a few pages tacked on here, a few pages added there. The freedom to add more material as it is needed is both one of the advantages and one of the dangers of publishing on the Web. Imagine a perfectly designed house, with a myriad of extensions tacked on any-old-how. The overall effect is reduced, but there's more space. If, however, expansion space is planned from the start, new wings can be added as they are needed, without breaking the original design. Additions need to be worked into the main body of the Web site.

THE PLANNING PROCESS

Planning a Web site is very similar to planning any other publication. You need to consider the audience, and the intentions of the publication. Who do you want to read it, and what do you want a reader to get from it? If you are not sure of whom your site is for, it may not be worth building. A consideration of the content, the style and the structure is as important for a Web site as it is for a book, a television programme or a CD-ROM. The time and thought spent on an appraisal of your intended audiences will help you reach them more effectively.

The process for planning a Web site can vary from site to site, but broadly it will cover a few key stages. The proposal for the site, whether it is a commercial site for a client, or a non-commercial site for, say, an art project, needs to cover the intentions of the site. A statement of what the site is going to be, what material it will cover, whom it is for, and how it is to be used, is a useful starting point that can help focus the later stages of Web building. A discussion of the possibilities of any interactive elements is useful at this stage. Interactive elements, such as search engines, data-basing, auto-response email, competitions or games, will need to be scripted in such a way that they can be built into the site. Is it possible to achieve what you are planning? Think about the intended effect of the site before you start, or you may not be able to plan your time and resources as accurately as you would like.

Once a proposal has been made, and the project has the go-ahead, you need to plan the structure and the construction of the site. Planning the production process requires a breakdown of team responsibilities.

Planning and production time will vary according to the nature of the site, but certain questions need to be asked in advance of the production period. You will not be able to answer all these questions now, but when you have worked through the book you will have a clearer idea of what is involved at every stage. All of this work may be done by a single person, or by a large team—but however many people are involved, enough time has to be allocated to produce a solid site.

- Who has overall responsiblity for the site?

- How time sensitive is the site? Do you have a deadline that is carved in stone, or is it fairly flexible?

- Who is to provide the content? Is it being created specifically for the site or adapted from elsewhere?

- Who is to be responsible for the structure of the site, the overall look and feel and the methods of navigation?

- Who is to write or adapt the text so that it is suitable for a hypertextual environment? How much time will this take?

- What about the graphics? Does the site need a large number of images converted into a form suitable for the Web? How much will need to be designed and produced specifically for the site? Who is responsible for the overall art direction?

- Who is responsible for the HTML authoring? How long will it take?

- How much programming is involved and how much will need to be created specifically for this site?

- Once the site is built, where will it live? Who will be responsible for maintaining the server?

- If the site needs to be checked over or approved by a client, how long will it take? At what stages should changes be considered?

- Who will be testing the site before it is published onto the Web? How much time will you allocate for fixing any problems?

- Is any fulfilment required—mailing brochures, for example, or filling orders? Can your organisation take the increased demand that may arise from visitors to your Web site? Is there someone who can respond to emailed questions?

- How much time can be spent publicising the site? Is the site going to be marketed through other media, or just online?

- Once the site is live, how frequently will the content and style need to be updated, added to or changed? How much time will be spent on the site every week?

Beyond the initial production process you must consider how much ongoing maintenance the site will require. Unless the site is intended as a short term, static event, time should be spent keeping the site live and fresh over its lifetime. Because it is possible to update a Web site at any point, sites that are left to stagnate can be worse than no site at all. Going to a "what's new on this site" page in July, and finding that it has been untouched since January will not encourage a reader to hang around. Time should be set aside for the upkeep of a site over time.

THE SKILLS AND TIME INVOLVED

If your site contains original content, you need someone to produce that content. If it contains content from another project, then all the elements will need converting to suitable forms and formats. If your site is going to include graphics, you will need someone who can design and produce them. You will need someone to author all the HTML so that your content can be published on the Web. If you need any interactive elements, you will need someone to program them, or someone who can work with ready made progamming. You will need someone who knows how to work with a Web server to get your site up and running on the World Wide Web.

The time will vary enormously between projects, but it is worth asking the production team how long they think they will need to build the site that you have proposed. The first Web project that you work on will be a useful learning experience, in that you will find out the proportions of time spent on each area of Web building. Production times will vary from other media, especially if the production team is new to the Web. Planning subsequent sites will be far easier, and many of the decisions you have to face about the production and planning process will be covered in more detail later in this book.

HANDLING THE CONTENT OF A SITE

When thinking about the content that you are planning to include in the site, there are numerous questions to be asked.

- Is your planned content suitable for a Web site?

- How do you expect a visitor to read and use the information that you provide?

- Is the site to be read at leisure, or as part of a learning process?

- What impact do you expect the information to have?

- Does the planned design of the site match the content, in a way that will make the content more appealing and more effective?

- How are you going to structure the information so that it can be used in the best way possible?

- Try to work out different ways in which a reader may want to use your information, and allow the variations to be built into the site. Is your content suitable for a casual reader, for a more determined reader or for both?

The answers to these questions will vary, but you need to consider all these problems when starting a Web site. Your answers will help to inform your Web site, and careful thought will increase your chances of a successful site.

Whether you are expecting your readers to be well versed in your subject matter, or newcomers to your ideas, a well designed structure and well written text will help them get more out of your site. If they can find their way around without problems, and find the information that they might be looking for, your site is well structured. The ideal site allows the reader to move seamlessly around the information in a way that suits her best.

Breaking the information down into chunks is a useful thing to do early in the production process. Although it is possible to have all the information you want on one page, it might not suit your material. Breaking the information apart into sections allows to you cover more, rather than less, ground. Identifying areas of the content that can stand on their own, and which need to be read in conjunction with other sections is the first step to building a strong structure. If one piece of data makes sense only if it is read directly after another, it should almost certainly be on the same page, so that the reader can see the immediate connection between them. You cannot rely on a reader following the next link to a crucial piece of information.

Hyperlinks mean that information is not fragmented, but sorted. Content should not be split apart just so that you can have a greater number of pages in your site, but so that a reader can move through the information in her own way. Wading through pages and pages of unrelated material is enough to try the patience of even the most tolerant Web user. Unlike reading paper, you cannot skim through a multi-page Web site to see whether it is of interest to you. Pieces of information, well connected by a sensible and transparent navigational system, can offer the reader the choice of path.

THE PAGES WITHIN YOUR SITE

Within a Web site, the pages are the only self-contained units. They have a top and a bottom, download in one go, and have a limited amount of content on them. Although a page could be linked to thousands of other pages, both within the same Web site and out to any other site, the page itself has its own limits. The lack of physical size restriction on a page adds significance to the amount that you choose to put on a page. The suggestion is that everything on a page is part of a single piece, and should be read as one. Although hypermedia encourages non-linear reading, the page is still usually read from one end to the other.

Reading a Web page is a different experience from reading a printed page. On paper you can see the whole page, including its physical boundaries. On the Web, unless you have a very large computer monitor indeed, it is unlikely that you will be able to see whole pages in the majority of Web sites. Unless it is clearly signalled, the place within a page can be lost, and the context of its surroundings are diminished.

Hyperlinks are the most obviously different thing on a Web page. They stand out a mile, and it is very common for a reader to scan the page for interesting links before pausing to read anything on the page. New readers, particularly, are more likely to hop from page to page, "surfing" the links without stopping to read the content. A well designed page is more likely to hold the attention longer. The links should, however, be clear and descriptive so that a reader can find the path they may want without having to fumble through a list of links all labelled "click here".

PAGE ORIENTATION

How are you expecting the reader to view your page? It can be important to remember that although computer monitors are usually landscape, the default setting for most Web browsers is portrait. The metaphor of the page comes from paper, not the screen. If you want to take advantage of the greater width of the monitor, you will need to indicate this to the reader, so that she can adjust the window of her browser accordingly. Asking a reader to work with the layout of your page may be no problem, but it is not something that you can do repeatedly.

Just because it is straightforward for a designer to vary the width from page to page, it does not follow that it is straightforward for the reader. If you expect a reader to shift the size of the window to a wide variety of widths on different pages of your site, you are going to have to provide a clear reason for doing so. Reading a book that needs to be turned on its side from time to time can be aggravating, and some readers may be tempted to ignore any pages that need adjustment. It is far better to decide on a single page orientation and width, and stick with it.

It is also worth remembering the size of smaller computer monitors. Find out what is the current average monitor size. Currently, the vast majority of monitors can display a total of 640 pixels in width and 480 pixels in height. You will, however, need to take menu bars, the browser window and buttons into consideration because you do not have the full 640 by 480 at your disposal. Forcing a reader to scroll from side to side as well as top to bottom will not facilitate ease of reading.

BALANCE

Once you have started to break up your information into chunks, with each chunk on its own page, look at them again and see how they stand up as individual pages. Many of these questions can only be asked once you have started to build your Web site, but they are worth bearing in mind as you start to pull the content together and break the information apart into multiple Web pages.

- Do your pages balance? Is there enough information on them in conjunction with any navigational devices, such as buttons, and explanatory material?

- How many pages are made up entirely of lists or indices?

- What is the purpose of each element on the page?

- How much is there for decorative purposes?

- How much material on one page is repeated elsewhere? It might make more sense to have one version of the information, and link to it each time it is needed than repeat the information in multiple pages.

- Pick one potential page at random out of the content. Does it make any sense on its own? If someone arrived there from outside, would they have any idea where they were?

Each page will need a clear title and a means of introducing its content and establishing itself within the larger framework of the whole Web site. Now is a good time to start thinking about how you are going to signpost your material. As you start to decide how to break your material down into individual pages, consider the purpose of each page.

- Does the information on a single page take the reader anywhere?

- Does the sense of it lead the reader on to another page?

- Is there enough to interest a casual reader?

- Does it provide anything useful or entertaining?

- Does it answer its own questions?

- Does each page have a clear role in the Web site as a whole?

The pages need not be totally dependent on each other, but there does need to be something to hold them together. A magazine may contain multiple articles, but can still feel like a unified whole.

Once your site is built, and on the World Wide Web, you will be able to track the number of visitors your site has received. You will be able to get a page by page breakdown which will help you assess your site. Some pages will be far more popular than others. Some may get no visits at all. You will need to ask why this is happening. It may be that some pages are far easier to get to than others. You may find that you have built some pages that cannot be reached at all, although careful modelling and planning will help prevent this. Perhaps some of your pages contain nothing at all worth coming back to. The information about your visitors will help you plan future changes to your site, to help balance the flow of movement around the site.

If some of your pages contain *necessary* information, but nobody is visiting them, you may not have provided enough paths to them, or you may have broken the material up too much. Once you have some information about how visitors use your site, information which can be gained from thorough testing, you can fix these problems and encourage readers to visit particular areas.

DECIDING WHETHER TO BUILD MANY SMALL PAGES OR A FEW BIG PAGES

A question you will keep returning to is how far should you break the site up into pages. During the planning time you will need to consider this as you refine your intentions for the site. Which is a more suitable size for a page—5k or 500k? The size of the pages will depend very much on the nature of the content. You will need to decide which is more suitable for the material itself, and for your intended audience.

An entertaining site for small children should have a very different format from a site aimed at archaeological researchers. Nobody would expect printed books to take the same form for such different audiences, but Web sites seem to be treated as if there were very few options. This is a brand new medium, yet people are imposing arbitrary limits on what can be done with it.

The size issue is a case in point. There is no one right answer, no right way to do something. The rules are still being written. If you think that your way works, and you can justify it, go with it.

One thing to consider, however, is the delay while a new page arrives. Hopefully the wait will decrease as general access speeds improve. Even with your Web site on a fast server, however, you have to be sensitive to the waiting periods and pauses that are part of reading through the Web. As you click on a link, and a new page is requested, there is a pause as the request is sent to the server, and the server responds and delivers the page. This process is repeated for every page. Regardless of the size of the page, there will be a pause as the request is sent and the server responds. Only after this do you have to wait for the content of the page to be delivered.

When planning page sizes you will need to consider the following:

- Would your audience rather wait for many small pages or one large one?

- Is there some text to read as the images download, or will the reader be staring at a blank page until 300k has come down the line?

- If there is a very large page, should you break it up with internal links and headings? This can help a reader navigate around the page without scrolling up and down searching for the correct paragraph.

- Long pages can be confusing, but careful planning can make them a good solution. With a smaller page, the reader will be able to see the content of the page as a complete unit.

- Small pages can encourage more activity on the part of the reader, who must make the decision where to go next more frequently. This may suit your material better.

There is, of course, no reason why you can't work with a mixture of lengths and densities of pages depending on the subject matter. Structure should work with the content, not against it.

If you are unsure of the best page sizes for your material, read through some Web sites, thinking about the flow of information. Do find that some sites are too broken up? Do some sites land you in acres of un-navigable text? Judging the right size of your chunks of information becomes easier as you work with Web publishing, and many of the issues involved are covered in more detail in later chapters.

CHAPTER 5

Finding a model and a structure for your Web site

Finding a model or a plan for your Web site is an important stage. This chapter explores different ways to approach this process, breaking away from rigid hierachical models to find more creative solutions. The planning of a site provides a solid foundation for construction, making the production period simpler to manage.

AVOIDING TREE DIAGRAMS

When you are planning a Web site, think about its shape. A flow chart, or a tree diagram can be a useful device for the initial planning—but it may not be appropriate as the ultimate model for your site. The lines on a chart can be taken too literally as the only linking options. It should be possible to make multiple flow charts, or route maps, through a site once the overall structure is planned. Breaking away from this model can open you up to different ways of moving around your information.

A tree diagram may be a clear breakdown of the hierarchy of information in a small site, but would limit the shape of the links if it was taken too literally. If the site was built in strict accordance with a rigid tree diagram it would be necessary to move up and down so many levels to move from side to side. Is the information really this disparate? There may be a better way of tying pages together which does not necessitate retracing your steps to get somewhere new. Do you have to move through the home page repeatedly? Do you need to move up one level in the hierarchy, then down one level to move between two pages on the same level? It would be easier to move directly between them. Do not use a tree diagram to represent all the links in your site, unless you plan to restrict movement between pages to a strictly heirarchical pattern.

A diagram of this sort may be more useful for planning the hierarchy of the folders and files that make up the site, than for mapping the possible movements of a reader. Hyperlinks do not need to follow directory hierarchy.

NEW WAYS OF MAPPING A WEB SITE

Mapping a Web site can help you plan routes through the information, and help you organise your content into the best form. Anticipating the flow of association can help you build a strong system of navigation for your readers.

The first step is grouping your chunks of information in an appropriate way.

- Which elements fit together?

- Which sections answer questions raised by other sections?

The pieces should fit together because of their meaning, not because of some arbitrary order that is dropped on top of the content. Think more about which information a reader might require to back up the current material, than about which page may have come next in a printed version that preceded your Web site.

- How do you anticipate a reader reacting to the flow of information?

- Can you anticipate a reader's next move, and provide a choice of relevant pages to link to?

- What will a reader want to see next?

A Web site can contain multiple routes, and multiple ways of reading through a site. There is no need to hold your readers to a single path. Group your information by sense, and provide a variety of roads through it.

Imagine your Web site as a physical space for a reader to explore—but do not limit yourself to a model that could exist in real life. Metaphors can become too neat to be of any use at all. If you are working with the idea of a house as a model for your site, with the content spread around the rooms—do you have to go through the hall each time you move from room to room? Why can't you move to any room directly? Metaphors can be useful starting points, but do not let them restrict your plans. Plan your information space, but do not be limited by physical laws.

DEVELOPING A MODEL FOR YOUR WEB SITE

Developing a model for your Web site is a useful stage in the production process. Although your readers may never be aware of the model that you have used, it can help the authors and builders to hold the shape of the web in their heads. An understanding of how the pieces fit together can help prevent dead ends and mistakes. It is far easier to work with a visual model of a site than with a cold list of files and folders. The aim of a good map is to help keep the production smooth, the site consistent, and the ways through it clear.

If your site is a complex one, the mapping process can help prevent over-linear models for reading. There are no quick ways around developing a model for your site, but it can help speed later stages up considerably. An understanding of the different areas of the site, and the way that they influence each other can assist the development of paths through the site that a reader may use.

What is the best model for your site? How is the information to be organised? How do you expect a reader to move around your site? Do you want to encourage visitors to move in certain directions? The links that you build into the site are the mechanism for moving a reader through the information. If you do not build a link to a page it will be cut off and remain unread.

Some information may need strong guidance for the reader, constant suggestions of the next place to go, while others may need to respond to direct queries.

If the site is based around a searchable database of information, the best model may be a form of soup. If you are not expecting anyone to read through your site, but rather to dip into it for specific information, is there any need to structure paths of reading? If the ingredients, the elements of contents, are loose within the site, accessible only through a search engine, you may not need to develop a complicated model for your Web. In this case it may be appropriate to let the reader enter an information request or query into a search mechanism, which responds with the information they need. Related information can be linked from the search result, but this type of web site has less need for a hard and fast structure. Web pages and hyperlinks can be built very much on the fly in response to a reader's needs.

If your content is designed to be read through and explored, a more ordered structure is appropriate. It can be useful to use index cards and pieces of string to develop a model. Prepare your index cards, by allocating one per page and writing something on it to indicate which page is which. Lay your cards out on a large space, and rearrange them until you are happy with the general structure. Lay out the cards so that related chunks of information are near to each other. Do not try to arrange them in straight lines and don't even think about a hierarchical structure. Once the layout feels right, you can start thinking about the links. Pieces of string and bits of sticky tape are useful indications of links. This will allow you to link cards that are next to each other, or on the other side of the room. Where the sense of the content necessitates a link to another page—stick on another piece of string.

By the time you have finished, your model will look appallingly messy. Don't worry about it. Your readers will never see you crawling about the floor with a ball of string in your hand. Stand back and look at the tangled jumble of *links* and *pages* that you have constructed.

- Are there any cards that have not been linked in to the whole?

- Why is this? Where in the site can these pages live? Should they be there at all?

- Can they be integrated more into the site? If they contain important information, perhaps they would be better if their information was included on a page that is more central to the activity of the site.

- Are there some pages that have many more links than others, even links from every other page? It might be worth shifting the cards around so that these are in the most accessible places of your model—whether that's somewhere in the centre, or closer to the edges.

Move the cards around on the basis of their links as well as their content, until your model starts to fall into something that can be understood.

It might be worth drawing the layout of the cards and making a few photocopies of the basic layout drawing. The links can be drawn onto any number of copies. If you were to draw every link onto the same piece of paper it would be almost impossible to read, however many different coloured pencils you used. Break the model down a little. Use copies and overlays to draw different levels of linking. Perhaps you could use one drawing to indicate the relationship between the different areas of the content, and another drawing to show common links. If you overload a single drawing, it could become unusable.

Mark any pages that are linked to all, or the majority, of other pages—these pages can be accessed by a standardised button or menu which appears on all pages. Map out a few sample routes through the pages, checking that you have built the appropriate paths. These drawings can be very useful when you plan the methods you use to help a reader navigate around a site.

Alternatively, you may find it easier to build a three dimensional model of your site. A tangle of cards and string does not always suggest the sense of space that your site may need. Molecule building kits, from chemistry class, can be a useful way of building a more solid model. The molecules give a strong sense of the connections between the pieces. The relation between different elements is as important as the elements themselves. Like the cards and the string, you will need to play around for a while to find the best use of connections and proximity. This type of modelling may not be as complete as a two dimensional map, unless you start sticking pieces of string on here as well.

Do not allow the metaphor to enforce an unsuitable structure on your site. Hyperlinks are more flexible than the bond between atoms. Your web need not conform to an expected or predetermined shape.

In Barcelona, in the crypt of the Sagrada Familia, is the model that Gaudi constructed as he was designing a church and its crypt for the Colonia Güell. The building was never finished, but the crypt is one of Gaudi's most inspired buildings. It looks wild and organic but has a superb logic that was made possible by the modelling process that Gaudi used.

Gaudi drew a ground plan of the crypt and hung a string from each point where a column would stand. These strings were joined with other strings for the position of each arch and vault. Small bags of lead shot were hung from the strings to represent the stresses that the columns would bear. The resulting mesh enabled him to work out the directions in which the stresses and strains would pull the columns if they were allowed to take their natural shape. He photographed the model and turned the pictures upside down to give a clear understanding of the natural positions that the columns would take. This allowed him to design a building that was based on the needs of the construction rather than the standard fat, straight, up-and-down pillars that most buildings rely upon. There are almost no right angles in the entire building.

Gaudi's experimentation with models enabled him to find the most suitable shape for his purpose. A visitor to the building may not have any idea of the underlying structure, but can appreciate the beauty and practicality of the design.

Look at subway maps, star charts, diagrams of agricultural land, architects' plans, anything that can help you visualise your site as a spatial structure. But if the metaphor you are using does not work—abandon it and find another one, or break and stretch the one that you are using. Look for new ways of mapping your site. The mapping process is meant to be useful, not constraining. Finding or developing a model that fits the project is far more effective than enforcing an existing concept on the content.

Metaphors and models can have their limits, but they can help you focus on the structure of your site. They can also assist the practical construction process. If you have a visualisation of the project, you will be able to carry the structure more easily in your head as you work.

Although you will need a strong model of your web site, it is unreasonable to expect your readers to see the same model. You have designed and built the site. You know how many pieces there are, and how they all fit together. You should not assume that a reader has the same knowledge as they arrive at your site. Even if you have offered a table of contents, and an outline of structure, why should readers be expected to hold that model in their heads? Reading a printed book is a different case. If the author refers to a chapter later in the book, the reader knows in which direction to look. There is a clear before and after within print media. In a non-linear web site, however, the idea of previous and next page can become meaningless. Just because you wrote one page before another it does not mean that the reader has read them in the same order, or has even read them at all.

Some web sites have buttons that not only link backwards and forwards but *up* and *down.* Up where? Are the publishers expecting the reader to know the shape of the tree diagram used by the information designer? Does it mean that the "up" page is up one level in the directory structure? Links should make sense in their own terms, and not require a working knowledge of the full structure of a site. The purpose of a complex model is to enable the information designer to provide simple navigation for a reader.

DIRECTORY STRUCTURES ARE NOT THE SAME AS WEB STRUCTURES

There is no need for your directory structure to follow your web structure, or your web structure to follow your directory structure. Setting up your files with descriptive names in a useful hierarchy is far more useful than enforcing an external structure upon them. You may find it easiest to base your directory structure on the structure of the web, but it is far from essential.

Later in the book, you will find how simple it is to move up and down a directory hierarchy using absolute or relative URLs. There is no need to shove several hundred HTML files and images loose in a single folder. It can help to print out a copy of the directory structure or window. Sort your files out and they will be easier to use.

CHAPTER 6

Design for the Web

This chapter looks at the role of graphic design on the Web, including the problems faced by designers, some of the attitudes towards design and a possible approach. The chapter also includes some ways of coping with the restrictions imposed by the technology and looks to find the best way around them. As with every other part of site construction, the more you know about how things work, the more you can achieve.

THE PROBLEMS

Good design is not a luxury. Design is an essential part of communication, yet all over the Web design considerations are being ignored and scorned. There are very few beautiful sites, and very few graphic designers working on the Web.

There are now millions of people using the Web every day. The accessibility of the Web is its biggest advantage and its greatest problem. The Web has developed at such speed it has had very little chance to catch up with itself. The Web was designed as a way of exchanging and sharing information between scientists and researchers. The initial demands placed upon the Web were very different from the demands of the general public. The logical structure of documents was preserved, and the appearance of Web pages was not of paramount importance. Current users are demanding graphical sophistication, but the Web cannot match the appearance of print, video or games. Web designers are struggling with the tools that were developed for sharing academic research.

A well thought out structure and well-written hypertext are essential parts of a Web site, but so is good graphic design. Design is not the only consideration, but it must be taken seriously. Because HTML was never intended to be used to control the look of a page, there are plenty of people who would argue that it must not be used to do so. Design may not have been the initial concern of Web developers, but it must become one now. There is no reason to exclude design considerations. Design assists the communication process.

Not everyone is a designer. Because the Web is seen as a *computer thing*, the IT department is often asked to take control of the design and build of Web sites. The support and assistance of the computer department of a company are very important— but do you really want them to art direct or design the most public face of your business?

Web browsers, on the whole, have been designed by programmers who may not have had any design experience. This can be seen as the cause of many of the problems that browsers have—the behaviour of graphics, the grey page and the colours of the links. There are more problems that stem from the limitations of HTML, and these are covered in later sections of the book.

There are deep problems facing anyone attempting to design a Web site. Browsers give the designer very little control over the behaviour of the page. Beyond the question of bandwidth and the size of images, there are questions of control:

- How can you design a page when you cannot predict the shape or size of the page from reader to reader?

- How can you flow text around images if you do not know the size of the type-face?

- How can you plan the overall tone of the page if you do not know what colour the background is?

Browsers are the first main problem that the designer has to face. Different browsers may treat objects on the page in a very different way, and the design of the browsers themselves is often problematic. There are solutions to some of these problems, and they are covered in detail in Section 3.

Browsers enforce their own design onto your site. Even if you had total control over your pages, they would still be framed by the browser. They would still be surrounded by the buttons, scroll bars and logos that are built in to the browser. This does have an impact on the look of the page. After spending a long time using the Web, you start to blank the browser interface out. You don't notice it so much. But try switching browsers. You will be more aware of the influence of the browser design. One way to reduce the impact of the browser controls is to avoid echoing any of the buttons. If you use a back button, readers may expect it to behave in the same way as the browser back button. Even if you want them to have a similar function, changing the names and the look can reduce confusion and separate the page from the window through which it is viewed.

There is no way to force a reader to use a particular browser, and the browser controls are in the hands of the readers. With Mosaic, for example, the reader can choose the typeface and the point size for *every single style*—from a top level heading to an address. There is no way that a designer can specify which typeface is used. How can you plan a page when you have no idea about the type? Some people would argue that this is a very minor issue. If so, we should ask why has type become so important in print. Type carries more than just the words—different fonts have different emotional resonance. Some seem more *serious* or weighty than others, for example. The relationship between the type and the graphics is crucial to a well-designed page. An inappropriate typeface can trash the intended effect of a page. But the main problem is one of legibility. Size, font, and leading are out of the control of the designer. Most browsers have a default leading based on the point size chosen by the reader, not on the x-height of the font. The lack of control over the vertical spacing of type on a Web page can make your text unreadable. Not only will it look terrible, the content will be lost as well.

The reader can stretch the browser window to the full width of a 21 inch screen, and there is nothing you can do about it. The variation in page width disrupts the flow of the text, makes aligned images behave very strangely, and makes the text very difficult to read. We are used to reading short lines of text on paper, but many readers will happily adjust their window to two or three times the comfortable width. If a line of text is too long, readers will lose their place in the text. Short lines are more conducive to smooth reading patterns. There are two points here—one is about handing some control to the designer rather than to the reader, but the other is to do with reading patterns and interface. Browsers seem to have been designed with very little attention to the user interface. There are so many problems with the interface, and page width is just one of them. This needs to be addressed by the browser developers. Perhaps there will be some way in which the window could be re-sized automatically according to the demands of the page and specifications of the designer.

Imagine you have to decide which colours should represent hot and cold. Would you choose blue for a *hot* link, and red for a visited link? Someone did. All the research into the cognitive effects of colour was ignored when link colours were written into the first graphical browsers. Blue is simply not an active colour. Look at your bathroom taps. Red is hot, blue is cold. Experienced Web users may have adjusted to using this interface, but the visual signals are confusing.

The Netscape extensions allow you some control over the colours of your links. If you use no other Netscape extensions, it is worth considering taking control over the link colours when you design and build Web sites. As a Web user you can adjust your default settings. Take the time to change your preferences. If controls are in your hands as a reader, use them to make the pages you view easier to read and use.

The standard grey background should also be trashed wherever possible. The contrast is too low. Most books and magazines are printed on white paper for a very good reason—it makes black text more legible. Images are also adversely affected by the grey background. Some browsers allow you to add a background colour or image to a Web page. There are hundreds of sites that have used this advance to make their sites illegible. Use it to *improve* the appearance and legibility of your sites instead. As a reader, if you can change the default setting of your background, do so. Grey is not the most effective colour.

The question of good taste and bad taste will be fought for many years. This is not about taste—it's about legibility. If you want to communicate your message with text—the text needs to be legible. There are occasions where illegible text has a function—but don't make your site illegible accidentally.

Designing for the Web, you will face more problems and more limitations than you would designing for print. Print has become very sophisticated, and print design is informed by hundreds of years of experience. The demands of Web design are not exactly the same, but there is no reason to discard everything that has been achieved in other media.

ACCESSIBILITY

Browsers behave in different ways and HTML is growing and being adapted. This affects the look and the accessibility of your site. Your site will not look the same each time it is viewed. There are too many variables. You cannot fix the appearance so that it looks the same for all readers. Even if all Web users used the same browser, there would still be problems. Computer systems handle colour palettes in different ways, monitor sizes vary, type and white space cannot be controlled with any degree of accuracy.

Beyond all these problems is the running argument about how the Web should be used. This is heavily tied in to the design question. The openness of the Web is very important. Information is accessible from all over the world. Hypertext and hypermedia allow you to publish your material into a global arena. But how open is open enough? Should you design and build your site so that everyone can see it, regardless of how that affects the appearance of your site? The Web is for everybody, but should everything be targeted low enough so that it is accessible to everyone? Should we be aiming at the lowest common denominator, the most beautiful site possible, or a working compromise? The issue of accessibility is an important one.

It is easy to dismiss readers who do not have access to graphical browsers because they are becoming a small minority. Some people are tied to non-graphical browsers, or to those browsers that allow the designer very little control. Some people choose to use them because they believe that design has no place on the Web. Should you factor these people into your design decisions?

There are different interpretations of the term "accessibility". To some people, accessibility is purely about whether someone can access the information contained in your Web page. To others it is about the accessibility of the information itself. Good design can make information more accessible to readers, and thus more useful. Presenting your message well will help your message have greater impact. Nobody doubts this in any other media. Why are there such big rows about it on the Web? Design is seen to be exclusive and privileged. Dry, semi-legible text excludes far more potential readers than well-presented material. Good design is a powerful communication tool. If it is possible to take control over the design of the page, what possible reason is there to refuse?

With the introduction of Shockwave, a plug-in for Netscape that adds real multimedia to Web pages, these questions are again becoming central to debate because of the increased sizes of pages. Web developers have to consider their audience and assess how far they can push the boundaries. If you are building a Web site you must consider how long a reader will have to wait for a page, and whether that page is worth the wait. You must also consider that there will be those who cannot see your all-singing all-dancing pages at all. What you choose to do depends very heavily on who you are trying to reach and what you are trying to say. It can be worth waiting a long time, if you end up with something that gives you great pleasure.

The introduction of graphical browsers pushed the Web to its current level of popularity. The inclusion of images moved the Web into a wider forum. The Web is no longer a plain text medium. Now that graphics have been allowed onto the Web, it is essential that we take them seriously. Adding a few pictures to a page is not the extent of design on the Web. There are limitations, but there is no excuse for not using every tool to hand.

HTML is not a sophisticated page layout language but it can be forced to do more than its developers expected. Some HTML is deemed incorrect—but if it works, why not use it? There is a difference between bad HTML and HTML that is used for specific reasons. Bad HTML is written by mistake, or through ignorance. Using HTML to achieve a particular visual effect is different. If you are aware that your page will behave differently with other browsers, is there a valid reason for not choosing to design for the browser that makes your page look best? HTML and browsers are quirky, but if you understand how they behave you should take advantage of that knowledge. If it looks gorgeous in one browser and still works in other browsers, perhaps you have achieved the best of both worlds.

The Netscape extensions are at the heart of this row. These extensions give designers the first tools to control the appearance of their pages. The Netscape extensions are not part of HTML. They may be added to HTML at some future date, but now they are of uncertain status. Obviously, Netscape supports the Netscape extensions, but other browsers are also starting to incorporate the Netscape tags. You can set the colour of the background, of the body text and the links. You can align images, and use tables to control the flow of the text. If the possibility is there, why not use it?

There are people who believe that you should not even try to design pages beyond a logical structure. You can preserve a logical structure within good design. There's more to a good page than a set of bullet points and a couple of headings. The Web is expanding beyond anyone's expectations. It is wrong to limit the possibilities. Why not take it as far as it can go. Learn how the medium works. Learn the limits and work around them.

THE STATE OF THE WEB

I talked to Mike Bennett, the creative director of a design company specialising in design for the Web. We talked about the state of the Web and the way in which designers approach the medium. All the quoted comments in this section are from Mike—this is not an interview as such, but a more general look at the questions of design on the Web.

KBC: *There are very few well-designed sites, because very few sites are approached with any thought for the design. The few sites that are well designed stand out a long way on the Web.*

MB: "Most sites on the Net, graphically speaking, are dull as ****.

"It's a fanzine medium full of kids having a bit of a play and programmers pretending to be graphic designers. I like the naivety of it all, but I don't think that there are many great sites out there and the mentality as yet has not had a chance to develop in terms of graphic design. The Internet is an unknown quantity and there is no such thing as an Internet designer. Not yet."

KBC: *Designers have not yet moved onto the Web in any significant numbers. Most of the design work is being done by people with little or no design experience or training. The experimentation and new solutions to old problems can be interesting, but rarely completely successful. The freedom of self-publishing is exhilarating but we're back to the earliest days of DTP.*

MB: "People are discovering the language and learning the medium. That's why at the moment, there are some really bad sites, because people are still learning to speak."

KBC: *Perhaps more damaging, however, is the idea that design has no place on the Web. There is, of course the problem of the bandwidth cost of graphics and the download delays. Text is a very efficient medium. Information can be transferred quickly and economically as text. Are graphics a luxury?*

MB: "All the 'nerds and geeks' who want to cut back on graphics are a dying breed because graphic design makes the Web more accessible; it's not yet an accessible medium.

"I don't think a text driven medium is the way to go forward. I think that a design driven medium, a graphics and film driven medium is what it's all about. There's a whole generation who have grown up on MTV and Nintendo who are very visually literate. They are bored by a flat text medium."

KBC: Even if you ignore the attitude of the anti-design brigade, the tools are primitive and there is very little control available to the designer. How much can be achieved within the limitations of the Web?

MB: "Graphic design has lost its direction because you can do anything with print. Graphic designers have to rethink what graphic design is when they are working on the Net."

KBC: The limitations a designer has to face may be frustrating, but it's worth spending time learning about the medium itself. The more that you know about the medium you're working in and the tools that you are working with, the more control you will have. It is a new medium that behaves in a new way, but that does not mean that all the lessons learnt elsewhere should be abandoned.

MB: "It's really no different from working in other media. It's about iconography, navigation, information and design. You're still designing fonts and graphics. Treat the medium as a medium. It's not a hybrid magazine, a hybrid video or a hybrid CD-ROM. I hate to say that form follows function, but you have to understand the content and you have to know the mechanics of the medium you're working in. You have to appreciate how to use the tools. You have to be intelligent about it. Strip it down to the bare essentials—good content, good design, good fun. Get the underlying message across."

KBC: Even though the Web is a new medium, there are clear patterns arising in how people approach common design questions. Graphics are often used to help reinforce navigational signals—most sites, for example, contain some sort of button bar. This is a very simple shorthand. Readers know how to use them. Clear navigation is an important part of the graphic design and the information design of any site. The obvious solutions are not always the best ones.

MB: "You have to think laterally and try to avoid the obvious answers. Experiment. Go for novelty and risk taking. Go crazy. If you get some good results, refine them."

KBC: There is the danger that designers will get stuck in a loop of experimentation without stopping to assess or refine their work before it goes public.

MB: "It's not like print where if people complain about the design, you've lost the client. If a site goes live and people complain you can change it. That's the beauty of it and the danger of it. Once they realise the implications of this, some designers will put things up on the Web too early and the attention to detail will go. They'll start adding things, and tweaking things and correcting things as they go. It can be too easy."

KBC: Designing to the level of what already exists on the Web is not going to take a site very far. You need to push the limits, without ignoring the questions of legibility and relevance.

MB: "It's all about relevance. You have to understand the content you are working with. You have to have an appreciation of the medium and an understanding of your general audience."

KBC: The Web is so large, that there is no single audience to consider. Your site will never appeal to everyone on the Net. There are hundreds of audience groups within the population of Web users, just as there are within the general population. Generalising about the "target audience" can be dangerous. Publishing a site onto the Web will not automatically make your site interesting. Be aware of your target audience, and design with them in mind. There are no rules. There is the experience of design in other media, but the Web has its own needs.

MB: "Designing for the Web is about having fun and pushing the limits. Understand what the limits are before you break them. Not many people understand them right now or they are not even prepared to explore. Treat the Web as a medium in itself."

THE APPROACH

Knowing the medium and knowing how to exploit the tools are the first stages in designing for the Web. Even if you are planning to concentrate on graphics, learning HTML will give you a serious advantage. If you know how Web pages are constructed, and how HTML behaves, you will be able to work with it and stretch it to the limits of the possible. If you are not intending to produce any graphics yourself, it is useful to know how a designer needs to approach her part of the task of building a Web site. You will almost certainly encounter designers who have no experience of Web design. If you understand what assistance they need to work with the medium, your sites will benefit.

If you know how each tag affects text and graphics, you will be able to choose the right tags for your purpose. You may choose to follow very strict HTML, and use tags only as the developers intended, but be aware of the options. With the prevailing attitudes to the Web, you will have to justify the use of HTML in non-standard ways. Using non-standard tags will always be contentious.

Think about how you would approach the design of the same content for print. What should be done differently. Which controls are not given to you? What control can you add? There are ways around many of the problems a designer faces. You need to know what is available, and what isn't.

Designing for the screen is not the same as designing for print. The resolution is far lower. Even high resolution monitors cannot match the clarity and detail of good print. Your graphics need to be 72 dots per inch. This is *very* low. An image can contain a maximum of 256 colours, and fewer colours will make them less memory hungry. Careful choice of palettes and time spent stripping images down will make a difference. Running your images through an automated conversion process may be quick, but the images may suffer. Check all your images.

Speed and beauty need to go hand in hand. If the graphics are over-large, readers may get frustrated by the download times and turn graphics loading off. This defeats the purpose of your fine graphics.

If you are setting the background colours in your site, make sure that you anti-alias your images with this colour in mind. If, however, the background colour is not displayed, your carefully anti-aliased images will probably look horrible. An image that has been anti-aliased on a white background, for example, will show a white border if it displayed on a grey background. If you expect the majority of your target audience to use browsers that are unable to work with background colours you may have to forgo anti-aliasing altogether. In this case, you may choose to work to the standard grey background instead.

As well as cursing the low resolution, learn how to make your images look as good as they can. Set up a test page of HTML as you work, and check your images with a browser. They will not necessarily look exactly the same as they do in your graphics software. Browsers do not handle colour palettes brilliantly, and you should be aware of cross-platform colour problems.

HTML is not a typesetting language, and you will not be able to control the type to the level you may have grown used to. You may, however, be able to exert some control over the white space on the page, the margins, the colours and the positioning of the elements on the page.

Using the heading tags in HTML, you can make text behave as a heading but you cannot control its appearance. Browsers treat headings in different ways, and some browsers allow readers to set the behaviour themselves. If you want more control over the relative sizes of the text, even if you cannot control the absolute sizes, the Netscape tags will be useful. These tags allow you to increase or decrease the size in relation to the default size of the body text. Combining this with bold text may give you something closer to the effect you want.

Be wary of overuse of the font size controls in Netscape. Increasing the size of the initial letter of a paragraph in no way approximates a drop cap. Drop caps can be very attractive, but *this method does not work.* The line spacing is thrown out, and the spacing of the initial line will be different from all the subsequent lines. If you want to use drop caps—use graphics. Make a small graphic for each letter that you want to use and align them carefully.

Almost all browsers support transparent images. You can use a completely transparent image to space out the elements on a page. The Netscape tags allow you to set the precise size of an image, even if the graphic itself is of a different size. Your transparent image can therefore be tiny—as small as a single pixel—and consume very little bandwidth. But you can set the blank to operate at whatever size you need, say two pixels high by ten pixels across. You can use this to pad something with white space, or to set an indent on the first line of each paragraph of text. This will, of course, look terrible if someone arrives at your page without loading the images. The icon that is used for a broken or missing graphic will be scattered around your page, messing up any alignments you have achieved with a small transparent image.

If you cannot control the length of a line of text, or the size of the type, it is very difficult to run text around graphics. Wrapping text on a Web page is fairly limited. All graphics are treated as rectangles, regardless of shape of the image itself. Text will not wrap around irregular shapes. You can use the Netscape tags to align an image to the left, the right or the centre. You can even allow some white space as a border around the image. But you can't be sure of how the text will flow around it. The controls do not go far enough, and you cannot depend on the page to behave as you expect.

If you are unsure of the chaos this can cause, try it out. Set up a page with a left aligned image, and a couple of paragraphs of text. Make it look really good, with the text and the graphic sitting really neatly together. Now use the browser's preferences to change the typeface and the size. Reload it and have a look. Now stretch the browser window to the widest possible setting your monitor will allow. It's not a pleasant experience. If it worries you that readers may see your pages looking like this, you will have to think very carefully before embedding images in your text.

There are some ways of controlling the maximum length of a line. Even if you cannot control the type itself you can contain it within certain boundaries. There is nothing within HTML that has been designed to set any margins on a page. There are several ways around this, with varying degrees of control. You can block quote your text. This will usually indent it on the left and the right, but some browsers may behave differently. If a reader is using Mosaic, for example, they may have set block quote to be displayed in a larger typeface, or in italics. You could use the line break tag to enforce line breaks where you want them. If a reader has set up their browser window so that it is too narrow to display the full line, it will wrap round so that you get a full line, then a couple of words, then another full line. This is probably not the effect that you were hoping for. You could preformat your text, but then you will be limited to a monospaced font like Courier.

The introduction of tables, and the Netscape extensions to tables, allow you to set some limits on the random behaviour of text on the Web. You can use tables to control the position of text on the Web page to a greater degree of accuracy. The standard table set-up allows you to align your text to the left, the right or to the centre of a table cell. You can also set the vertical alignment to the top, middle or bottom of the table cell. Thankfully, no-one has thought of using justify as an alignment option. This would be the very last thing that Web design needs.

You can use tables to set up columns of text, or to add white space to a page. With the Netscape extensions, you can control the width of the elements within your tables. This means that you can set a column of white space, then a column, followed by another column of white space. It's not a simple way of setting margins, but it works.

The details of most of these methods require thorough knowledge of HTML and are covered at the end of Section 3: Advanced HTML.

CHAPTER 7

The interface issue: navigating a Web site

This chapter covers the importance of consistency, the need to test and re-test a Web site, as well as ways of integrating a good navigation into your site. The chapter points out some of the common weaknesses and ways to weed them out.

Coming up with a useful navigation interface can require careful thought. Plan an overall style for your site—consistency helps readers' orientation. Changing the signals will only confuse a reader who is trying to move around your web site. If you are using any graphics as navigational buttons—do they match the overall look and feel of the site? If someone comes to your site without the ability to view graphics, will they be able to find their way around?

Hyperlinks are the lifeblood of the Web. Poorly designed links are no use to anyone. If the reader has no idea what is on the other side of a link, or has no sense of the content of the site, you will have lost them. Links, as far as possible, should be self-explanatory and seamless.

DON'T CLICK HERE

There are few things more annoying than a page that is a sea of click here links. Find a page like this, there is no shortage, and scan down the page quickly. Hyperlinks always stand out more than regular text, because of the change in colour, the under-lining or any other method that your browser uses to signal the presence of a link. All you can see is click here. Going back to find out which "here" goes "where" can be confusing and annoying.

You can build your links into the fabric of the content to a far greater extent. If you feel the need to say "for more information about this subject click here" you need to rewrite your text. Turn your sentences around, so that the link becomes an integral part of the regular flow of the text. There is no need for the text you use for the link to be an addition—work the link into the existing text.

Make your links descriptive. Use the links to indicate what is on the other side. "Here" says nothing at all about the page in question. Try to keep your links as consistent as possible. If you have six links on a page, all sounding different, and they all go to the same page, you will confuse your readers. Well thought out link text will help readers find the best way around the web site. You can use this text to encourage a reader to go in a particular direction. Repeating key links and backing them up with graphical links, say a button for the home page or for the help page, will make it more likely that a reader will follow them.

If your links are useful, they will be used. Help the reader to anticipate the content. Do not expect the reader to have a visual model of how your web site fits together.

How do you go back to a place you haven't been?

There are some web sites that have a string of buttons along the bottom of each page. This can be very useful, if the buttons are clear and descriptive. Many of them, however, are labelled *up, down, back* and *next*. This can be worse than useless.

Making assumptions about the path that a reader has followed, especially if there is more than one possible route, is crazy. There have been times when I've clicked on a "back" button, only to be landed on a page that I've never been to before. How can you go back to a place that you've never been? Assuming a certain direction, or allowing only one route through a web site, is fundamentally limiting. You have no idea whether a reader has come in through the "front door" or "home page" or whether they have just arrived. To impose your model upon them is misguided.

Pointing up or down is equally meaningless. How does a reader know which pages are on which levels of your hierarchy? You may have planned and designed your web site around a perfectly formed tree diagram, but please remember that the reader does not have access to that diagram. Describe the directions a reader can move in. Provide as many clues as possible to help them find their way. Use descriptive names for pages and sections of your web site. A reader does not know what is in "Chapter three" unless you tell them. It is difficult to flip through a web site as you would flip through a book, to have a quick look at the contents and the structure.

Help the reader by giving her a sense of the range of the content, and the size of the web. If you pick up a book, you know how long it is. It has a physical size. As you read a book, you know exactly how far through it you are, and how much more you have to read. If a reader comes to your web site, and finds a couple of interesting pages, she will have no idea whether there are two more pages, or 20,000 more, unless you point it out. Give a clear indication of the other areas of your web site.

Do not limit these indications of scope to your home page or your front door. You may be happier if all your readers were to come through a single door into your site, but every single page in your site has an URL. Every page has an address, so every page can be an access point. You may advertise one URL all over the place, but other people may build links to the inside of your site. People may pass around the URL of a particular page to check out. You cannot reasonably control the means of access to your site. When someone turns up in the middle of your site, it is important to help them orient themselves as quickly as possible. If you give them no idea of what is in the rest of the site, or how they might find it, they will leave. If you want people to read through your web site, you will need to help them find their feet.

Clear, descriptive titles on the pages are useful. Signposts and clearly labelled links will help a reader find their way into and around your site. Names for different sections or areas of the site can help indicate the range of content, and its uses. A consistent graphical style will help establish the boundaries of your site. The more help that you give a reader, the more useful they will find your site. It is important, however, not to overload a reader's senses. If every page is signalled as prominently as the others, the choice of which page to link to can be rather overwhelming. If some pages are more important than others, and you want to encourage a reader to visit them, signpost these ones more clearly than the others.

Another useful way of indicating a reader's place within a larger site is to use real maps. Provide a small map with a "you are here" arrow to give visitors an idea of the scale of the site, and of their place within it. This need not be a page by page representation of the whole web site. A general indication of area can be very useful. Making such a diagram active, turning it into a clickable image map, means that it not only helps the reader find where they are in the site, it can provide a direct link to another area.

DESCRIPTIVE NAVIGATION, ICONS AND BUTTON BARS

A strong navigational system, whether it's text based, graphics based or a combination, can be as important as good content. The most interesting content on the Web is no use if a reader can't find it. Time spent working on helping the reader by providing sensible navigation can make all the difference. Look carefully at the map you have produced of the structure and think about the routes that you want a reader to take, and about the information that a reader may want to find.

Develop a set of navigational icons or buttons that refer directly to the content rather than to your own scheme of up and down. Be as consistent as possible, if your home page is titled *base camp* or *contents* or *front door* reflect that in your icons, rather than using the conventional picture of a house. Do not feel obliged to have a home page at all.

If you are using a button bar or a map as a navigational scheme, keep it in the same style as the rest of your graphics. Don't abandon your sense of balance and design just because you're working an a new medium with new needs.

As far as possible, keep the size of the graphics down. Large graphics can overwhelm a small computer monitor. If your graphics are large in memory terms, they will take a long time to download over the Net, and lose some of their functionality. If the navigational graphics put too heavy a load on the page, they are defeating their own purpose.

Consistency is very important. Because the reader cannot see the whole Web in one go, and therefore cannot see her own place within the site, she needs to be given clear signals that do not change. If you change the signposts around, the reader may be confused and disorientated. Sometimes, you may want to disorientate the reader by stripping away the clues and signposts. Some sites are suitable for a form of playfulness, where the reader is forced to hunt for links and maps. This should be done for a particular effect, however, rather than as a matter of course.

A clear naming scheme, giving each page a descriptive and useful title is the first step towards a solid navigational system. The more signs that you can give your readers to let them know where they are in the site, the better. Combining this with a coherent set of buttons or menus will assist the reader's use of the content.

THE MODEM FRIENDLY WEB SITE

Until there are some major changes in the technology that delivers the content of a Web site to a reader, it is important to consider the speed of your site. If you make unreasonable demands on bandwidth, you could lose a large number of potential readers. Although many Web readers are on fast connections and direct lines, a considerable proportion are using relatively slow modems and dial-up accounts. A site that seems slick and quick on a fast line can take an unbelievably long time to arrive by modem.

Think about the balance of your pages:

- How much of the bandwidth is taken up by content, how much by the navigational scheme, and how much by decoration?

- How large are your graphics? Have you taken the time to strip them down to the smallest size possible without sacrificing image quality?

- Can you justify the size? Would you wait ten minutes to download a copy of your logo? Readers will tolerate long delays if they believe that they will get something worth waiting for.

- If you need to have a large number of heavy bandwidth images on a page, is there some way that you can warn people first, so that they know what they are going to be waiting for?

If you are unsure of how long your Web site might take to download on a slow line, test it on one. Test every page, preferably when you are in a hurry. If you start to get annoyed by the waiting times, you can be certain that a reader will. You know what you are waiting for, there are no surprises when the full page has arrived. A long wait, for something that does not interest you, is likely to make you look elsewhere. If a page is taking too long to come down, a reader will probably scan the page for an interesting sounding link and move on. There are ways of exerting a certain amount of control over which parts of the page download first, which are covered in later chapters. Ask yourself the question—is this page worth the wait? If you're not sure, ask someone else to test the site for you. Consider the readers on the slowest lines, and your site will be fantastically fast for readers on a fast connection.

TESTING AND CHECKING A WEB SITE

A good Web site should contain no broken links. A reader should never have to face the dreaded *URL not found* message or anything else that leads them to a non-existent page. Some time spent checking your links can spare you the ire of a reader who has faced a barrage of error messages. Once your site is built, check all your links. If your browser will let you, mark all links as unfollowed, and go through every page of the site. If a link has been used, the colour will have changed (or it will be marked as followed in some way according to the browser). If you find an unfollowed link, test it. Fix all the broken links—it may just be a typo in your HTML file, or you may be pointing to a non-existent page. Something as small as a missing quote mark, or misplaced slash can break a link. Missing quote marks can cause particular problems. Check your site with more than one browser, because some are more forgiving of small mistakes.

It is important to double check all the links that are anchored on images rather than text, particularly if you have a number of image maps, or images set with no borders. These do not provide the useful visual clue of whether or not a link has been followed. If you do not find the broken links, you can be sure that your readers will.

CHECK THE CONSISTENCY OF LAYOUT

As you go through page by page testing the links, keep an eye on the layout and the graphics. Check that all your pages are consistent. If most of your pages have a button bar at the top, for example, check that any that don't are missing them for a good reason. If some of your images have a text alternative, make sure they all do. Jump at random about the site, and check that the site holds together visually. If you are in any doubt, check again.

BETA-TEST WITH SOMEONE OUTSIDE THE WORKING TEAM

Recruit someone outside the production or design team to help you check your web site. Ask them to record their thoughts, ideas and problems as they read through the site. Ask them to find their way around, without your help.

- Did they find the site clear?

- Do they find what they are expecting on the other side of a link?

- Can they understand any icons you have used?

- Did they miss any areas of your site?

- Were they aware of the full range of the site?

- Were they ever confused about how to find their way?

- Did the information flow in a satisfactory way?

Testing the site with someone who has not been involved in the production process can give you some valuable insights into your information design. If the tester runs into difficulty at any point, consider why they did, and what you can do to improve the situation.

Ideally, you should do some early tests with members of your intended audience. Find out how they react to the site. Watch carefully to see which parts of the site are most popular. Ask what is missing, what else they would like to see. Check that they understand how to use the site.

The ultimate readers of the site will have different needs and varying levels of interest in your content. If you can smooth their passage through your Web site, you can enhance their reading experience. A well designed structure, with clear descriptive links and strong signposting allows the readers to find their way without having to fight. Give your readers the tools they need, and they will get more from the Web site that you have built.

The more attention to detail in the planning stages, the more smoothly the production period will run. Before you start to mark up any text with HTML you should have a clear idea of what you are trying to achieve and how you are going to do so. The picture of the site that you form early on will help inform the construction process. HTML is easy to learn, but HTML alone will not build an excellent Web site.

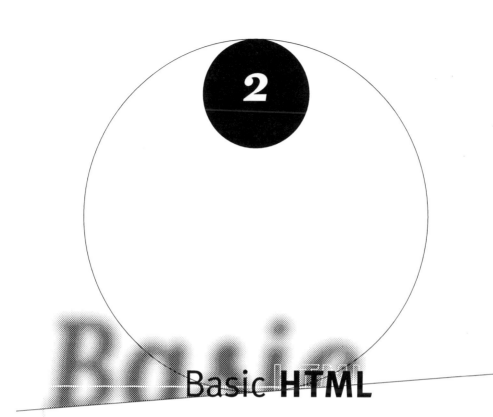

2

Basic HTML

CHAPTER 8

Why learn HTML?

HTML is a simple mark-up language. At first sight, the jumble of text and tags enclosed in angled brackets may be hard to interpret, but it is a simple system to learn. You don't need to be a programmer to work with HTML. Do not be scared by the unfamiliarity of direct mark-up.

Knowing more about the mechanisms of the medium will help you work with it. You may never need to write any HTML, but knowing how to do so will give you a sense of how hypermedia fits together. The more you can learn about the underpinnings of the medium, the more you will be able to get out of it. If you know the rules, you will know how to stretch them, or work within them. If you work through the following sections of this book, "Basic HTML" and "Advanced HTML", you will be able to build the web site that you want. Publishing on the Web is a very rewarding experience, and the tools that you need are straightforward. Learning the basics of HTML, the string of tags that you will use to mark up a web page is only the starting point. You also need to think about the nature of the medium itself.

This is a new medium. If you learn how to work with it you can help shape its potential.

Isn't there a program that can do that?

There are four main types of software that can help you build a Web site:

- page creation tools, that try to give you a WYSIWYG approach;

- HTML editors that allow you to drop tags onto your text;

- filters that convert from a word processor or page layout package into HTML;

- and text editors that require you to type your own HTML but offer other tools that are useful.

Writing HTML by hand can be tedious. It requires a high level of concentration, and accurate typing to check that every last bracket, quote mark or slash is in place. Stick with it. Allow enough time to check your pages, and proof-read your typing. You may find it easier to work with an editor or filter, but when you are learning it is worth the extra effort to type the tags yourself. Constructing pages from scratch will give you more of a feel for the texture and the workings of HTML and hypermedia. Once you are comfortable with HTML, you might find it quicker to type it in yourself, alternatively you may prefer to use a filter, converter or editor. Even if you find yourself working with an HTML editor, it can sometimes be quicker to add the occasional tag by hand.

HTML and page editors

This is only a very brief look at what Web building tools and HTML editors and filters can do. There is more information about specific programmes in the appendix, along with details of where to find them.

HTML editors allow you to add tags to a page of text and images without having to type them yourself. Often you will have a floating palette of tags to work with, or a pull down menu—clicking on the tag you want inserts it into the page. Some allow you to write in your own tags as well, or to add extra tags to the standard set built into the editor. Some are accurate, others are not. Some have a checking facility, others don't. Most of these editors are becoming more sophisticated, allowing you more control or less direct involvement with HTML, but rarely both.

HTML editors usually require a working knowledge of HTML, but provide a short cut by letting you add ready-made tags. Some HTML editors let you apply a style to a chunk of text, and the editor maps it to a predefined HTML style. For example, you can make a selected passage of text italic, and the editor will automatically add the correct tags at the start and finish of the selection. To make full use of them, however, you will need to know some HTML. Most of them are designed for creating individual pages, rather than managing the development and upkeep of a large site.

If you are interested in trying one out, there are plenty available for all platforms, and many of them are shareware. You may find that they suit the way that you work, or you may find it quicker to do it yourself.

HTML FILTERS

In addition to the editors, there are filters and converters available that can help you prepare web pages. Usually they will map style sheets from a word processed document to a predetermined set of HTML tags. Some filters are more flexible than other. If you have large amounts of pre-prepared text in Quark, or Word, for example, you may find that you can save time by working with a filter. Some filters require a knowledge of HTML, but most have a more "hands off" approach. If you want to add extra tags to a filter, you will usually have to write them in yourself. As with the editors, there are plenty available, both as commercial software or as shareware.

WYSIWYG PAGE CREATION TOOLS

WYSIWYG page creation tools are the most recent addition to the site builder's armoury. The great advantage of these is that they allow you to experiment with the look of a page without having to fiddle with swapping large numbers of tags around. They are mostly designed for people who do not want to get their hands dirty with HTML code, and some of them do that job very well. Again, however, there are disadvantages with this hands off approach. These tools are becoming more sophisticated, and they will offer more and more to people who want to build a Web site, rather than just create a home page.

TEXT EDITORS

The best solution at the moment may be to find a good text editor that you are comfortable with. Flexible systems that allow you to run a search and replace over multiple files are extremely useful. Some text editors support macros and scripting which can help you manage the construction of a large or complex site. The ability to search and replace a string of text in a large group of files at once, for example, or change a batch of file names, will save you a great deal of time. Text editors often have plug in modules that allow you to use them like a specially designed HTML editor. Even if you use a filter or editor to build your site, you may find that a good text editor will help you manage your site as it continues to grow or be updated. Used in combination with another tool that allows you to experiment quickly and easily, this gives you a visual solution matched with detailed control over your hypertext.

SURELY IT WILL GET BETTER?

When you are learning HTML, it is a very good idea to start by typing the tags in yourself. This will fix them more firmly in your memory. Many HTML authors continue to work in a text editor, rather than using a filter or editing package. Most current HTML software is slightly clunky and limited. HTML and hypermedia are developing so fast, that the software is lagging behind. If you want to work with the boundaries of the possible, there are few applications to help you out. If you want to be able to work with all the most recent additions to the Web, with all the multimedia elements that are being added, you will need to write at least some of the HTML yourself. Keeping your hand in by writing your own code sometimes, even if not always, will give you the chance to experiment and sketch out new ideas on the Web.

Obviously, this situation will change. Web authoring software will become slicker and more complete, and most people will never need to touch raw HTML. Even as it develops, however, I still recommend learning HTML. Even if you only learn the basics, it will give you a more solid understanding of the mechanisms that underpin the medium.

CHAPTER 9

The basics

This chapter will get you started with your first page of HTML. Starting from the basic page elements of title and body, text and hyperlinks, you will have the foundations for any Web site.This chapter also covers basic formatting, including lists, paragraph and line breaks and basic text styles.

If you have looked at a page of complex HTML, you may have been a little over-whelmed by the jumble of tags and text. The construction of HTML is, however, very straightforward, and if you start from the basic structure, and work through the more advanced options, a sample like that in figure 1 will soon hold no terrors for you.

```
<IMG SRC="images/strip.gif" WIDTH=450 HEIGHT=8 ALT="divider">
<P ALIGN=CENTER>
<A HREF="think/index.html" onMouseOver="window.status='Think - in-
depth coverage of current issues in media' ; return true">think</A> -
<A HREF="talk/index.html" onMouseOver="window.status='Talk - contact
us by email, phone or on foot' ; return true">talk</A> -
<A HREF="find/index.html" onMouseOver="window.status='Find - delve
into our large archive of information' ; return true">find</A>
</P>
```

Figure 1: Scary HTML

One of the good things about HTML is that you don't need expensive or complex software packages to help you create a Web site. All you need is a basic text editor, such as Simpletext on the Mac, Notepad in Windows or your favourite word processor. You may choose to use an HTML editor or filter when you are building sites, but I would recommend writing the tags yourself as you learn. As you go along, remember to save your work as text only. You will need a browser to check your work.

All the screen shots in the following examples were taken using Netscape 1.1 or above on a Macintosh. As you try things out for yourself, the appearance of the examples will vary, depending on which typeface, which browser and which computer you are working with as you write and test the HTML.

THE NEED FOR CORRECT HTML

HTML may be rather tricky to type, but it is a straightforward language, and you should find it easy to learn. Strive for correct HTML as far as possible and if you are going to break the rules, do so knowingly. Some browsers are very forgiving, and will ignore mistakes and non-standard tags, but others will behave very strangely. There are some tags that all browsers know how to interpret—the basic structural tags that made up the first version of HTML—but other tags may have been developed since a browser was released. Although most browsers are built to skip past unknown tags, this will become more problematic.

Including as much basic information as possible will ensure that the largest number of browsers will be able to read and display your Web site. If you want to use a large number of non-standard tags, you should probably consider building a more rigidly correct version of your site if you do not want to exclude large numbers of potential readers. It is important to remember that the number of tags within HTML is limited, and you cannot start adding your own. If you want to develop new tags, you will need to develop a browser that can read them. This will change in the future, with the introduction of style sheets that will allow you to create new styles along with the information the browser needs in order to display them.

There are currently some tags, mostly experimental ones from Netscape (see Section 3: Advanced HTML), that are liable to be changed, or removed. If you use these now, it is likely that you will have to go through your site and remove them at a later date. If you are aware of the status of the tags that you are using, you may be able to save yourself a great deal of time in the future.

The example files in this chapter are part of a small working Web site. As you work through this section of the book, try the examples youself. Type in the HTML, save the file, and open it up with a browser. As you work on the HTML, save your changes and reload the page in the browser to see their effects. Trying the examples and typing up the HTML will help you remember how the tags fit together.

GETTING STARTED

HTML requires you to tag or mark up the different parts of your document. The tags are the instructions that tell the browser about the structure of the document—for example, which bits are headings and which bits are body text. The browser interprets the parts of the document, and displays them according to its own settings.

Tags start and finish with an angled bracket and contain an HTML element, like this: ‹ELEMENT›. Most tags work in pairs, with a forward slash (/) added to the closing tag. Any block of text surrounded by a pair of tags will be affected by them. A pair of tags will look like this:

‹ELEMENT› the text affected by the tag ‹/ELEMENT›

For example, everything surrounded by the tags ‹TITLE› and ‹/TITLE› is treated as the title. The pairs of tags affect all the text that they surround.

Some tags are *empty* in that they are used on their own and are not used to contain a chunk of text. A tag such as ‹BR› produces a line break, and ‹HR› adds a horizontal rule across the web page. They do not affect a block of text, and therefore have no need for a corresponding closing tag.

HTML is case insensitive. It doesn't matter whether you type ‹HEAD›, ‹Head› or ‹head›—the browser will interpret it in the same way. You may find it convenient to keep your HTML tags in upper case. Although this has no effect on their functionality, the upper case tags will stand out more on the page and this may make the editing process slightly easier.

‹HTML› ‹HEAD› AND ‹BODY›

There are two main parts to any HTML document—the head and the body. The head section contains information about the document, whereas the body contains the document itself. The information in the head of the HTML document is not displayed on the page itself, but gives instructions to the browser that affect the whole document, such as the title. The head area of the HTML file is marked with ‹HEAD›‹/HEAD›.

The body contains the text of the document and the tags that instruct the browser how to display it. The body of the HTML file is delineated with ‹BODY›‹/BODY›.

These are the starting point of every HTML document, along with the tags that mark the beginning and end of the HTML code.

```
‹HTML›
‹HEAD›
head elements go here
‹/HEAD›
‹BODY›
body elements go here
‹/BODY›
‹/HTML›
```

The head area of the HTML file can contain complex instructions that affect the behaviour of the page, but the most important element to include here is the title.

‹TITLE›

The title of your page is a useful identifying device. Within your Web site, it will help a reader differentiate between the range of pages, and once your site is live the title will appear in indices and catalogues. Within a subject search, the title of your page will often appear on its own, without any of the text of the document. A descriptive title will therefore help a reader to decide whether to visit your site.

Your title should be concise, but as descriptive as possible. It needs to make sense out of context, and give a clear indication of the contents of the page. Within the context of this book, "About the Author" has some meaning, on the Web it would have very little.

"History and Architecture of Oxford" could be a more useful title than "History", "Oxford" or "Page 17". "Section 2: Learning HTML" would make more sense than just "Section 2". (Meaningful titles are those that make sense even when separated from the content of their parent document.)

Adding a title to the basic framework of an HTML file, your document would look like the following example:

```
<HTML>
<HEAD>
<TITLE>History and Architecture of Oxford - Introduction</TITLE>
</HEAD>
<BODY>
</BODY>
</HTML>
```

(You cannot add any hyperlinks or other HTML tags to a title.) The title is not part of the page, and trying to make it bigger or smaller will just create garbage tags:

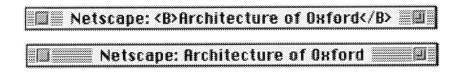

Figure 2: The title bar - with and without garbage

(The title will not display as part of the web page itself, although most browsers do display the title somewhere in the window. If you want the title of the document to appear as part of the page, you will need to reproduce it in the body of the document, perhaps as a heading.)

COMMENTS IN HTML

You can add comments to your HTML file, which will not be displayed as part of the web page. It can, for instance, be useful to note the last time a file was updated, and by whom, in the HTML source. This can be a useful way of keeping track of different versions of your HTML files. You can use comments to explain the HTML and layout that you have used to other people who may need to work with the file, or to leave reminders for yourself. Your readers will not see this on the page, but anybody working on the HTML will. Although not strictly necessary, each line of comment should be marked separately.

‹!--this is a comment--›
‹!--comments are not displayed by the browser--›

SAVING YOUR FILE

When you save an HTML file, remember to save it as text only, without any formatting from a word processor or page layout package. Give your file a useful name that has some correspondence with the title of the document.

You will need to add an extension to the file name, so that a browser can recognise it as an HTML file. So when you save the file add .html (.HTM in DOS) to the file name—for example, gargoyle.html or GARGOYLE.HTM. If you are working on a DOS/Windows 3.1 machine you will need to adapt both your file names and some of the HTML to accommodate the eight.three file naming convention. If you are using a Mac, a UNIX machine or Windows 95, you should be able to use the examples without changing the names of the files.

Be careful with mixed case filenames. Macs, UNIX machines and Windows 95 are case sensitive, so if your HTML file refers to homepage.html and the file is called HomePage.HTML—you will get a "file not found" message. To save confusion, keep your filenames either uppercase or lowercase, rather than a mixture of the two.

PUTTING TEXT ON THE PAGE

The current example, although a valid piece of HTML, is an empty file. As yet, there is nothing within the body section of the page. If you were to open it up with a browser, the window would be empty apart from the title bar. The first thing to do would be to add a heading, and then some text.

HEADINGS

The way that headings work is a good example of how HTML is concerned with structure rather than appearance. Headings are set by level of importance, not by point size, spacing or any other specific means of display. Headings range from ‹H1›, a top level heading, down through various levels of subheading to ‹H7›. The level of heading does not denote point size, but the logical structure of the document. Remember that browsers display HTML in different ways, and just because one browser varies the size of headings it does not mean that they all do.

Using particular levels of heading to achieve a particular appearance can backfire, and your document may become meaningless in some browsers. Use your headings according the structure of the document. Top level headings should be marked with ‹H1›‹/H1›, second level headings with ‹H2›‹/H2› and so on. It is not a good idea to skip levels just to achieve a particular display. You may use as many of each level of a heading as you need on a single page. You may, for example, have a single ‹H1›‹/H1› but six ‹H2›‹/H2› headings, but you should not do this just to make your text big and bold. There are other ways of controlling font size, with Netscape specific tags, and these will be covered in the next section, "Advanced HTML".

Use the top level of heading, ‹H1›, to add a title that will be displayed on the web page, in addition to the document title. Sub-headings can be added later, once we have some text on the page.

```
‹HTML›
‹HEAD›
‹TITLE›History and Architecture of Oxford - Introduction‹/TITLE›
‹/HEAD›
‹BODY›
‹H1›The History and Architecture of Oxford‹/H1›
‹/BODY›
‹/HTML›
```

‹P› AND THE WAY THAT TEXT BEHAVES

Text may seem to behave rather strangely in HTML. Add the following text to the existing HTML file:

text can behave

in rather odd ways   in HTML.

This

may

come as

a

surprise.

Save the file and open it with your browser, and it should look something like the example in figure 3.

text can behave in rather odd ways in HTML. This may come as a suprise.

Figure 3: A browser will not read your carriage returns or extra spaces

Without tags to provide formatting instructions, all the text will flow together into one paragraph. You may have formatted the text with carriage returns, spaces and five different typefaces but the browser ignores this information. A browser will not read your carriage returns or any extra white space you add to your HTML. There is one exception to this rule—preformatted text, which will be covered later in the chapter. Because HTML is concerned with the structure, rather than the appearance, of a web page, additional white space is seen as unnecessary. If you feel that the space is essential to your page, it can be added, with blank images or preformatting but this is not necessarily under-stood to be correct HTML.

Text can, however, be broken up into paragraphs. Whilst some browsers will add a line of blank space between paragraphs, others may indent them. Do not use paragraph breaks to try to space out your text—additional paragraph breaks will just be ignored by the browser.

The way that paragraphs are marked is currently under discussion. Early versions of HTML used a single ‹P› tag to indicate a paragraph break, whereas future versions of HTML will almost certainly use a ‹P›‹/P› to enclose a paragraph. It is probably a good idea to start using the paired paragraph tags now, to prevent a longwinded process of replacing them all in the future. The pair will become more significant with HTML 3.0, when it should be possible to align text to the left, right, or centre. This can already be done with the Netscape tags, in anticipation of HTML 3.0.

The main difference at the moment occurs in browsers which add a line of blank space to indicate a paragraph break. Formerly, ‹P› was used to end a paragraph, but with the paired tags, ‹P› is used at the start of the paragraph. The space will therefore be added before the paragraph. Most browsers will simply ignore the ‹/P› tag if they do not require it.

Go back to the example HTML file, and add a couple of paragraphs of text, marking them with pairs of tags.

```
‹HTML›
‹HEAD›
‹TITLE›History and Architecture of Oxford - Introduction‹/TITLE›
‹/HEAD›
‹BODY›
‹H1›The History and Architecture of Oxford‹/H1›
‹P›
The city and the University of Oxford are inseparable. The construction of
Oxford Castle in 1070 was quickly followed by a rapid development of the
city as a centre of learning. The influx of scholars and the foundation of the
first colleges went hand-in-hand with the growth of the city as a commercial
centre.
‹/P›
‹P›
"This Oxford, I have no doubt, is the finest City in the world" (Keats)
‹/P›
‹P›
Oxford is a living city. Its history and architecture span hundreds of years, but
```

the city continues to thrive and grow. The colleges and university buildings
are an integral part of the city.

‹/P›

‹P›

This web site is an exploration of Oxford, from the colleges to the rivers,
from the museums to the carworks.

‹/P›

‹/BODY›

‹/HTML›

The text is now broken up into logical paragraphs, rather than flowing freely
together (figure 4).

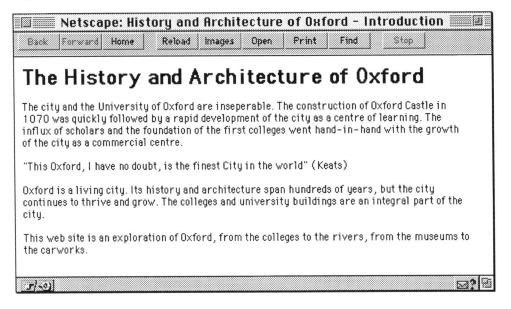

Figure 4: Paragraphs

In general you will not need to add paragraph tags to other elements—such as lists
or addresses—because they have their own built in spacing. Headings should not be
broken spaced with paragraph tags—paragraphs are part of body text.

Line Breaks

It is possible to break a line of text, without forcing a paragraph break, by adding a ‹BR› tag. It is most useful for breaking the text where the sense requires it, in an address for example. This is an empty tag, and has no corresponding end tag. Remember that a reader may have her browser window set more narrowly than you expect, and the text may already have flowed to another line. Using ‹BR› to try to line up elements of a page will rarely work, as you cannot anticipate the typeface or width of window that a reader will use. We will come back to this problem of line length and line breaks in the next section.

Horizontal rules

Adding a horizontal rule to the page can help break your page up into clear sections. Just as with any other element, over use will weaken the visual impact. Rules are added with the tag ‹HR› which needs no closing tag. By default the rule is the full width of the page. The Netscape extensions to HTML allow a greater degree of control over the rules, and this is covered in the next section of the book.

Lists

Lists are an excellent way of ordering information within a web page, particularly if you want to provide a menu, or focus a reader's attention on a selection or series of items. There are four types of list: ordered, unordered, menu and definition lists. Ordered lists have numbered items, unordered lists have some form of bulleting before each item. Some browsers will use roman numbers, some arabic numbers, some will use solid bullets, others hyphens or asterisks. Netscape specific tags allow you to control this to a certain extent, but there is no guarantee that these extensions will be carried over into HTML 3.0.

Menu lists are suitable for lists of short items, as they run across, rather than down, the page. This form of list seems to be used less and less.

Ordered and unordered lists behave pretty much in the same way, with the list itself marked at top and bottom and each list item marked with an ‹LI› tag.

Try the following example: (as seen in figure 5)

```
<HTML>
<HEAD>
<TITLE>Index of Oxford Colleges</TITLE>
</HEAD>
<BODY>
<H1>Oxford Colleges</H1>
<P>
Oxford's colleges, in alphabetical order, with the date of their foundation:
<UL>
<LI>All Souls' College (1483)
<LI>Balliol College (1263)
<LI>Brasenose College (1509)
<LI>Christ Church (1525)
<LI>Corpus Christi (1517)
<LI>Exeter College (1314)
<LI>Green College (1979)
<LI>Hertford College (1874)
<LI>Jesus College (1571)
</UL>
</P>
</BODY>
</HTML>
```

If you wanted to suggest an order of importance, or a sequence, you could turn this into an ordered list by simply changing the <UL></UL> to <OL></OL>. Menu lists are marked with <MENU></MENU> tags, and each list item is marked with an <LI> tag.

Lists can be "nested" within lists. If you choose to use sublists within your lists you can, and it is possible to mix ordered lists with unordered lists.

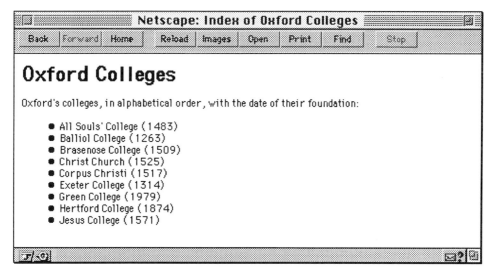

Figure 5: An unordered list)

DEFINITIONS

Definition lists are slightly more complicated, in that they involve a greater number of elements. Definition lists are made up of definition terms, ‹DT›, and their definitions ‹DD›, and need tags to indicate the beginning and the end of the list itself, ‹DLx/DL›. This type of list is particularly useful if you want to include a glossary, or a summary of general information.

Definition lists are put together like this (see figure 6):

‹HTML›

‹HEAD›

‹TITLE›Oxford Colleges‹/TITLE›

‹/HEAD›

‹BODY›

‹DL›

‹DT›Merton College

‹DD›Founded in 1264, Merton was the first of the permanent institutions that grew into what we now know as colleges. Walter de Merton endowed the college with enough land to ensure a good income and a secure future.

‹DT›New College
‹DD›New College, founded in 1379, was the first college designed around a quadrangle. It was intended, in the words of its founder, William of Wykeham, to be "a house of community which could vie in the splendour of its buildings and the dignity of its corporate life with the great capitular and monastic establishments."
‹/DL›
‹/BODY›
‹/HTML›

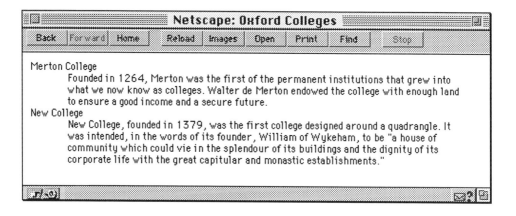

Figure 6: A definition list

    Lists contain their own line breaks and vertical space, and it is considered incorrect to add additional space with paragraph tags or to have multiple ‹DD› for any one ‹DT›.

BLOCKQUOTE

Most browsers will treat a blockquote in the same way, by indenting the whole block on both the left and the right. Whilst this is designed to differentiate a quoted passage of text, it can be a useful device for adding a small margin to the whole page. This is not strictly correct HTML, but it is a fairly attractive trick.

The whole passage can be marked with <BLOCKQUOTE></BLOCKQUOTE>.

This is the only form of margin control that is available in current versions of HTML. Netscape and HTML 3.0 include a method of aligning text to the left, right or centre, and some other browsers support centred elements. Adding margins of white space to a page can be achieved with more precision using tables. These methods are covered in more detail in the next section: "Advanced HTML".

LOGICAL STYLES AND PHYSICAL STYLES

The appearance of a logical style is controlled by the browser's style definitions, rather than by the author. Physical styles, on the other hand, involve hard formatting, where the author can specify the appearance of the text. The levels of heading, from <H1></H1> to <H7></H7> are a good example of logical style. You control the structure behind the appearance, but not the final display of the text.

The choice of logical or physical style is very much down to the HTML author, or designer. Soft formatted logical styles are more in keeping with the nature of HTML, but physical styles give you more control over the finished look of the page.

<CITE>, <EM>, AND <STRONG>, <CODE>, <SAMP> AND <KBD>

A citation is tagged with the <CITE></CITE> pair, and is usually displayed in italics. <EM></EM> emphasises the tagged text and usually displays as italics. <STRONG></STRONG> produces a stronger emphasis on the selected text, and often displays as bold text.

<CODE></CODE> is used to produce source code listings, and <KBD><KBD> to show keyboard input. <SAMP></SAMP> is related to keyboard and code, in that it is used to show sample output. These tags are rooted very strongly in the computer oriented background of the Web. I assume that these will be used less frequently as the Web becomes

less focused on itself. They may be very useful, however, for teaching material and demonstrations of code.

‹PRE›

Everything enclosed within the ‹PRE›×/PRE› tags is displayed as is, in monospaced type. This is the exception to the HTML rule—every carriage return and space you enter is displayed on the Web page. Preformatting is a very useful method of laying out a page that requires text to be lined up in columns, or in a simple table.

This is included as a logical rather than a physical style, even though preformatting gives you the most direct control over the appearance of the text. Although the text may appear in Courier on your machine, however, it may appear in any other monospaced font on another platform. You have control over the placement of each character, but *not* the typeface or the size.

Be aware that a line will not break unless you include a carriage return. If your lines are very long, they will not flow to the next line, and readers will have to scroll back and forth to see the whole line.

If you feel that you need to add a few lines of white space to your page, you can do so with preformatting. Again, this is against the general ethos of HTML, but it can be very useful and it is widely used. Other HTML tags can be included within a pre-formatted block, but not ‹P› or ‹BR› because line breaks and paragraph breaks are controlled within the preformatted text itself.

‹I›, ‹B›, ‹TT›, ‹U›, ‹S›

Italic and bold are the most widely used physical styles. All the text included within ‹I›×/I› will be displayed in italics, whatever the browser, and everything tagged with ‹B›×/B› in bold. Nesting the tags like this ‹B›×I›×/I›×/B› to produce bold italics will rarely work, and most browsers will display the text in either bold or italics.

‹TT›×/TT› displays text in a monospaced font, and should be used to indicate type-writer output.

‹U›×/U› and ‹S›×/S›, underline and strikeout, are not widely implemented as they are proposed HTML 3.0 tags. They may work with some browsers.

ADDING CONTACT AND DATE INFORMATION WITH ‹ADDRESS›

Adding contact information to your Web site is considered good practice. Although not strictly necessary, it can provide a useful contact address for the person responsible for the technical upkeep of the Web site. It can also be used to indicate copyright information, a design credit, and a publication date. There is no need to include this information on every page of your site, but there should be some contact details on the more prominent pages. At the very least, provide an email address for the "Web keeper" responsible for the smooth day to day running of the site—the first person to contact if there are any problems.

Anything contained within ‹ADDRESS›‹/ADDRESS› usually displays in small type, and often in italics.

‹ADDRESS›Katie Blakstad-Cooke, email: katie@question.co.uk‹/ADDRESS›

THE STORY SO FAR...

Adding some formatting to the earlier example of HTML, we can produce something like that shown in figure 7. The HTML used to produce this formatting is:

```
‹!--http://www.question.co.uk/oxford/index.html--›
‹HTML›
‹HEAD›
‹TITLE›History and Architecture of Oxford - Introduction‹/TITLE›
‹/HEAD›
‹BODY›
‹H1›The History and Architecture of Oxford‹/H1›
‹P›
```

The city and the University of Oxford are inseparable. The construction of ‹B›Oxford Castle‹/B› in 1070 was quickly followed by a rapid development of the city as a centre of learning. The influx of scholars and the foundation of the first colleges went hand-in-hand with the growth of the city as a commercial centre.

‹/P›

‹P›

‹I›This Oxford, I have no doubt, is the finest City in the world‹/I› (Keats)

‹/P›

‹P›

Oxford is a living city. Its history and architecture span hundreds of years, but the city continues to thrive and grow. The colleges and ‹B›university buildings‹/B› are an integral part of the city.

‹/P›

‹P›

This Web site is an exploration of Oxford, from the ‹B›colleges‹/B› to the ‹B›rivers‹/B›, from the ‹B›museums‹/B› to the ‹B›carworks‹/B›.

‹/P›

‹HR›

‹ADDRESS›Katie Blakstad-Cooke (email: katie@question.co.uk)‹/ADDRESS›

‹/BODY›

‹/HTML›

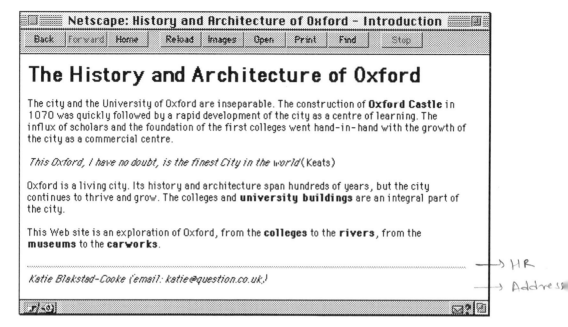

The History and Architecture of Oxford

The city and the University of Oxford are inseparable. The construction of **Oxford Castle** in 1070 was quickly followed by a rapid development of the city as a centre of learning. The influx of scholars and the foundation of the first colleges went hand-in-hand with the growth of the city as a commercial centre.

This Oxford, I have no doubt, is the finest City in the world (Keats)

Oxford is a living city. Its history and architecture span hundreds of years, but the city continues to thrive and grow. The colleges and **university buildings** are an integral part of the city.

This Web site is an exploration of Oxford, from the **colleges** to the **rivers**, from the **museums** to the **carworks**.

Katie Blakstad-Cooke (email: katie@question.co.uk.)

→ HR
→ Address

Figure 7: A simple page of HTML with basic formatting

PUTTING THE HYPERLINKS IN YOUR HYPERTEXT

Without any links, your Web pages may be beautiful, but they won't be hypermedia. Constructing a hyperlink is a very simple process—you need to create the link text, and something to link to. There is a strange ambiguity here—"link" refers to both the underlined text on the Web page, and to the linking process. "Link" is both noun and a verb. Where possible I will refer to the "link text" or "link graphic" to refer to the clickable hotspot.

The first stage in creating a link is to choose the link text. This should be as descriptive as possible, and preferably part of the general flow of text. At all costs, avoid using "click here" or "click on this button" as a link. Think carefully about the assumptions that a reader will make about the link destinations. Try to give them the clearest possible idea about what is on the other side of the link.

‹A HREF›‹/A›

The tags used for creating the link text are ‹A HREF›‹/A›. This pair of tags anchors the hypertext reference to the enclosed text. To turn this into an active link, you need to include the destination URL in the tag:

‹A HREF="new.html"›New College‹/A›

The enclosed text would be displayed on the web page as a link, with underlining or a change of colour, and would link to the file new.html when clicked. The file needs to be on the local machine, in the same directory or folder as the linking file, index.html. Linking to other folders and other levels in the directory structure is covered later in this section. Add this link and others to a current example.

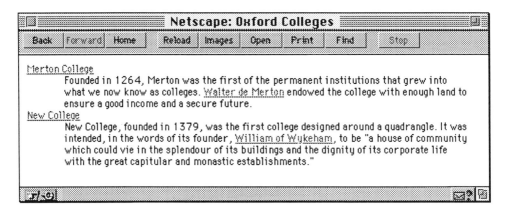

Figure 8: Hyperlinks

```
‹HTML›
‹HEAD›
‹TITLE›Oxford Colleges‹/TITLE›
‹/HEAD›
‹BODY›
‹DL›
‹DT›‹A HREF="merton.html"›Merton College‹/A›
```

‹DD›Founded in 1264, Merton was the first of the permanent institutions that grew into what we now know as colleges.
‹A HREF="waltermerton.html"›Walter de Merton‹/A› endowed the college with enough land to ensure a good income and a secure future.

‹DT›‹A HREF="new.html"›New College‹/A›
‹DD›New College, founded in 1379, was the first college designed around a quadrangle. It was intended, in the words of its founder,
‹A HREF="wykeham.html"›William of Wykeham‹/A›, to be "a house of community which could vie in the splendour of its buildings and the dignity of its corporate life with the great capitular and monastic establishments."
‹/DL›
‹/BODY›
‹/HTML›

If you want to embolden the text of any of these links with ‹B›‹/B›, these should be nested within the link tag because you are making the bold text a link rather than making a link bold. There are two schools of thought about this order, but this way seems to make more sense.

If you include any space between the tags and the link text, the spaces will be link text as well. This can produce a rather ugly result, with underlined space at either side of the link text.

‹A HREF="wykeham.html"› William of Wykeham, ‹/A›

would be displayed as in figure 9.

Including punctuation within the link text, say a final full stop, can also be rather unattractive although it is sometimes necessary to preserve the sense. Restrict the link text to the key phrase, and check that there are no stray spaces.

You are obviously not restricted to building links to your own Web pages. You can link from your site to any available page on the World Wide Web. If you know the URL of the destination page, you can build the link. The best way to check that you have the correct form of the destination URL is to copy it from your hotlist or bookmarks, or from the page itself, and paste it into your HTML file.

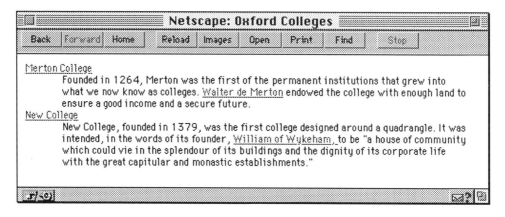

Figure 9: A badly formed hyperlink

If you want to link to an external site, you need to include the full URL in the link, including the *protocol*. If you are linking to another page on the Web, this will be hypertext transfer protocol, or HTTP.

The link will look something like this

‹A HREF="http://www.question.co.uk/ismcomics/index.html"›index of creators involved in Ism Comics‹/A›

This provides the full URL of a particular page, which is all the information necessary to build a working link to the page in question.

If you are linking within your own site, once you have a link, and some link text, you need to set up a destination. Obviously, you can build several HTML files first, and then add links between them. The links in the current examples refer to individual colleges from an alphabetical list. In the next example, the main file is worcester.html. If we set this file up now, we can start to add images and more complex linking.

<!--www.question.co.uk/oxford/colleges/worcester.html-->

```
<HTML>
<HEAD>
<TITLE>Worcester College, Oxford</TITLE>
</HEAD>

<BODY>
<H1>Worcester College</H1>
<P> Worcester is one of the most beautiful colleges in Oxford.
</P>
<P>
Walking through the front gate, you are aware of Worcester's
<A HREF="history.html"> diverse history</A>. To the left of the pristine
<A HREF="quadhistory.html">quad</A> is a row of mediaeval cottages, to the
right a remarkably well proportioned classical eighteenth century range.
Turning around, you can see Hawksmoor's library, and Wyatt's chapel and
hall.
</P>
<P>
At the end of the <A HREF="gardens.html">gardens</A>, by the lake, is the
Sainsbury building, one of Oxford's more successful modern buildings.
</P>
<HR>
<ADDRESS>Katie Blakstad-Cooke, email: katie@question.co.uk</ADDRESS>
</BODY>
</HTML>
```

CHAPTER 10

Using images in your Web site

This chapter covers the use of images in your Web site — how to prepare them and how to add them to the page. There are some decisions that you will need to make about how you use images in your site and one of the most important things to remember about graphics on the Web is that they are larger than text, and take longer to download. Do your graphics have a purpose — as information, navigation or the general look and feel of the site, or are they purely decorative? Use graphics, but do not use them just because you can.

Good graphics can turn an interesting site into a stunning site, but you must be prepared to spend time preparing your images to get the best results. You will not have the controls and level of quality you may be used to in other media, but you must always aim to produce the best and most effective graphics possible within the limitations.

THE CHOICE OF FORMATS: GIF, GIF OR GIF

On the whole, the only format that browsers can display is CompuServe GIF, or Graphical Interchange Format. Whilst this may mean that you have to convert a large number of graphics, it does mean that your images can be displayed across all platforms, and require no external software to view them. All browsers that can handle graphics can display GIFs. Some browsers can also display JPEGs, a format that allows more control over the level of compression, better colour and greater efficiency, but for the widest possible audience you will need to use GIFs.

To display your images to best advantage, they will need to be set to 72 dots per inch. It is possible to save your GIF at a higher resolution, but browsers will try to display it at 72 dpi. Using an image of a higher resolution will probably make it look worse, particularly if it is just a couple of dots out.

Most comprehensive graphics software packages should be able to produce GIFs, although you may need to adjust some of your settings (for example to 256 colours, or indexed colour). Read the software documentation for specific details about how to save your images as GIFs. There is more information later in this chapter about preparing the best looking GIFs.

ADDING AN IMAGE TO A PAGE

Once you have saved an image into the appropriate format, you can add it to any of your Web pages. The example here is a small photograph of the library and cottages in Worcester College, library.gif. The suffix .gif may not be necessary for all browsers at the moment, but it is good practice, and will help you keep track of your files. If you are working with a large batch of images the suffix enables you to see the format at a glance and know which images you have already converted.

The tag needed to display this image on the page is:

```
‹IMG SRC="library.gif"›
```

This tag requires no corresponding closing tag, as it does not directly change any text. This inserts the image, library.gif, which is in the same folder as worcester.html, wherever the tag is on the page. Adding this to the example file, the HTML is changed as follows, with the results shown in figure 10.

```
‹HTML›
‹HEAD›
‹TITLE›Worcester College, Oxford‹/TITLE›
‹/HEAD›

‹BODY›
‹H1›Worcester College‹/H1›
```

```
<IMG SRC="library.gif">
</BODY>
</HTML>
```

Figure 10: Worcester College library IMG SRC

In this case the image sits on its own line, but images can be placed "inline" so that they sit within the text. (Figure 11)

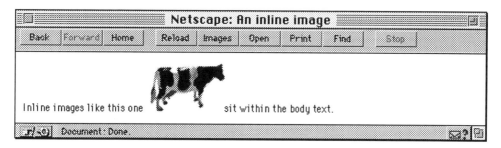

Figure 11: An inline image

Without using Netscape specific tags, you have very little control over the alignment of your images. The basic alignments within HTML affect the vertical rather than the horizontal and do not allow for text flow around the image. The possible attributes you can add to the image tag are ALIGN=TOP, ALIGN=BOTTOM or ALIGN=MIDDLE, for example:

<IMG SRC="lake.gif" ALIGN=TOP>

These affect how the inline images sit relative to the line of text. The ALIGN attribute is optional, and the default is bottom.

There is no limit to the number of images that can be added to a page, but remember to consider the demands you are making on the bandwidth. If a reader has to wait a long time to view all the graphics, they may take the first interesting link out rather than waiting for them all to download. The quicker your graphics, the more they will be seen. There is a compromise involved—you may need to sacrifice large or very detailed graphics in the interests of speed.

<ALT> AND ALTERNATIVES TO IMAGES—WHY BOTHER?

Not everyone will see your images. Some people are still using text only browsers, either for the speed or because of the limits of Internet access provision. This is becoming a smaller and smaller percentage of Web users. More significantly, some people move around the Web with their graphics capability turned off. Downloading text only makes a considerable speed difference, which is significant if you are on an expensive dial up account.

Some people only download the images when they reach a site where they believe that it is worth their time and bandwidth to do so. Even on a fast connection, there are people who leave images turned off until they have a particular reason to view the graphics. There are a few people who believe that the use of graphics is in general a bad thing for the Web. This is a patently silly idea, but it is worth remembering the bandwidth "cost" of your graphics.

Most browsers can display a text alternative to an image, which you can use to explain the image to a text-only reader. A well chosen text alternative may persuade the reader to download the images, or make it clear that the image is purely for decoration and has no real relevance to the page. It can be useful to include the size of the image in this text, so that the reader can anticipate the time it will take to download.

Any amount of text can be added into the ALT attribute, but no additional HTML tags.

‹IMG SRC="library.gif" ALT="photo of the library and cottages, 9k"›
‹IMG SRC="garden.gif" ALT="photo of the college gardens and lake, 10k"›

USING AN IMAGE AS THE LINK

Images, as well as text, can be used as the *hot spot* for a link. The link is set in exactly the same way, but rather than enclosing the link text with the anchor, you surround the image:

‹A HREF="gardens.html"›‹IMG SRC="garden.gif" ALT="photo of the college gardens and lake, 10k"›‹/A›

The image will be surrounded with a border to indicate that it has an active link. If you are working with transparent images (see later in the chapter), this can defeat the purpose of the transparency. There is a way to remove the border, or change its thickness, but only by using Netscape specific tags. Assuming that you will have a border displayed around your images, be careful not to include any stray spaces in this group of tags—an extra tail on the image can look very sloppy.

If you have an image and some text linked to the same destination, linking the text and the image separately looks better than one link around both items. A single link will add a rather unsightly join between the two items.

‹A HREF="gardens.html"›‹IMG SRC="garden.gif" ALT="photo of the college gardens and lake, 10k"›‹/A›
‹A HREF="gardens.html"›Worcester Gardens‹/A›

will look better than

‹A HREF="gardens.html"›‹IMG SRC="garden.gif" ALT="photo of the college gardens and lake, 10k"› Worcester Gardens‹/A›

SHOULD YOU WARN ABOUT THE SIZE?

Something that seems to be rather uncommon at the moment is any indication of the sizes of images that people are using in their web sites. If you include large graphics, it might be a good idea to warn your readers about the size. A small note in brackets, (75k gif of Radcliffe Square) for example, is enough to assist your readers. Obviously, the smaller the image is, the faster it will download.

REUSING GRAPHICS

If you reuse the same graphics throughout your web site, they will not need to be downloaded separately for each page. Most browsers will *cache* any downloaded graphics, unless they are above a certain size, and then reuse the cached version rather than downloading it repeatedly from the server. When an image is cached, it is stored locally, on the reader's computer. Each time the image is reused, it is pulled from the local hard disk rather than from the remote Web server.

To benefit from this, it is important to remember to use not just the same graphic, but the same graphics file. If you use several versions of an identical graphic, they will be treated as different graphics.

This caching of images can save a great deal of time, and it is worth taking advantage of this feature. The more smoothly your pages can download, the greater their visual impact. If you develop a standard set of buttons and page furniture to use throughout the site, once they have been downloaded the first time, they will drop into subsequent pages very quickly. There is a small delay as the images redraw, but it is considerably less than reloading them from the server. A Netscape feature—frames—which is explained in "Section 3: Advanced HTML" allows you to leave some areas of the page intact, removing the need even for the delay that stems from redrawing. Anything that you can do to speed the loading of a page, without damaging the appearance of the page, you should consider.

Colours and palettes

A GIF can contain its own palette of 256 colours, but you can choose to use fewer. The fewer colours you use, the smaller the graphic will be. The less information a graphics file contains, the less space it will consume. The best way of reducing the colours in your image is by reducing the pixel depth—that is by using a 3 or 4 bit image (8 or 16 colours), rather than an eight (256 colours) bit image. Even using a 6 bit image (64 colours) can make a considerable difference. The graphics software you use to produce your images should give you the option to adjust the number of colours. There are software packages that can give you a high level of control over this, and let you adjust the individual colours used. If it is at all possible to reduce the number of colours in your image without affecting its quality—reduce the colours.

Keeping a consistent colour palette on a page, if not on the whole site, can also speed up your image loading, and prevent strange colour variations and unpleasant dithering as each image loads. Browsers, on the whole, can support a maximum of 256 colours on a single page. These colours are allocated on a first come, first served basis. The first images to load on the page will claim the allocation of colours. Later images, if they require a different palette, will be dithered in an attempt to fit in with the palette established by the earlier images.

One way around this is to make sure that all the images you plan to use on a page share the same palette of fewer than 256 colours. Again, you will need to set these limits in your graphics software, rather than controlling them from the HTML file. You could, for example, paste all the images you plan to use into a single Photoshop file, then switch to index colour/adaptive with no dithering. This will establish a palette to accommodate all your images. Check the quality of each part before continuing. Once you have your palette, you will need to return to the individual image files and index each palette to this preset palette. Do not attempt to cut out pieces from the super-graphic, because they will not look as good.

Some time spent optimising your images for the Web can make your site speedier to download, and better looking overall. Careful choice of colour palettes as you create the images will allow you to retain the quality without over-burdening the reader's bandwidth.

GIFs and JPEGs

All graphical browsers can display GIFs on Web pages, but some can also display JPEGs. JPEG is a graphics file format with adjustable levels of lossy file compression. When you create a JPEG, you can choose the balance of compression and quality depending on your needs. JPEGs can contain millions of colours, rather than having an upper limit of 256 colours.

Not all browsers can display inline JPEGs. They may be downloaded, saved and viewed in an external helper application but they will not be displayed on the Web page. Until JPEGs are accepted as an additional standard for the Web, if you want to ensure that your images are an integral part of the page you should stick to using GIFs.

You may, however, want to provide links to JPEG images outside the main pages. If you have a small thumbnail GIF on a Web page, you can build a link to a larger, higher quality JPEG version for interested readers to download. This does not put any additional demands on a casual reader, but can be a good way of distributing high quality images across the Web.

If you want to provide a link to an external JPEG, you can reference it like this:

```
<A HREF="sheldonian.jpeg"><IMG SRC="sheldonian.gif" ALT="16k gif of the
Sheldonian Theatre, linked to 100k JPEG"></A>
```

Clicking on the small GIF will download the larger JPEG to a new page of its own.

TRANSPARENCY

Almost all graphical browsers support transparent images—that is they can support the GIF 89a format. Rather than being constrained to a rectangular image, you can define a custom outline by making the image *background* transparent. The image is still treated as a rectangle on the page, even though the displayed image may be irregular or round. After setting the background of the image to a single colour, you can choose to remove that colour, so that the background colour of the browser window shows through as in figure 12.

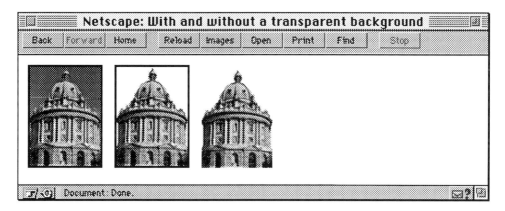

Figure 12: A regular image, and the same image with a transparent background with and without a border

One rather neat trick that you can use is complete transparency. If you create an image of a single colour, and set that colour to transparent, you will have a completely invisible image. This can be used to add white space to your page. The only downfall of this trick occurs if a reader arrives at the page with images turned off. Instead of a clear space, they will see the icon for a broken GIF. Only if they load the images will the image disappear. Remember that you can strip down the image's palette to only one bit (2 colours). This will keep the size down to a minimum.

There are plenty of shareware applications that enable you to set your transparent colour with a single click of the mouse. There is more information about these utilities in the appendix. The ability to make images transparent is already being built into high end graphics software.

CHAPTER 11

More about Links

This chapter goes into more detail about hyperlinks, how to decode them and how to construct them, allowing you to build and control more complex Web sites.

THE ANATOMY OF AN URL

Before using many-layered directory structures, you need a clear understanding or how URLs are constructed. Every page on the World Wide Web has a unique address, in the form of an URL, or Uniform Resource Locator. Usually pronounced "earl", sometimes spelled out U. R. L. A typical example might look like this:

http://www.question.co.uk/oxford/bodleian/radcliffe.html

The basic structure of an URL is:

protocol://www.company.com/folder/file.html

Working backwards, from right to left, the URL is fairly easy to understand. Each element of the URL is separated by a forward slash, each of which indicates another level in the directory hierachy. The final element of the address (file.html) is the individual file—an HTML file, an image, a movie or a sound. The level directly above that is the folder that file is in (folder). Above that can be any number of folders, and some URLs can be extremely long. The preceding part of the URL is the domain name, or name of the host machine (www.company.com). This will often start with "www" to indicate the connection to the Web. Web servers do not need this prefix, but is fairly common. This part of the URL can give a good indication of the physical location of the machine. A ".co.jp" domain is a company in Japan, for example, and ".ac.uk" would be one of the universities in Britain, equivalent to the ".edu" ending elsewhere in the world. Most companies in the US use a ".com" domain, although this is not exclusively American.

The protocol (http) is the method of delivery—on the Web it will almost always be hypertext transfer protocol, http. Other areas of the Internet can be accessed through the Web using protocols such as *ftp* (file transfer protocol), *gopher,* or *news.* These will be covered in more detail later in this chapter.

ABSOLUTE AND RELATIVE PATHS

When linking to other HTML files, or image files, you can use either absolute or relative paths. An absolute path uses the full URL of the file in question, for example:

<IMG SRC="http://www.question.co.uk/oxford/bodleian/radcliffe.html">

An absolute path pinpoints the specific file, regardless of where the tag is used, and will always be the same from anywhere on the World Wide Web. Relative paths, on the other hand, locate the file in relation to the position of the current file.

Say, for example, that the HTML file radcliffe.html was in the folder bodleian in the folder oxford. (If you have any trouble visualising the directory structure used in these examples, see figure 13 for a screen shot.) If you wanted to build a link to the file sheldonian.html in the same folder, bodleian, the link tag would look like this:

<A HREF="sheldonian.html">

If, instead, you wanted use the image radcliffe.gif which was inside the folder images, also inside the folder bodleian, the link tag would take the following form:

<A HREF="images/radcliffe.gif">

The forward slash is used to move down one level in the directory structure. The file, radcliffe.html, is at the same level as the folder, images, and the image file radcliffe.gif is inside it. The absolute URLs of these files are:

http://www.question.co.uk/oxford/bodleian/radcliffe.html
http://www.question.co.uk/oxford/bodleian/sheldonian.html
http://www.question.co.uk/oxford/bodleian/images/radcliffe.gif

If you wanted to link from the file radcliffe.html to a file on a "higher" level of the directory structure, colleges.html, where the absolute URL was:

http://www.question.co.uk/oxford/colleges.html

you would need to use a tag like this:

‹A HREF="../colleges.html"›

The "../" is used to instruct the browser to request a file from the next level up in the directory. Without the "../" the browser would try to download the file from the same directory level as the current file. If you use repeated "../" the browser is instructed to move up one level for each "../". For example:

‹A HREF="../../search.html"›

You can use a relative path to move up a couple of levels, and then down a different branch of the hierarchy.
If you wanted to link from

http://www.question.co.uk/oxford/bodleian/divinity.html

to

http://www.question.co.uk/oxford/colleges/new/chapel.html

your link tag would take the following form:

‹A HREF="../colleges/new/chapel.html"›

This has moved up one level of the directory structure, then down through the folder colleges into the folder new for the file chapel.html.

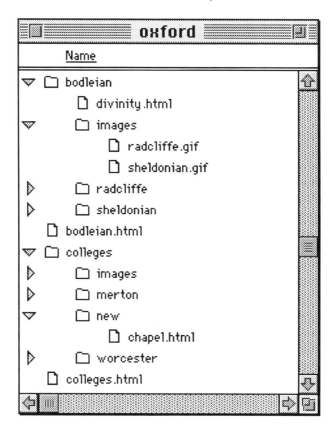

Figure 13: The directory structure for these examples

Once you have a clear picture of the structure of your file directory, relative paths are very easy to use. You may find it useful to draw a diagram of the hierarchy structure. If you keep a print out of the directory window to hand as you build the Web site, you shouldn't have too much trouble working with the hierarchy.

The great advantage of relative over absolute paths will become clear if you ever have to move your Web site from one machine to another. If you build the site on one machine, and then transfer it to another when you want it to go "live", you will have to change every single one of your links if you have used absolute paths. If you have used only relative paths, the whole site can be moved without any alteration.

LINKING TO A SPECIFIC PLACE IN A DOCUMENT

By specifying a target point, it is possible to build a link that goes not to the top of the linked page, but to a particular point on that page. This can be particularly useful when you are working with very long pages that may need a little more in the way of navigation. You can build a link to a later point in the text, for example, or a footnote. It is possible to link to a target within the same page, or from one page to another.

Setting the target point is the first step. The target point can be either text or an image. As with any other hyperlink, the link itself can also be either text or an image.

The target point is tagged with a name:

```
<DL>
<DT><A NAME="hawksmoor"><B>Nicholas Hawksmoor</B> 1661-1736</A>
<P>
<DD>Nicholas Hawksmoor is the most famous student and disciple of the
great Renaissance architect Sir Christopher Wren. Hawksmoor's most famous
Oxford buildings are the main quad, hall and chapel of Queen's College
(1710-19); the Clarendon Building at the Oxford University Press (1713); the
library at Worcester College (1714) and the north quadrangle at All Souls'
College (1720-35). He is also well known for his series of London churches.
</P>
```

The link to a target is very similar to that used for linking to another file, but with the addition of a hash mark, #. If the target was on the same web page as the link, the link would be formed like this:

‹P›

Certainly the most impressive of these buildings is
‹A HREF="#hawksmoor"›Nicholas Hawksmoor's‹/A› library, which rises above
the cloister in an elegant windowed facade.
‹/P›

If this link was clicked, there would be a jump to the target point that you have set.
If the link was on a different page from the target, the target name (#name) follows the
path to the file:

‹P›

Certainly the most impressive of these buildings is
‹A HREF="../../architects/index.html#hawksmoor"›Nicholas Hawksmoor's‹/A›
library, which rises above the cloister in an elegant windowed facade.
‹/P›

This links to the target hawksmoor in the file index.html, which is in the folder
architects at the same directory level as the folder colleges.

PUTTING IT ALL TOGETHER

Read through the following HTML file, quadhistory.html, comparing it to the examples
so far. Have a look at figure 14 which shows this file as a web page viewed with
Netscape. The final appearance would vary if it were viewed in another browser, but
the basic structure would remain the same.

Once you have a basic grasp of the structure and the tags used, read through the
breakdown that follows. Notice that there are some tags that haven't been covered
yet—these will be explained very soon.

‹!--http://www.question.co.uk/oxford/colleges/worcester/quadhistory.html--›
‹HTML›
‹HEAD›

\<TITLE\>The History of Worcester's Main Quad\</TITLE\>

\</HEAD\>

\<BODY\>

\<BLOCKQUOTE\>

\<H1\>The History of Worcester's Main Quad\</H1\>

\<PRE\>\</PRE\>

\<P\>

Worcester College is built on the site of Gloucester College, which was founded in 1283 as a college for Benedictine monks. The mediaeval cottages (\<A HREF="images/cottages.jpeg"\>60k jpeg\</A\>) on the south side of the main quad are the most substantial surviving part of Gloucester College. They are among the oldest residential buildings still in use in Oxford.

\</P\>

\<P\>

In 1539, the college was dissolved during the Dissolution of the Monasteries under Henry VIII, and the site was unused for academic purposes until 1560. This year saw the foundation of Gloucester Hall.

\</P\>

\<P\>

\<IMG ALIGN=LEFT SRC="images/northquad.gif" ALT="photo of North Quad, 10k"\>

The next substantial addition to the college came in 1714, when Thomas Cookes, a Worcestershire baronet, provided the college with a large benefaction. This led to the refounding of the institution as \<A HREF="worcester.html"\>Worcester College\</A\> and the construction of the eighteenth century buildings on the north and south sides of the quad.

\</P\>

\<P\>

Certainly the most impressive of these buildings is \<A HREF="../../architects/index.html#hawksmoor"\>Nicholas Hawksmoor's\</A\> library, which rises above the cloister in an elegant windowed facade. Its grandeur is reinforced by the slope down to the sunken quadrangle. In 1536, Sir George Clark guaranteed the importance of the library with a gift of his collection of books and manuscripts. These included a large proportion of the drawings of ‹A HREF="../../architects/index.html#jones"›Inigo Jones‹/A› and a wealth of papers covering the history of England during the period of the Commonwealth.

‹/P›

‹P›

At the same time, work was in progress on ‹A HREF="../../architects/index.html#wyatt"›James Wyatt's‹/A› hall and chapel, which lie beneath the libary. Through lack of funds, these were not completed until the 1770s. The same financial embarrassment had a surprisingly positive effect. The mediaeval cottages, which were to have been demolished to make way for a second classical building, survived intact and contribute to the beauty of the quad.

‹/P›

‹P ALIGN=CENTER›

‹A HREF="../../index.html"›index‹/A› |

‹A HREF="../../maps/index.html"›maps‹/A› |

‹A HREF="../../colleges/index.html"›colleges‹/A› |

‹A HREF="../../search.html"›search‹/A›

‹/P›

‹PRE›‹/PRE›

‹P›

‹ADDRESS›Katie Blakstad Cooke, email

‹A HREF="mailto:katie@question.co.uk"›katie@question.co.uk‹/A›

‹/ADDRESS›

‹/P›

‹/BLOCKQUOTE›

‹/BODY›

‹/HTML›

Back | Forward | Home | Reload | Images | Open | Print | Find | Stop

The History of Worcester's Main Quad

Worcester College is built on the site of Gloucester College, which was founded in 1283 as a college for Benedictine monks. The mediaeval cottages (60k jpeg) on the south side of the main quad are the most substantial surviving part of Gloucester College. They are among the oldest residential buildings still in use in Oxford.

In 1539, the college was dissolved during the Dissolution of the Monasteries under Henry VIII, and the site was unused for academic purposes until 1560. This year saw the foundation of Gloucester Hall.

The next substantial addition to the college came in 1714, when Thomas Cookes, a Worcestershire baronet, provided the college with a large benefaction. This lead to the refounding of the institution as Worcester College and the construction of the eighteenth century buildings on the north and south sides of the quad.

Certainly the most impressive of these buildings is Nicholas Hawksmoor's library, which rises above the cloister in an elegant windowed facade. Its grandeur is reinforced by the slope down to the sunken quadrangle. In 1536, Sir George Clark guaranteed the importance of the library with a gift of his collection of books and manuscripts. These included a large proportion of the drawings of Inigo Jones and a wealth of papers covering the history of England during the period of the Commonwealth.

At the same time, work was in progress on James Wyatt's hall and chapel, which lie beneath the libary. Through lack of funds, these were not completed until the 1770s. The same financial embarassment had a surprisingly positive effect. The mediaeval cottages, which were to have been demolished to make way for a second classical building, survived intact and contribute to the beauty of the quad.

index | maps | colleges | search

Katie Blakstad Cooke, email katie@question.co.uk

Figure 14: quadhistory.html viewed with Netscape

The first line used in this HTML is a comment. Nothing contained in the comment will display on the page, nor will it affect the function of the page. The comments are useful to the production team, who will need to keep track of the URL of each page. Printing out the HTML, this will be the only indication of the file name, and its place within the directory structure. Some site builders put the URL on the Web pages themselves.

Although this is very useful, it is not always appropriate, especially in sites intended for a non-technical audience. Other comment lines in the HTML could include a note of when the page was last updated, and by whom.

The page is set up as an HTML file with ‹HTML›‹/HTML› and divided into head and body sections with ‹HEAD›‹/HEAD› and ‹BODY›‹/BODY›. The head section only contains the document title, in this case "The History of Worcester's Main Quad".

The title is repeated on the page with a top level heading. There are no subheadings on this page.

Each paragraph of the page is tagged top and bottom with ‹P›‹/P›. Remember that you cannot add additional white space with repeated paragraph tags, or line breaks. Your browser will ignore any extra ‹P› tags.

The page contains a link to an external JPEG image of the cottages. Clicking on this link will download the JPEG that has been specified. There is a main image on the page, aligned to the side of a block of text. Image alignment is covered in a later section. The image is sourced with the ‹IMG SRC="URL"› tag, and alternative text is supplied with the ALT element. The alternative text will be seen only if the image is not displayed. The text is used here to indicate what the picture is and how large it is.

This page contains several links, although some of them are going to the same destination page. The link in the third paragraph of the main text is to a Web page that includes an introduction to Worcester college. The file worcester.html is in the same folder as the current file, quadhistory.html. The next paragraph has two further links, each linking to a different target point on the page architects.html. These target points have been specified with ‹A NAME="target name"› on the destination page. Each link here will jump to the specific point on the page where that particular architect is discussed. The graphics are sourced from a sub-folder, images, within the current folder, worcester.

The site-wide links at the end of the page are separated from the content with a couple of lines of white space. This is acheived using preformatting. Everything contained within the ‹PRE›‹/PRE› tags is displayed within the page—including every space and every carriage return.

Most of these links are to Web pages that are on different levels of the directory structure. The "search" link, for example, is two levels up from the current file, loose at the same level as the folder colleges. The "maps" link points to a page inside the maps folder, which is also two levels up from the current file, at the same level as the folder colleges.

The site wide navigation links are followed with an address, that contains a name and email address for the person responsible for the Web site. This strand could also be used for copyright information or a date. The email address has a "mailto" link which is covered next.

LINKING TO OTHER PARTS OF THE INTERNET FROM THE WEB

As the Internet has grown, various methods of storing and accessing information have been developed. Almost all of these can be accessed via the World Wide Web. You can, for example, access ftp file archives, news groups and email through hyperlinks.

One of the most useful aspects of the Internet has to be email. The immediacy of contact that email provides is an excellent crossover point between the telephone and the letter. On the Web, email can provide a point of contact with the authors, designers and publishers of the site, or the Web keeper responsible for the technical running of the server. If an email link, or "mailto" is built into a page, readers are encouraged to respond. You can ask for feedback, field questions or just establish contact. Building an email link into your site is very simple.

A mailto is a variation on the standard ‹A HREF› tag and takes the following form:

You can email comments to:
‹A HREF="mailto:katie@question.co.uk"›katie@question.co.uk‹/A›

Clicking on this link on the page would bring up an email message window, or launch the reader's email application, depending on the browser. It is worth including a text version of your email address, just in case the mail link is broken, or the server is down.

Accessing other areas of the Web, such as ftp sites, news groups or gopher space, is as simple as providing a mail link. You need to know the full URL, including the protocol, just as you do when you are linking to any external resource. If for example you wanted to build in a link to a related news group, the link would be:

news://name of newsgroup

and an ftp link would be:

ftp://full address of the ftp site/folder/

Once you have clicked on this sort of link, a new Web page will appear showing the postings to the newsgroups, or the directory structure of the ftp site. If your ftp link points to a particular file, rather than to a directory, the file will start to download automatically. If you are providing a link to a piece of downloadable software, you should give an indication of which platform it is for, and its size:

‹A HREF="ftp://address of the site/pub/mac/invaders.sea.hqx"›Invaders‹/A›
(Mac version 120k)

Chapter 12

Forms

Forms allow the reader to interact directly with the Web page. By filling in a form, a reader can request information, provide details about themselves, vote, make an order. Forms make a Web page a two way experience. This chapter will lead you through the stages of constructing a form, from a very simple text entry box to a more sophisicated form made up of a mixture of multiple choice selections.

The most common forms on the Web at the moment are probably feedback forms and registration forms. Feedback forms allow readers to give their opinion about something, usually the content of a Web site. This gives the readers a valuable voice. Ideally, there will be someone on the other end who will read the comments submitted through the form and act upon them. Without some response, the form becomes meaningless. Using forms, Web developers can canvass opinion and encourage direct feedback. Filling in a form is very quick and simple, and unless you are asking unneccessarily personal questions, most readers are very happy to take the time to give their opinion. The immediacy of contact that Web forms provide is a great advantage. Readers can send a message without leaving the site itself, with no fussing about checking the address, finding paper, an envelope, stamps or dealing wth the postal service. A message sent through a Web site is fast and simple for a reader to use.

Forms can be used for anything that requires an exchange of information. Forms can be used to trigger different sorts of results—a phone call from technical support, a delivery of pizza, a personalised Web page created on the spot. As a reader, forms give you input; as a developer forms give you contact with your audience.

WHAT MAKES FORMS WORK?

A reader fills out a form, and then submits it using a button that is usually marked "submit". The contents of the form are then sent on in a way that has been specified by the developer, in the ‹FORM› tag. The contents of the form are passed on to an URL, where they are usually handled by a script that has been set up on the server. The script you use depends on how you intend to use the information from the form. The simplest method is to gather the text that the user has entered, and email it on to the relevant person.

Forms will not work without a script, although it is unlikely that you will need to write the script yourself. There are dozens of ready made freeware, shareware and commercial scripts available, and you should be able to find one that suits your needs and your server. Some of the sources of ready made scripts, or tutorials if you want to do it yourself, are covered in Section 4: Beyond HTML and in the appendices.

Some browsers do not support forms. If you would like to provide a feedback option for readers who may be using a browser that does not support forms, you should provide an email alternative. Use a mailto link, and make sure that the relevant email address is clearly marked on the page. This applies only to older browsers — forms are now part of "standard" HTML, rather than the proposed HTML 3.0 changes, or Netscape extensions.

Forms can be added to any page of HTML, and you should not dispense with the basic framework of head and body or any other layout and design that you are using.

BUILDING FORMS WITH HTML

The starting points for any form are the ‹FORM›‹/FORM› tags to mark the extent of the form on the page. Without these tags, the form will not work. You can use multiple forms in a single page, but be careful not to confuse your readers. You cannot have one form within another.

You need to specify what should be done with the user's input. The ACTION and METHOD elements contain instructions for the use of the form. The ACTION always points to an URL. In this case the URL is that of a script to process the form and return the results to me. The METHOD specifies which protocol is used to send the form's contents to the URL. The default METHOD is GET, but you will almost certainly use

POST. The action and the URL will vary according to the server and the script being used to process your form. What happens to the information within the form depends on the script—it could be emailed to you, for example, or added directly to a database. If you do not plan to write the scripts yourself, check with the person who will be if you are unsure about the action or the method.

A reader will enter information into this form by typing into the text input boxes.

```
<HEAD>
<TITLE>A simple text entry form</TITLE>
</HEAD>
<BODY>
<H1>A simple text entry form</H1>
<P>
This form has a single box. Please type in your favourite word.
</P>
<FORM
ACTION="http://www.question.co.uk/ismcomics/cgi-bin/mail-form"
METHOD="POST">
<P>
my favourite word: <INPUT NAME="word">
</P>
<P>
You can now <INPUT TYPE="SUBMIT" VALUE="submit"> your word
</P>
</FORM>
</BODY>
</HTML>
```

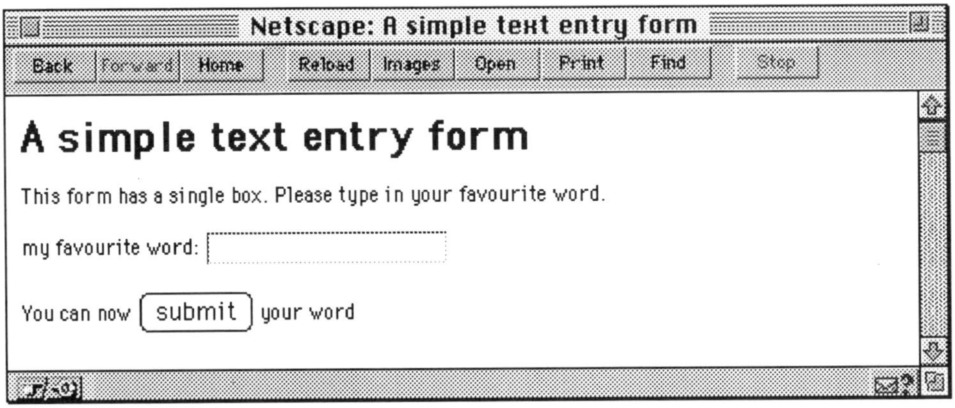

Figure 15: A simple text form

The input box is a simple, single line in which a reader can type. Although the text box is fairly short, readers will be able to type in as many characters as they need. The text will scroll off out of view as the reader continues to type.

This field is given a NAME, which should have some connection to the field's content, to distinguish it from other fields. The NAME allocates a name to the input field. If the filled in form is being converted to a text file and emailed back to you, or added to a database, this information can be very useful. Choose a meaningful name.

To use any other form of input, such as a check box or a submit button, you need to specify which TYPE of input you want to use. The button at the end of the form is a standard submit button, set by adding the TYPE=SUBMIT element to the INPUT tag. The VALUE of a submit button is displayed on the button itself. You could, for example, use something like ‹INPUT TYPE="SUBMIT" VALUE="send it"› or ‹INPUT TYPE="SUBMIT" VALUE="blast off"› instead. If you would like to offer readers the chance to clear the form and start again, you can add a RESET button:

‹INPUT TYPE="RESET" VALUE="clear"›

If the reader presses this button, all the information they have added to the form will be removed.

You can have multiple text entry fields in a single form. Each text entry field has a distinct NAME attribute.

```
<HTML>
<HEAD>
<TITLE>A simple text entry form with multiple text fields</TITLE>
</HEAD>
<BODY>
<H1>A simple text entry form</H1>
<P>
This form has three boxes. Please use them to type in your favourite things.
</P>
<FORM
ACTION="http://www.question.co.uk/ismcomics/cgi-bin/mail-form"
METHOD="POST">
<P>
my favourite word: <INPUT NAME="word">
</P>
<P>
my favourite colour: <INPUT NAME="colour">
</P>
<P>
my favourite hat: <INPUT NAME="hat">
</P>
<P>
You can now <INPUT TYPE="SUBMIT" VALUE="tell me"> or
<INPUT TYPE="RESET" VALUE="forget it">
</P>
</FORM>
</BODY>
</HTML>
```

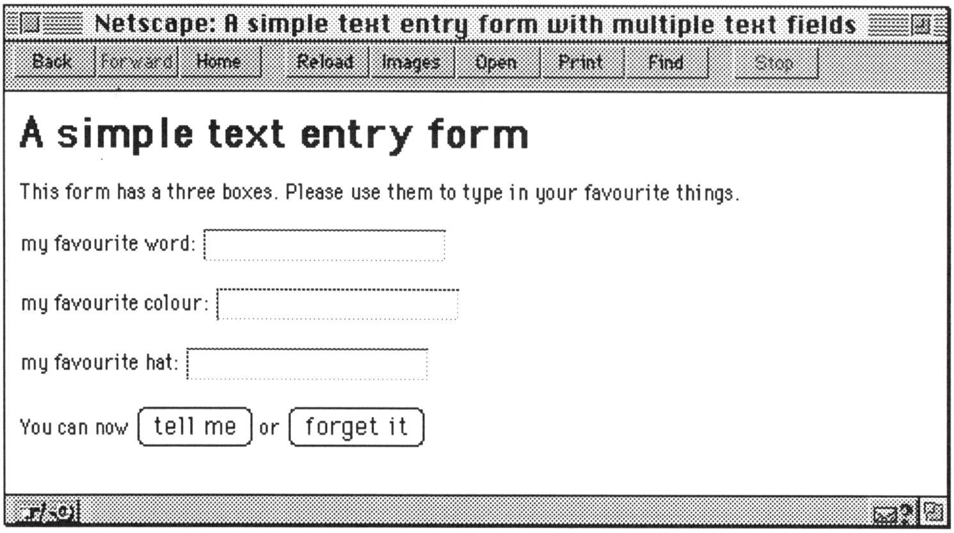

Figure 16: A simple text form with multiple text fields

You can choose to set the size of the text input boxes. In the next example, the "who are you" section contains examples of input boxes, which allows the reader to type in her name and email address. The SIZE is measured in pixels, and sets the length of the input box.

The length of the box has nothing to do with how many characters a reader is able to type. If you want to set a maximum, MAXLENGTH sets a limit on the number of characters that can be entered into a text input box. In this example, the size and the maximum length are the same, but they need not correspond. It might not be a good idea to set the MAXLENGTH shorter than the size as it can be disconcerting for a user if she cannot type up to the end of the box.

This example uses preformatted text to line the boxes up.

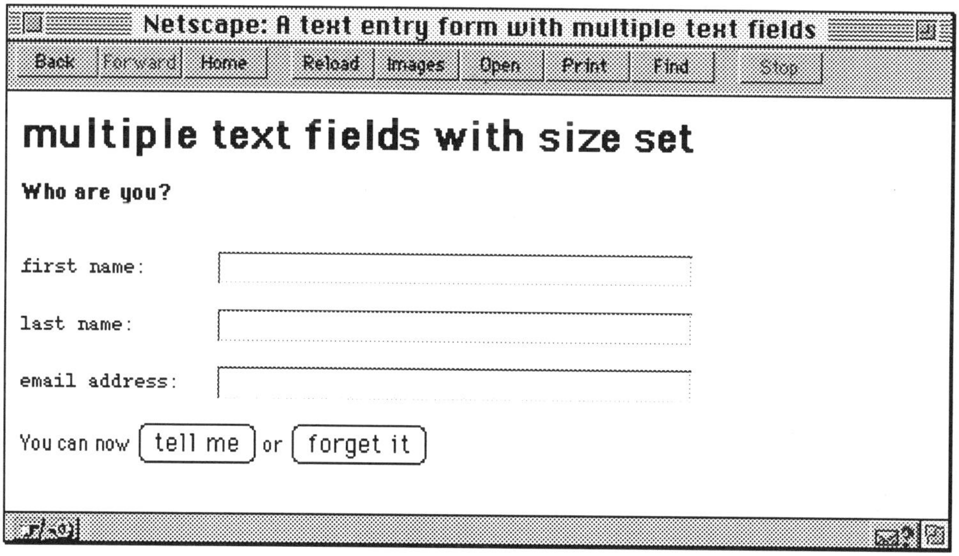

Figure 17: A simple text form with multiple set length text fields

```
<HEAD>
<TITLE>A text entry form with multiple text fields</TITLE>
</HEAD>

<BODY>
<H1>multiple text fields with size set</H1>
<FORM
ACTION="http://www.question.co.uk/ismcomics/cgi-bin/mail-form"
METHOD="POST">
<P>
<B>Who are you?</B>
</P>
<PRE>
first name:      <INPUT SIZE=40 MAXLENGTH=40 NAME="name">
```

```
last name:       <INPUT SIZE=40 MAXLENGTH=40 NAME="last">

email address:   <INPUT SIZE=40 MAXLENGTH=40 NAME="email">
</PRE>
<P>
You can now <INPUT TYPE="SUBMIT" VALUE="tell me"> or
<INPUT TYPE="RESET" VALUE="forget it">
</P>
</FORM>
</BODY>
</HTML>
```

CHECKBOXES AND RADIO BUTTONS

Checkboxes are a simple way of gathering information. Readers do not have to type anything, they can just click their mouse on the appropriate boxes. By default, the checkboxes appear on the page unchecked, and the reader can check as many as they need to. The NAME for each checkbox can be the same, or can vary from box to box.

```
<HTML>
<HEAD>
<TITLE>talk to Ism Comics</TITLE>
</HEAD>
<BODY>
<H1>Talk to Ism comics</H1>
<FORM
ACTION="http://www.question.co.uk/ismcomics/cgi-bin/mail-form"
METHOD="POST">
<P>
<B>Who are you?</B>
</P>
```

```
<PRE>
first name:      <INPUT SIZE=40 MAXLENGTH=40 NAME="name">

last name:       <INPUT SIZE=40 MAXLENGTH=40 NAME="last">

email address:   <INPUT SIZE=40 MAXLENGTH=40 NAME="email">
</PRE>
<P>
<B>Which parts of the site have you visited?</B>
</P>
<P>
<INPUT TYPE="checkbox" NAME="visits" VALUE="comics"> the comics
anthology <BR>
<INPUT TYPE="checkbox" NAME="visits" VALUE="biogs"> the artists'
biographies <BR>
<INPUT TYPE="checkbox" NAME="visits" VALUE="background"> the
background information
<BR>
</P>
<P>
You can now <INPUT TYPE="SUBMIT" VALUE="send"> your answers or
<INPUT TYPE="RESET" VALUE="clear"> the form.
</P>
</FORM>
</BODY>
</HTML>
```

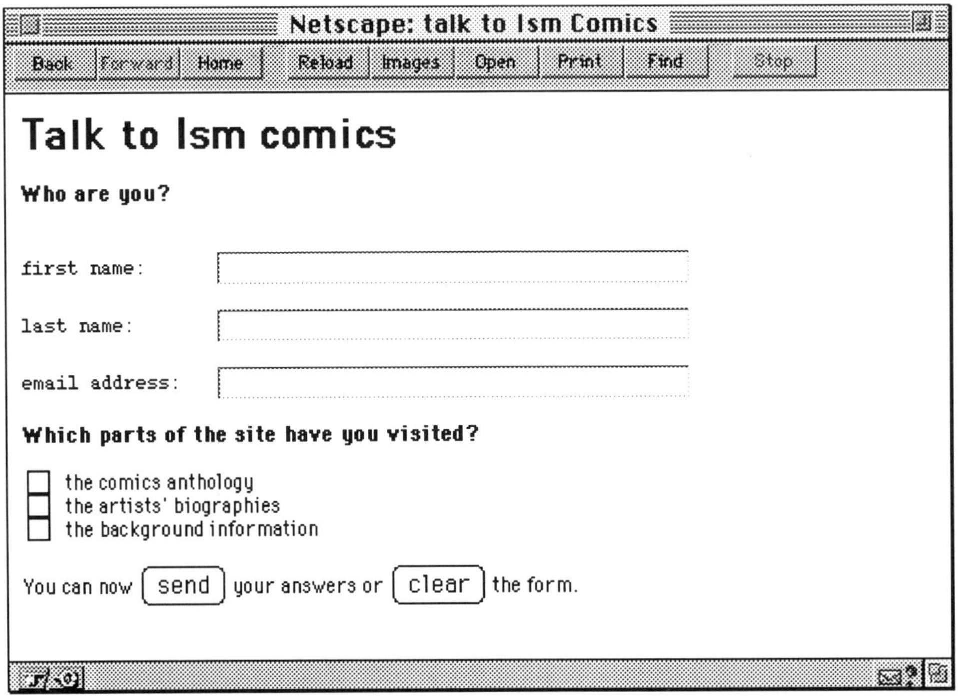

Figure 18: Form with checkboxes and text entry

Some questions may require a single answer from a range of choices, in which case radio buttons might be more suitable. If the buttons have the same NAME, they are treated as a group and readers may only choose one radio button from a single group.

In the following example, there are two sets of radio buttons.

```
<HTML>
<HEAD>
<TITLE>talk to Ism Comics</TITLE>
</HEAD>

<BODY>
<H1>Talk to Ism comics</H1>
```

```
<FORM
ACTION="http://www.question.co.uk/ismcomics/cgi-bin/mail-form"
METHOD="POST">
<P>
<B>Who are you?</B>
</P>
<PRE>
first name:      <INPUT SIZE=40 MAXLENGTH=40 NAME="name">

last name:       <INPUT SIZE=40 MAXLENGTH=40 NAME="last">

email address:   <INPUT SIZE=40 MAXLENGTH=40 NAME="email">
</PRE>
<P>
<B>Would you like us to email you some more information?</B>
</P>
<P>
<INPUT TYPE="radio" NAME="info" VALUE="yes"> yes
<INPUT TYPE="radio" NAME="info" VALUE="no"> no
</P>
<P>
<B>have you visited the site before?</B>
</P>
<P>
<INPUT TYPE="radio" NAME="visits" VALUE="no"> No, I've not been here
before <BR>
<INPUT TYPE="radio" NAME="visits" VALUE="once"> Yes, I've been here
once before <BR>
<INPUT TYPE="radio" NAME="visits" VALUE="all"> Yes, I live here <BR>
</P>
<P>
```

You can now ⟨INPUT TYPE="SUBMIT" VALUE="send"⟩ your answers or
⟨INPUT TYPE="RESET" VALUE="clear"⟩ the form.
⟨/P⟩
⟨/FORM⟩
⟨/BODY⟩
⟨/HTML⟩

You can set checkboxes, radio buttons and text inputs so they have a default setting. These are set by adding the CHECKED element to the input tag. Text input default
values are set by adding a VALUE to the input tag. The tag ⟨INPUT SIZE=40 NAME="user-
name" VALUE="guest"⟩ would be displayed with the word "guest" already filled in.

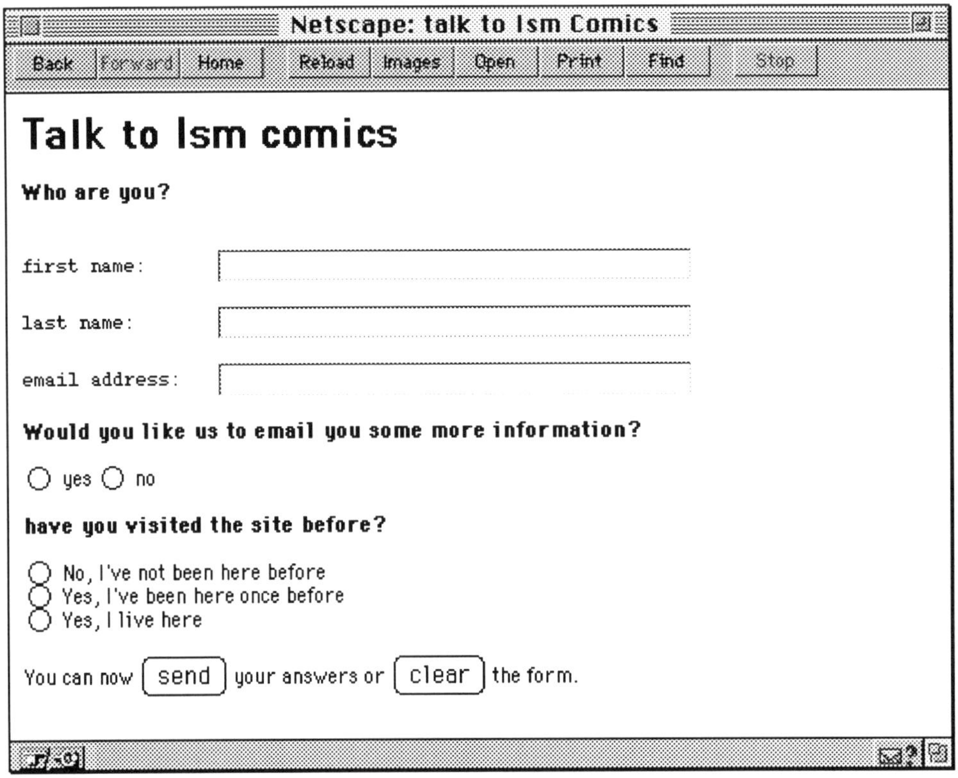

```
╔══════════════════════ Netscape: talk to Ism Comics ══════════════════════╗
║  ┌──────┐┌─────────┐┌──────┐  ┌──────┐┌──────┐┌──────┐┌──────┐┌──────┐┌─────────┐  ║
║  │ Back ││ Forward ││ Home │  │Reload││Images││ Open ││ Print││ Find ││  Stop   │  ║
║  └──────┘└─────────┘└──────┘  └──────┘└──────┘└──────┘└──────┘└──────┘└─────────┘  ║

    Talk to Ism comics
    Who are you?

    first name:      ┌──────────────────────────────────┐
                     └──────────────────────────────────┘
    last name:       ┌──────────────────────────────────┐
                     └──────────────────────────────────┘
    email address:   ┌──────────────────────────────────┐
                     └──────────────────────────────────┘

    Would you like us to email you some more information?

    ◯ yes ◯ no

    have you visited the site before?

    ◯  No, I've not been here before
    ◯  Yes, I've been here once before
    ◯  Yes, I live here

    You can now [ send ] your answers or [ clear ] the form.

╚═══════════════════════════════════════════════════════════════════════════╝
```

Figure 19: A form with two sets of radio buttons

SELECTION MENUS

You may want to offer a selection of choices in the form of an option menu, like this:

```
<HTML>
<HEAD>
<TITLE>a pop up menu</TITLE>
</HEAD>

<BODY>
<H1>a pop up menu</H1>
<FORM
ACTION="http://www.question.co.uk/ismcomics/cgi-bin/mail-form"
METHOD="POST">
<B>How old are you?</B>
<SELECT NAME="age">
<OPTION>under 18
<OPTION SELECTED>18-25
<OPTION>25-35
<OPTION>35+
</SELECT>
<P>
You can now <INPUT TYPE="SUBMIT" VALUE="send"> your answers or
<INPUT TYPE="RESET" VALUE="clear"> the form.
</P>
</FORM>
</BODY>
</HTML>
```

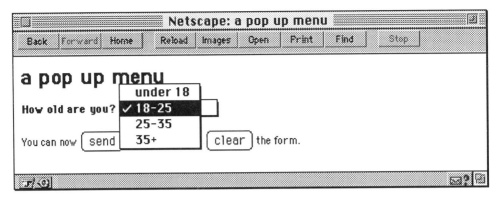

Figure 20: A pop up menu

The menu is set with the ‹SELECT›‹/SELECT› tags, and each option in the selection list is started with ‹OPTION› There is no corresponding ‹/OPTION› tag. You can set any of the options as a default, by adding SELECTED to the option in questions. If you do not include SELECTED, the first option on the list will be set as the default.

This selection list is displayed as a pop-up menu, but you might prefer a scrolling selection. You can set the list to a scrolling box by adding the SIZE element to the ‹SELECT› tag.

```
‹HTML›
.‹HEAD›
‹TITLE›a scrolling menu‹/TITLE›
‹/HEAD›

‹BODY›
‹H1›a scrolling menu‹/H1›
‹FORM
ACTION="http://www.question.co.uk/ismcomics/cgi-bin/mail-form"
METHOD="POST"›
‹B›How old are you?‹/B›
‹SELECT NAME="age" SIZE=4›
‹OPTION›under 18
```

```
<OPTION SELECTED>18-25
<OPTION>25-35
<OPTION>35+
</SELECT>
<P>
You can now <INPUT TYPE="SUBMIT" VALUE="send"> your answers or
<INPUT TYPE="RESET" VALUE="clear"> the form.
</P>
</FORM>
</BODY>
</HTML>
```

The SIZE is set to four, so all four options are displayed. If you set the SIZE to less than the number of options, the reader will need to scroll up and down to view the full list.

Only one of the options may be chosen. By adding MULTIPLE to the SELECT tag, readers will be able to choose more than one of the available options. You can also set multiple defaults within a selection menu.

```
<HTML>
<HEAD>
<TITLE>multiple options within a scrolling menu</TITLE>
</HEAD>

<BODY>
<H1>Talk to Ism comics</H1>
<FORM
ACTION="http://www.question.co.uk/ismcomics/cgi-bin/mail-form"
METHOD="POST">
<P>
<B>Which of the following would you like to see as part of Ism?</B>
</P>
```

```
<P>
<SELECT NAME="see" MULTIPLE SIZE=8>
<OPTION>longer comics
<OPTION SELECTED>more comics
<OPTION>more colour comics
<OPTION>more European comics
<OPTION>more Japanese comics
<OPTION>more American comics
<OPTION SELECTED>more background information
<OPTION>shop listings
<OPTION>more detailed biographies
<OPTION>artists' sketch books
</SELECT>
</P>
<P>
You can now <INPUT TYPE="SUBMIT" VALUE="send"> your answers or
<INPUT TYPE="RESET" VALUE="clear"> the form.
</P>
</FORM>
</BODY>
</HTML>
```

TEXT AREAS

In some parts of the form you may want to ask the reader to type in their comments. In this case, a multiple choice form built from radio buttons or check boxes is not suitable. The simple text entry fields do not encourage anything beyond a simple answer, and they can run to only one line. You can, however, give readers a larger space in which to type.

The area for text entry is set with the <TEXTAREA></TEXTAREA> tags. The size of the area is set in rows and columns.

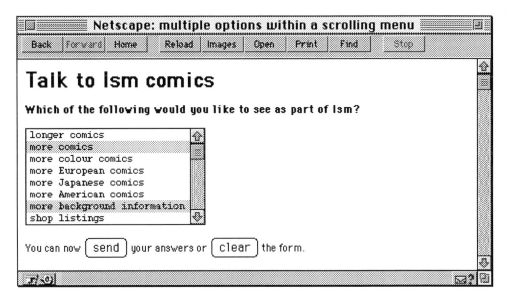

Figure 21: Multiple selection options

```
<HTML>
<HEAD>
<TITLE>text areas for comments</TITLE>
</HEAD>
<BODY>
<H1>text areas for comments</H1>
<FORM
ACTION="http://www.question.co.uk/ismcomics/cgi-bin/mail-form"
METHOD="POST">
<P>
<B>If you have any general comments, please type them here:</B>
</P>
<P>
<TEXTAREA NAME="comments" ROWS=6 COLUMNS=60></TEXTAREA>
</P>
```

‹P›

You can now ‹INPUT TYPE="SUBMIT" VALUE="send"› your answers or

‹INPUT TYPE="RESET" VALUE="clear"› the form.

‹/P›

‹/FORM›

‹/BODY›

‹/HTML›

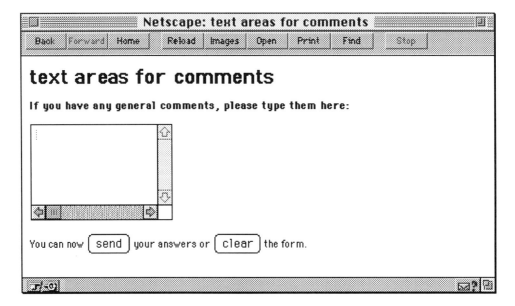

Figure 22: Text areas for comments

You can add some text of your own, which will appear inside the text entry area:

‹TEXTAREA NAME="comments" ROWS=6 COLUMNS=6o›

please type your comments here

‹/TEXTAREA›

PUTTING IT ALL TOGETHER

When you are building a form, think about which input type suits your purposes best. This form contains several of the input options, based on the type of response needed. The "who are you" section uses a definition list so that the input boxes line up without having to use preformatted text.

```
<HTML>
<HEAD>
<TITLE>Talk to Ism Comics</TITLE>
</HEAD>
<BODY>
<H1>Talk to Ism Comics</H1>
<FORM
ACTION="http://www.question.co.uk/ismcomics/cgi-bin/mail-form"
METHOD="POST">
<P>
We would like to know a little about you and what you think about Ism
Comics.
If your browser does not support forms, you can email your comments to
<A HREF="mailto:katie@question.co.uk">katie@question.co.uk</A>
</P>
<BLOCKQUOTE>
<P>
<B>Who are you?</B>
</P>
<DL>
<DT>first name:
<DD><INPUT SIZE=40 MAXLENGTH=40 NAME="name">
<DT>last name:
<DD><INPUT SIZE=40 MAXLENGTH=40 NAME="last">
```

```
<DT>email address:
<DD><INPUT SIZE=40 MAXLENGTH=40 NAME="email">
</DL>
<P>
<B>How old are you?</B>
<SELECT NAME="age">
<OPTION>under 18
<OPTION SELECTED>18-25
<OPTION>25-35
<OPTION>35+
</SELECT>
</P>
<P>
<B>Would you like us to email you some more information?</B>
</P>
<P>
<INPUT TYPE="radio" NAME="info" VALUE="yes" CHECKED> yes
<INPUT TYPE="radio" NAME="info" VALUE="no"> no
</P>
<P>
<B>Have you visited the site before?</B>
</P>
<P>
<INPUT TYPE="radio" NAME="visits" VALUE="no"> No, I've not been here
before <BR>
<INPUT TYPE="radio" NAME="visits" VALUE="once"> Yes, I've been here
once before <BR>
<INPUT TYPE="radio" NAME="visits" VALUE="all"> Yes, I live here <BR>
</P>
<P>
<B>Do you normally read many comics?</B>
```

\</P\>

\<P\>

\<INPUT TYPE="radio" NAME="reader" VALUE="frequent"\> Yes, I often read comics \<BR\>

\<INPUT TYPE="radio" NAME="reader" VALUE="create"\> I don't just read comics, I make them too \<BR\>

\<INPUT TYPE="radio" NAME="reader" VALUE="sometimes"\> I read comics sometimes \<BR\>

\<INPUT TYPE="radio" NAME="reader" VALUE="creator"\> No, I don't often read comics \<BR\>

\</P\>

\<P\>

\<B\>If you do read comics, where do you normally buy them?\</B\>

\</P\>

\<P\>

\<INPUT TYPE="checkbox" NAME="buy" VALUE="shop"\> a comic book shop \<BR\>

\<INPUT TYPE="checkbox" NAME="buy" VALUE="book"\> a regular book shop \<BR\>

\<INPUT TYPE="checkbox" NAME="buy" VALUE="borrow"\> I usually borrow them

\</P\>

\<P\>

\<B\>If you have any general comments about the site or the comics, please type them here:\</B\>

\</P\>

\<P\>

\<TEXTAREA NAME="comments" ROWS=6 COLUMNS=60\>\</TEXTAREA\>

\</P\>

\<P\>

You can now \<INPUT TYPE="SUBMIT" VALUE="send"\> your answers or

```
<INPUT TYPE="RESET" VALUE="clear"> the form.
</P>
</BLOCKQUOTE>
</FORM>
<P>
Thanks for taking the time to fill out this form, we appreciate your feedback.
</P>
</BODY>
</HTML>
```

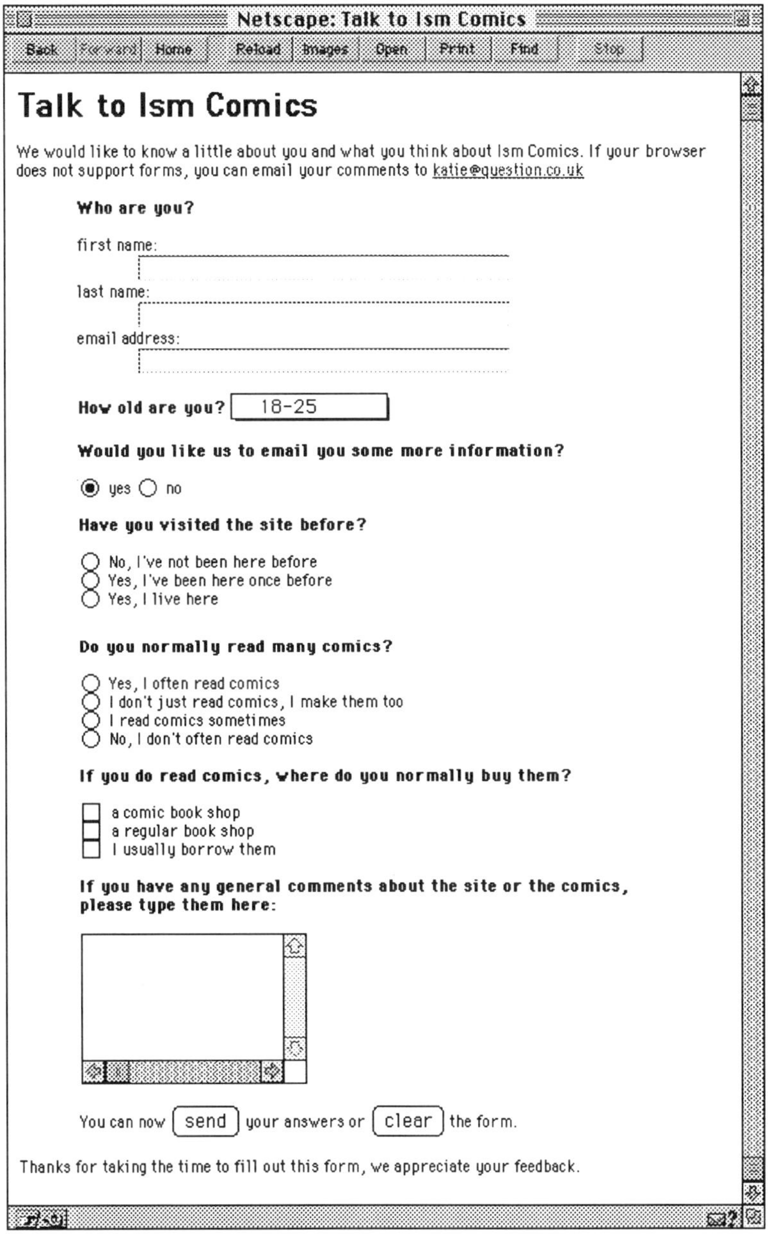

Back | Forward | Home | Reload | Images | Open | Print | Find | Stop

Talk to Ism Comics

We would like to know a little about you and what you think about Ism Comics. If your browser does not support forms, you can email your comments to katie@question.co.uk

Who are you?

first name:

last name:

email address:

How old are you? 18-25

Would you like us to email you some more information?

◉ yes ○ no

Have you visited the site before?

○ No, I've not been here before
○ Yes, I've been here once before
○ Yes, I live here

Do you normally read many comics?

○ Yes, I often read comics
○ I don't just read comics, I make them too
○ I read comics sometimes
○ No, I don't often read comics

If you do read comics, where do you normally buy them?

☐ a comic book shop
☐ a regular book shop
☐ I usually borrow them

If you have any general comments about the site or the comics, please type them here:

You can now [send] your answers or [clear] the form.

Thanks for taking the time to fill out this form, we appreciate your feedback.

Figure 23: A form with checkboxes, radio buttons and text areas

CHAPTER 13

Using a graphic as an image map

As a reader, you will almost certainly have come across a large number of image maps. An image map is a graphic that has multiple links within it.

Using a graphic as an image map is very straightforward. Rather than building single links on individual images, you will be setting areas *within* an image as hotspots. Once you have chosen a suitable graphic you need to go through a process of mapping areas of the graphic to URLs—turning them into links.

Each pixel of the graphic is specified by a pair of co-ordinates. By marking the boundaries of your hotspots, all the enclosed pixels can act as links.

The easiest way of setting up your image maps is to use a mapping application, such as WebMap on the Mac. There are a range of map applications available for all platforms and most of them are shareware, and some graphics packages like Fractal Painter 4.0 include a mapping feature. Load your GIF into the application and select areas of the image. Most applications will allow you to select rectangles, circles, ovals or irregular polygons. The boundaries of each hotspot will not be displayed on the graphic when it is displayed as part of a Web page. To indicate the hotspots visually you will need to do so on the graphic itself. The example in figure 24 shows one way of signalling the positions of the hotspots.

Once you have chosen the hotspots on the image, each one can be mapped to an URL. You should also set a default URL, for the areas not covered by the hotspots. Usually you will need to set these to absolute rather than relative URLs. The sets of co-ordinates and their corresponding target URLs need to be saved in text form, as a "map file". Figure 24 shows a map application with the selected hotspots and their URLs. Figure 25 is a .map file.

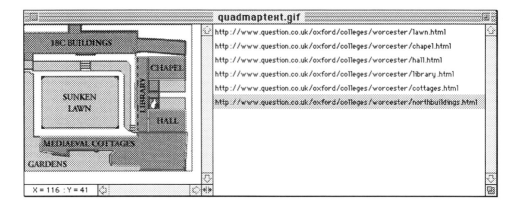

Figure 24: WebMap

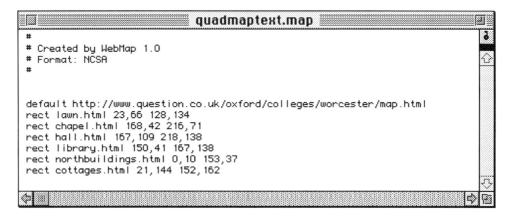

Figure 25: The .map file from figure 24

The mapping application will give you a choice of format, as there are two types of map—NCSA and CERN. Check with your server documentation, your Web keeper, or server administrator, which one you will need to use. You should also be aware that the line wrapping required by some UNIX machines will vary from the line wrapping, or line breaking on the platform that you are using. The application may give you the option to save to a UNIX compatible format. Again, it is worth checking with the web keeper if you are unsure.

The text file should be saved with a .map suffix. This is the map file that contains all the information for your image to work as a clickable image map. It will, however, do nothing on its own.

This method refers to server side image maps, that is maps that require a map file on the server in order to work. Netscape 2.0 and HTML 3.0 allow for client side image maps, maps that run without a server. These are covered in later chapters.

‹ISMAP›

The image itself needs an extra element in its tag: ISMAP. This is added in the following way:

```
‹IMG SRC="images/quadplan.gif" ISMAP›
```

This instructs the browser to treat the image as a map, but it still needs to be connected to the map file. This is added as if it were a normal hyperlink:

```
‹A HREF="../../../cgibin/quadplan.map"›
‹IMG SRC="images/quadplan.gif" ISMAP›‹/A›
```

This may or may not work, depending your particular server. To test your map you will need to open the page which it is on using the Web server protocol, http. The map will not function if you open the page as a local file. You may need to provide a direct reference to the script that will run your map file. Running MapServe.cgi (a Mac based map script) under MacHTTP the above example would look like this:

```
‹A HREF="../../../cgibin/MapServe.cgi$quadplan.map"›
‹IMG SRC="images/quadplan.gif" ISMAP›‹/A›
```

(assuming that the MapServe script was in the same folder as the .map file). If you are unsure of how to run your maps, check with your server administrator about the precise set up that you will need. Different map set ups will require different syntax, so the link to the map file will vary.

CHAPTER 14

Audio and video

Although you can include audio and video in your Web site, you should be aware of the current limitations upon them. Netscape 2.0 allows for the inclusion of Live Objects within a Web page, including QuickTime videos. Other than this, however, it is not possible to play the audio or video clips from within a Web page itself. The file will be downloaded, saved onto the reader's hard disk, and played through an external helper application. Most browsers allow readers to set the sound and video players of their choice. It is very difficult to integrate sound and video into a Web site without the ability to play them directly from the browser.

The other main problem with sound and video is the size. Video files, particularly, can be very large. Even a few seconds of video can run to several hundred k. Sound is smaller, especially if it is not extremely high quality, but is still considerably larger than text or graphics. Certain formats produce smaller files, but this depends on the compression systems that are part of the file formats themselves and cannot be controlled from the HTML.

DON'T MAKE VIDEO ESSENTIAL

Until there are significant inprovements in access speeds, it is unwise to make video essential in your Web site. The majority of Web users will not download long clips, unless they have a very good reason to do so. Video is seen very much as an optional extra, something that is fine as long as you have a fast or free connection to the Internet. If the video sections are necessary parts of your publication, there may be a better way of distributing the video that you can use in conjunction with your Web site. Do not underestimate the bandwidth of the postal system!

This said, well chosen video can add a great deal to your site. Make sure that video is the best medium for the information, however, rather than using it just because you have some material on video. A sequence of stills can be as effective as video, and requires far less bandwidth. But if you need to show how something moves, video is certainly the best option. Video is also the most understandable medium and does not require high levels of literacy to communicate complex visual messages.

Audio files are smaller, but the same considerations apply. Does the sound file take advantage of the medium? If the clip contains spoken word material, would a transcript be more effective? The use of music or examples of pronunciation are hard to replace with text.

The development of *Real Audio* allows almost real-time playback of sound files. Currently this can work only with fairly low quality audio, but the impact of immediate delivery is considerable. The sounds are played as they arrive, with only a small time lapse. This still requires an external sound player, but the file does not have to be completely downloaded before it can be played. If you want to include Real Audio in your Web site, you will need to use the Real Audio server software. Delivering Real Audio, or any other real time sound, is considerably harder on the server than on the receiver and requires a great deal of free bandwidth.

It is very important to mark video and sound clips with an indication of their size, format and platform compatibility. Video files can run to many megabytes, and readers will have to consider the time they might take to download.

If you want to include a few video files in your Web site, the simplest format is probably QuickTime. If you have created your QuickTime file on a Mac, it will need to be *flattened* so it will be playable on both Apple and IBM compatible machines (if they are equipped with the necessary player software). Most QuickTime programmes can flatten a file. The file should be given a name of no more than eight characters, to ensure the cross platform compatibilty. You need to add a ".mov" suffix to all your QuickTime files.

Most high end video generation and editing software for both Apple and Windows has a wide range of useful output options and allow you to control the level of compression. Allow yourself plenty of time to experiment with video to see the different effects and file sizes that are generated by different compression settings. Aim to get the best looking video possible at the smallest possible file size. Producing video files for the Web requires more time and more attention to detail than you may expect.

To include a video clip in a web page, you will need to build a hyperlink to it. The link to the clip in this example is anchored to a set of stills from the video itself. This helps to give the reader an idea of what the video is. Each still has a separate link to the same clip. On the page, this means that each graphic will have its own outline, rather than an all-encompassing group link. The size and length of the video is noted in the text version of the link.

```
<A HREF="video/row.mov"><IMG SRC="images/row1.gif" ALT="still image of
rowing, linked to movie"></A>
<A HREF="video/row.mov"><IMG SRC="images/row2.gif" ALT="still image of
rowing, linked to movie"></A>
<A HREF="video/row.mov"><IMG SRC="images/row3.gif" ALT="still image of
rowing, linked to movie"></A>
<P>
This series of images is taken from a video clip demonstrating the
<A HREF="video/row.mov">movement of the rowers</A> and their blades. This
QuickTime clip is 30 seconds long and 1.6Mb in size.
</P>
```

The most common formats for audio files on the Web are probably ".au" and ".aiff". There are large numbers of shareware and commercial players that can handle these formats on any platform. Sound clips are linked to a page in the same way as video.

There is a wide range of formats available from ".wav" to ".snd" and ".avi" to ".mpg"—if you want to include a fairly high concentration of video and audio you should probably talk over the options with a digital a/v specialist.

CHAPTER 15

Getting it all online

Once you have built your Web site, it will need to live on a Web server. This chapter is a very brief introduction to some of the things you will need to consider when getting your site online and does not cover how to configure a server.

Your Web site will need to live on a properly configured server that needs to have a permanent connection to the Internet, so that the site can be accessed at any time. A professional Web site cannot be run from a dial up account.

The server hardware can be a Mac, a PC or a UNIX machine, and there is server software available for all platforms. You should be aware that the machine will need to be maintained by someone with a fairly high level of technical expertise. It can be useful to set up your own machine with the server software, even if you do not intend to use it as a live Web server. Running HTTP on your own machine will allow you to test any image maps or other scripts before transferring your site to its final destination. If you are working on a Mac, it is very easy to install and configure WebSTAR, for example. There is a great deal of information available on the Net about setting up your server. Some of the sources are listed in the appendix.

You may choose to run your live Web server in-house, or use the services of a third party. There are many companies, from Internet access providers to Web production houses, that rent or supply maintained server space.

The files that make up your Web site will need to be stored on the Web server, and there are various methods for getting them there. If the Web server is part of your local network, you can transfer them directly. If the server is at a remote location you may be able to upload your files by ftp. If this is the case, you will need to obtain ftp access to the server. If you have any queries about this process, you should contact the server administrator.

Make sure that there is someone with the ultimate responsibility of checking that the correct versions of files are being loaded onto the server. Once the site has been uploaded onto the server, check *all* the pages, *all* the graphics, *all* the links and *all* the forms and other interactive elements. Once the site is live, it is extremely important that none of your links are broken. You may be able to protect your site from outside access while you are going through a testing and approval process. Your server administrator should be able to set up password protection for you.

If you are using space on someone else's server you may not need your own domain. If you want or need your own address, however, you will need to check that your domain name is correctly registered and set up. The domain name is the main address of your web site, and helps to give it an identity. Contact InterNIC for information about registering a domain (see the appendices for their URL), or ask your server administrator for more details.

If you want people to access your site using an URL such as:

http://www.question.co.uk

without a specific file name (filename.html), you can set the server up so that they receive the default page. This can vary from server to server but may be index.html, home.html or default.html. You will need to check the appropriate default names with the server administrator.

When your site goes live you will want to publicise it to a certain degree. You will probably want your site to be listed in the catalogues, listings and search engines that readers use to find information online. Visit the main search engines and check their guidelines for submitting a new site. There are several resources that allow you to submit your site to all the major listings from a single form. The URLs for some of these resources are in the appendices. This can be a great time saver but you may find that your site benefits from a more selective and controlled approach. Make sure that you allow enough time in your production and post-production schedule to make your site known.

Once your site is on a Web server and connected to the Internet, you will have published your Web site. It is hard to express the immense pleasure that you will feel when you receive your first email response from a visitor to your site.

3

Advanced HTML

HTML 3.0 and the status of the Netscape extensions

This section of the book covers the new tags and the new possibilities added to HTML by the Netscape extensions and HTML 3.0. These additions to HTML allow the Web developer far more control over the appearance and behaviour of a Web site.

If you have spent some time on the Web you will have seen plenty of pages that go far beyond the basic HTML covered in the previous section. If you are using a recent version of Netscape (1.1 or above) you will be able to view the variations of colours, backgrounds and alignment of text that many people have been implementing in their sites. These are already a fairly established part of Web design.

Netscape 2.0 goes far beyond the changes implemented in earlier versions—including more tags as well as fundamental changes to the behaviour of Web pages with the introduction of frames, client side image maps, live objects like Shockwave and JavaScript. This section covers the Netscape extensions to HTML, and some of the proposed changes that will be introduced with HTML 3.0. The changes introduced with Netscape 2.0 are at the end of this section rather than with the more established changes earlier in the section. The Microsoft Internet Explorer introduces further tags, and other elements, but these are not covered in this section.

WHAT IS HAPPENING WITH HTML 3.0?

At the time of writing, the specifications for HTML 3.0 are still in a draft or proposal stage. There are new drafts and proposals being prepared on an ongoing basis. To check the current status of HTML 3.0 you will need to refer to some of the resources covered in the appendices.

Although liable to change, HTML 3.0 should allow web designers to align text, flow text around images, overlay images, build image maps that do not require server based scripts to run them, and build tables. Several browsers already support tables and they are becoming fairly common on the Web. Something else that will become more important with future versions of HTML is the implementation of style sheets and DTDs (Document Type Definitions), a means of defining tags on the fly.

HTML 3.0 is being specified by the working group of the W3 consortium, but when it comes down to it, the adoption of any new form of HTML is based on consensus. There is no single governing body that controls the Web. Open standards are in everybody's interest. If HTML is consistent across the Web, the universality of the Web will remain. One of the main ideas behind HTML was to make information available as widely as possible, on as many platforms as possible. Any narrowing of this field will start to eat away at the edges of the Web.

The Web is changing, however, as it is drawn further and further into the commercial realm. If the choice is between universally available information with minimal gloss, and widely available information with all the whistles and bells—which one do you think might win? There are already signs of the fragmentation of the Web—with some browsers being built around proprietary code. Will it become necessary to read different parts of the web with different browsers?

It remains to be seen how far commercial pressure will influence the ultimate shape of HTML and thus the Web itself.

What is the status of the Netscape extensions?

HTML 3.0 and the Netscape extensions are not the same. Although some of the new Netscape tags will be carried over into future versions of HTML, and some of the extensions are based on HTML 3.0, there are some that will clash with *correct* code.

Netscape began to introduce additional tags with version 1.0, tags that could only be displayed by the Netscape Navigator browser. These tags, which were christened *extensions,* have an uneasy place within HTML. They are mostly designed to give a designer a greater degree of control over the appearance of the Web page, but this can be seen as being against the ethos of HTML. Should HTML be used to structure a document or display it? Good design can help the information structure of a document.

Giving designers more control over the look of the Web is not necessarily a bad thing.

The Netscape extensions have made some members of the Web community very unhappy, but they have become very popular with large numbers of Web developers. There are very few recent sites that do not take advantage of some of the extensions. Some of the elements introduced with Netscape 2.0, frames for example, go a long way further than HTML 3.0 and may result in sites that are completely Netscape specific.

Netscape is not the only company that is introducing browser specific tags, but they have gone further than anyone else, with a greater take-up by Web designers. The Netscape Navigator has become by far the most popular browser, and this has major implications for the future of HTML. How many of the Netscape extensions will be included in HTML 3.0? Netscape wants their extensions to be available to other browsers, but some of them clash with the proposed additions to HTML. The problem here lies not in the effect of some of the tags, but in the tags themselves. Hopefully the differences will be ironed out and a single form of HTML decided upon.

Netscape's tags have gained popularity and widespread use because they offer a higher degree of control over the appearance of the page. Hopefully these needs will be addressed by future versions of HTML and the variations in code will start to converge. The Netscape extensions have been designed so that they do not "break" other browsers, so most browsers will simply ignore them.

All the Netscape extensions are experimental and there is no guarantee that any of them will remain valid, even within Netscape. If you use the Netscape tags you will be doing so at your own risk. You can achieve some very effective page and site designs using these tags, but you may have to strip them out and replace them if they become obsolete. Keep abreast of the latest developments. Try the experimental tags and use them to design the best sites possible, but be aware of their status.

Throughout this section, wherever the Netscape tags are discussed, remember that their effects can usually only be viewed with the Netscape browser. Some of the proposed tags from HTML 3.0 are supported by current browsers, and more will be adopted once the final version is announced.

CHAPTER 16

New tags and new possibilities

This chapter covers Netscape extensions and the tags that are part of HTML 3.0 that are already starting to be implemented by current browsers. This chapter explains how to control the alignment and size of text and images, the colour and pattern of the back-ground, and the behaviour of rules. There is more information about other proposed parts of HTML 3.0 in a later chapter. The major changes introduced with Netscape 2.0 are not included in this chapter, because they are not yet so widespread on the Web.

ALIGNING TEXT

The only way of aligning text until Netscape 2.0, was by using the Netscape ‹CENTER› ‹/CENTER› tags. Any block of text, any image or other page element enclosed within these tags will be centred in relation to the browser window. Netscape 2.0 now supports the use of ALIGN in combination with the paragraph tag.

The proposed HTML 3.0 alignment tags allow you to align page elements to the left, right or centre with the tags:

‹P ALIGN=LEFT›

‹P ALIGN=RIGHT›

‹P ALIGN=CENTER›

Headings can be aligned in the same way, by adding the ALIGN element to the heading tag:

<H2 ALIGN=RIGHT>

<ALIGN=JUSTIFY> will also be included, justifying the text where possible. If it is not practical to justify the text it will be aligned to the left. Without control over the spacing of words and letters, however, justification is probably not a good idea.

The default alignment is to the left.

This alignment is supported by Netscape 2.0, as is <DIV> which is covered later. If you just want to centre elements, however, and you believe that the majority of your audience will be using a version of Netscape 1, you may be better off working with the <CENTER> tag. The ALIGN tags are more stable, and you should plan to implement these as more and more people can see the effects.

HORIZONTAL RULES

The Netscape extensions offer a surprising amount of control over the appearance of the horizontal rule. The width, thickness, alignment and shading can all be specified very precisely.

The WIDTH of the line can be set as a percentage of the width of the page, or as an absolute width measured in pixels. The thickness of the line can be specified in pixels with the SIZE attribute, and the alignment by adding ALIGN. The rule can be drawn as a solid line without the 3D shading if you add NOSHADE to the <HR> tag.

The tag

<HR ALIGN=CENTER SIZE=3 WIDTH=50%>

would add a centre aligned, 3 pixel thick rule that ran 50% of the width of the page as displayed by the browser window.

Fixed width rules can be useful if you want to suggest the optimal viewing size of your page. If your rule is 500 pixels wide, for example, the reader may be encouraged to set her browser window to display a page at least 500 pixels wide. The default rule is the width of the page as displayed in the browser window.

HTML 3.0 will allow you to use an image as a horizontal rule.

BACKGROUNDS AND COLOURS

Netscape allows a considerable degree of experimentation with the colours of a page. When coloured backgrounds and type were introduced with Netscape 1.1, they were a very welcome addition to Web design tools. Most people were starting to get rather tired of the standard light grey background of the browser window. The new background controls enabled the Web designers to add solid colours, patterned backgrounds and coloured type to their sites. Many browsers now support background colours and images, as well as text colours.

While working with background and text colours and images, you should be aware of the order in which a browser loads the different elements. Netscape 2.0 switched the loading order around. The new order is background colour, text, images, background image rather than the old order of background colour, background image, text and images. If you are using a dark background image with light text, you will need to make sure you have set a background colour to match the image, or the text will be impossible to read before the background image has loaded. This can look very strange.

All the background and text controls are added to the ‹BODY› tag.

BACKGROUND GIFS

A tiled image can be added to the background of a Web page by adding the element BACKGROUND to the ‹BODY› tag. As with any image on a Web page, the graphic needs to be specified with either a relative or an absolute URL.

```
<BODY BACKGROUND="images/texture.gif">
```

would use the image texture.gif as a background for the page. The image will be tiled to fit the full extent of the page as it is displayed in the browser window. If the graphic is smaller than 60 pixels by 60 pixels, the browser may have problems displaying it. Some versions of Netscape will replace an image that is too small with a solid black background, which can make your web page rather difficult to read.

Each background GIF is loaded only once, and used repeatedly from the cache to fill each page where it is used. It is still important to keep the size of this image down because the content of the page cannot be loaded until the background is complete. Waiting for a complicated background image on a slow connection can be extremely annoying.

Make sure that your background image does not render your text illegible. You may need to adjust your text colour to balance the page. There are dozens of sites that have such complex backgrounds their text is completely unreadable, even with contrasting coloured text. A background of solid colour, or a subtle texture can be the most effective addition to your page.

BACKGROUND COLOURS

It is currently possible to control the colour of the background without using a tiled GIF. The advantage here is that there is no loading time, and so no delay before the content of the page can be downloaded. There is some doubt about whether this will be supported in future versions of Netscape.

Rather than using the BACKGROUND element, you will need to use BGCOLOR. The colour itself is specified using "hexadecimal" notation to set values for the red, green and blue combination that make up a colour on screen. Hex is a computer friendly method rather than a human friendly one, and it does take some getting used to.

The colour is set with BGCOLOR="#RRGGBB" where RR, GG and BB are hex notations of colour values. Each part of the colour can be set to a value from 0 to 255. You should be able to get a numerical value for your chosen colour form your graphics software. You will then need to convert each part of this value to hex. The easiest way of doing this is to use one of the widely available shareware hex calculators, or a more graphical tool like ColorHEX.

As an indication the RGB setting for white is 255, 255, 255 in decimal and FF, FF, FF in hex. The decimal setting for black is 000, 000, 000, and the hex is 00, 00, 00. If you wanted to specify a white background for your web site, you would need to include the tag

‹BODY BGCOLOR="#FFFFFF"›

on each page.

Try setting up a sample page of HTML and experimenting with different settings in BGCOLOR. Rather than choosing a background colour in your graphics software, try playing with the hex settings to get a feel for the variations you can achieve. Some of the more visual page creation tools, like PageMill allow you to experiment with background images and colours very simply although you should check the results on other computers and with other browsers. Be aware of the limited palette available, and the problems of cross-platform colour palettes.

TEXT COLOUR

As you vary the background colour, or the background pattern, you may find that the text on the page becomes illegible or just less attractive. There are Netscape specific tags that enable you to change the colour of the main text and the colour of the links. More and more browsers now support these tags. Again, you will need to use hex for this. Using colour is covered in more depth in Chapter 18 "Taking Control of the Page with the Netscape Extensions" later in this section.

You can only change the colour of the whole page, however, and cannot specify the colours of particular paragraphs without using the new tag introduced with Netscape 2.0.

The controls for setting the text colour are added to the ‹BODY› tag as follows:

‹BODY BGCOLOR="#RRGGBB" TEXT="#RRGGBB" LINK="#RRGGBB"
ALINK="#RRGGBB" VLINK="#RRGGBB"›

In each case RRGGBB is the hex for your chosen red, green and blue combination. TEXT specifies the colour of all the text on the page that is not a link. LINK is the colour of unfollowed link text, or the borders of unfollowed link graphics. When you hold down the pointer on a link, the link changes colour to show that it is active. This colour is set with ALINK. The colour of previously visited links is set with VLINK.

You can use the type colour settings with a background GIF, with BGCOLOR, or without either of them. The colour settings are not global, and apply only to the page where they are set. If you wish to use your colour settings throughout your Web site, you will need to specify them on every page.

You can choose to specify any or all of these settings. If you change one and not the others, the reader's default settings will be used to display all those that you have not specified. Remember that a reader can choose to override your colour choices, but not to remove any background GIF that you are using.

If a reader views your pages with a browser other than Netscape, they will not necessarily see the colours that you have specified, nor will any background images be displayed. If you are using Netscape colour control tags throughout your site it is a good idea to check the appearance in another browser and on another platform.

It is also worth checking the legibility of your site using Netscape but with a greyscale monitor. Check the site on different platforms to ensure that your chosen colour palette is stable across different system palettes. The more you are designing a site for a particular browser, the more carefully you should check your site with others.

IMAGES

The Netscape specific tags allow a Web designer to control the appearance of the images to a far greater degree. Text can be flowed around images, the size of the borders can be specified, and in general they can be integrated into the page far more. There are still problems with the precise alignment, however, and it is impossible to control the precise flow of text around graphics.

Netscape treats images as a valid part of Web design, rather than a luxurious add on. There are a considerable number of additions to the IMG tag, and the tag lines can get extremely long, as in this example:

‹IMG LOWSRC="logo1.gif" SRC="logo2.gif" ALIGN=LEFT HSPACE=5
VSPACE=10 WIDTH=200 HEIGHT=100 BORDER=0›

Keeping track of such long tags can be rather tricky. Type carefully and check each element as you add it. Hunting for an error in a page full of such tags can take a while.

Remember that the effect of these tags will only be displayed when viewed with Netscape. Other browsers will ignore the additional tags and act only on the familiar ones.

IMAGE ALIGNMENT AND RUN-AROUND

The alignment of images on the page is controlled by adding an ALIGN element to the image tag. Unlike standard HTML, the Netscape tags allow for horizontal alignment as well as vertical alignment. If you wanted to align an image to the left margin of a block of text, the tag would look like this:

‹P›
‹IMG ALIGN=LEFT SRC="images/northquad.gif" ALT="photo of North Quad, 10k"›
The next substantial addition to the college came in 1714, when Thomas Cookes, a Worcestershire baronet, provided the college with a large benefaction.
‹/P›

The image is aligned to the left of the text, and the text flows around the image, as in figure 26. If you wanted to set it to the right of the text, you would need to use the element ALIGN=RIGHT.

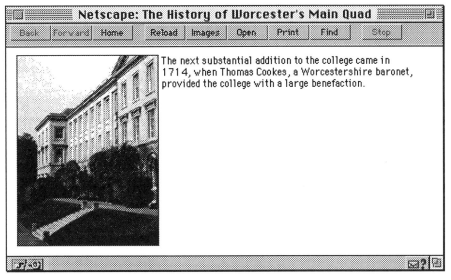

Figure 26: A left aligned image

Left and right aligned images fit into the first available space on the page. This can produce some rather strange effects, so it is worth experimenting with the layout of the page until you get the balance that you want.

Text will flow only around a rectangle and it is not yet possible to force text to flow around irregular images. All images are treated as rectangles.

Unless you specify run-around space the text will sit very close to the graphic. The amount of vertical and horizontal run-around can be set in pixels with VSPACE and HSPACE. In this example, a ten pixel border of white space is set around the image:

```
‹P›
‹IMG ALIGN=LEFT HSPACE=10 VSPACE=5 SRC="images/northquad.gif"
ALT="photo of North Quad, 10k"›
The next substantial addition to the college came in 1714, when Thomas
Cookes, a Worcestershire baronet, provided the college with a large
benefaction.
‹/P›
```

There is more control over the flow of text, and the possibility of overlaying one element on top of the other as part of HTML3.0. This is covered in more detail in Chapter 20 "HTML 3.0 in more detail".

‹BR› AND ‹CLEAR›

With the addition of text flow around images, some changes were made to the line break tag, ‹BR›. By adding CLEAR=LEFT to the ‹BR› tag, the line will be broken and not restarted until there is a clear space by the left margin after left aligned image. ‹BR CLEAR=LEFT› will break the text, restarting it only when the right margin is clear of right aligned images. ‹BR CLEAR=ALL› moves the text down to a point where both margins are clear of aligned images. The effects of this tag may not always be exactly what you expect. Check your work repeatedly with a browser as you work.

The CLEAR tag in HTML is slightly different. The tag can be used within the text and does not need to be part of the ‹BR› tag. In HTML 3.0 you have slightly more control over the behaviour of clearance, because you can specify the minimum space that is needed. You can use the CLEAR tag to specify that the text will flow alongside the image if there is enough space for it. If the space is not there, the text will be pushed to the next clear space on the left or right margin as specified. The minimum width can be specified in pixels or in "en". En size is determined as half the point size of the type on the page.

If you were to specify CLEAR="30 en" the next block would be moved down until there is at least 30 en units free. If you used CLEAR="120 pixels" the next block would move down until there was the minimum width of 120 pixels free. This is slightly more adaptable than CLEAR on its own.

BORDER

If you use an image as the anchor point for a link, the image will be given an outline to indicate its status. This can ruin the effect of a graphic, particularly if you are using transparency, or want to play with "hidden" links. The Netscape tags allow you to control the thickness of the border that is automatically displayed.

By adding a BORDER element to the image tag, and specifying the thickness of the border in pixels, you can remove the border altogether, or change its appearance considerably.

<IMG SRC="logo.gif" BORDER=1>

would add a pixel wide border to the image logo.gif, even though it is not being used as a link graphic.

<A HREF="gargoyle.html"><IMG SRC="images/gargoyle.gif" BORDER=0></A>

would display the image gargoyle.gif without a border even though it is a link graphic.

Adding a border to an unlinked image can be very useful if you are using a strip of separate images as a button bar. Assuming that all the buttons are the same size, if all the images but one are acting as links, the unlinked image will be out of alignment with the others. This is because it does not have the couple of extra pixels padding that a border provides. Adding a border will lift the image up into line with the others. The border will not be displayed in the same colour as the link images, and unless it is viewed with a black and white monitor it should be quite clear that there is a difference between them.

If you have removed the border from a linked image, the border will still be displayed by other browsers that do not support the border tag. This can be rather annoying if the image is transparent, because the shining blue border will be added to the enclosing rectangle of the graphic.

SPECIFYING SIZE

The size of the image is specified in pixels, using the HEIGHT and WIDTH elements in the image tag. Specifying the size of an image has two main uses—one controls the loading order of the page, the other the appearance of the graphic.

As a page downloads, the browser has to allow the correct amount of space to display a graphic before continuing with any text that follows. The browser starts at the top of the page, and works down. If there is an image at the top of the page, the image must be downloaded before the text. Some browsers behave differently, loading the text first, then the graphics, but usually, the size of the graphic cannot be set until the graphic itself is completely downloaded.

If the browser is given information about the size of the graphic, however, it can leave a correctly sized space and continue loading the text. The images can then be filled in as they download. As the images download, the visitor has something to read, and does not have to wait until the page is complete.

By specifying the height and width of an image in pixels the browser can allocate the correct amount of empty space on the page.

<IMG SRC="vaults.gif" HEIGHT=82 WIDTH=67>

Most general purpose graphics utility software will give you the exact size of the image in pixels. The image vaults.gif is 82 pixels high and 67 pixels wide. A space is left for the image, which will later be downloaded into a correctly sized hole. Using a browser other than Netscape, this advantage will be lost and the page will be downloaded in the normal way.

The size specification can, however, be used to scale an image. If the size is set to anything other than the actual size of the graphic, the graphic will be scaled to fit the specification. In a browser other than Netscape, however, the image will be displayed actual size, so be wary of changing the size too dramatically. If you are scaling the image at all, make sure that you check its appearance with another browser.

INTERLACING

If you have spent any time on the Web with Netscape as your browser, you will have seen images that appear to fade in, gaining resolution in waves. This effect is produced by using interlaced images. Rather than downloading the image a line at a time, the browser is able to display sets of equally spaced lines. On each "pass", more detail is filled in between the existing lines, and the images appear to come into focus. Netscape goes through four passes to display the image. This can produce a very attractive effect but is not always appropriate.

A standard feature of most GIF creation software is the ability to save the image with interlacing. Rather than saving the data of the image line by line, the image is saved in interlaced form. As an image is downloaded and decoded, the lines are displayed by the browser in the order that they are saved. Interlacing is not a new effect but was used on a far wider basis with the spread of Netscape.

The image will be displayed normally in any other browser. If an interlaced GIF is used on the Web, the final display will be the same across all graphical browsers. Netscape can display the interlaced graphic as it comes through, but browsers that do not support interlaced GIFs will still be able to download it without trouble. The difference is that Netscape displays the process of the decoding of the image, and some other browsers do not.

Interlacing can be used on any GIFs, including those that you use for backgrounds. Some people frown on this, even though it takes no longer for the image to download. There can be problems using interlacing in combination with transparency, particularly when you have set a background image or colour. Some releases of Netscape have trouble drawing the edges of an interlaced transparent image, leaving mess feathered around the edges of the graphic. Recent releases seem to have fixed this problem, although it is wise to be aware of this quirk and avoid combining the two effects if you believe that your audience may be using the more troublesome releases of Netscape.

The high res/low res trick

Another extension that Netscape added to the IMG tag was LOWSRC. This can be used to load a low resolution image to the page, that is later replaced with a high resolution version:

<IMG LOWSRC="quad.gif" SRC="quad2gif">

On the first pass, Netscape will download the image specified with LOWSRC. Once the page has completely loaded, the image specified with SRC will be loaded. If the reader has remained on the page, they will see the initial image replaced with another. If it is the same image, it will appear to fade in. If the low res image is part of the high res image, the high res section will appear to drop in behind the image that is already on the page. To achieve this effect you may want to avoid interlacing the high res image. The display size of the image will be the same, even if the two versions of the graphic are a different size. The space on the page is allocated to the first version downloaded, and the second image is scaled to fit the space if there is any variation.

Although the LOWSRC element was introduced to allow a low resolution version of the same graphic to be downloaded initially, there is no reason that you can't use a different image altogether. The image you specify with LOWSRC will be downloaded first, and later replaced with whatever graphic you specify with SRC. It will be displayed at the same size as the LOWSRC image, but need not be the same graphic. You can achieve some really strong effects using two different graphics, rather than two versions of the same one, as in figure 27.

This element can be used in combination with any other of the Netscape extensions to the IMG tag. If you set both the HEIGHT and the WIDTH, both the images will be scaled to fit the image box. The images can be aligned to the left or the right. Either, or both, of the images can be interlaced GIFs, or normal GIFs. The low res/high res replacement can also be used with inline JPEGs, or any combination of GIF and JPEG.

Any other browser will ignore the LOWSRC element, and simply download the main image, at its own size.

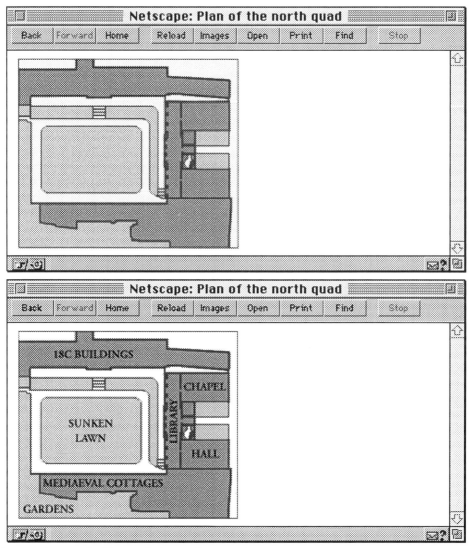

Figure 27: An example of low res/high res with two similar images

Inline jpegs

Netscape and some of the other browsers can now display JPEGs as inline graphics, rather than requiring the reader to view them with an external "helper" application. This is a definite improvement, because JPEGs are more efficient in terms of file size and can a produce a better looking image. These are added to the page in the same way as GIFs:

⟨IMG SRC="image.jpeg"⟩

Playing with Font size

With version 1.1 of the browser, Netscape introduced some tags that allow you some control over the size of the type on the page. Netscape assumes a range of seven possible sizes, from one to seven. This does not correspond to a particular point size, but works on relative sizes with the base size set up by the reader. The default type size for body text paragraphs is 3, although this can be changed.

The type size is adjusted with the ⟨FONT⟩⟨/FONT⟩ tags. Assuming a base size of three, the type can be increased to the next size up with either:

⟨FONT SIZE=+1⟩⟨/FONT⟩

or

⟨FONT SIZE=4⟩⟨/FONT⟩

The size can be decreased by specifying a size smaller than the base size, or by using

⟨FONT SIZE=-1⟩⟨/FONT⟩

The base size of the type can be changed to any size within the one to seven range using, for example:

‹BASEFONT SIZE=4›

The ‹FONT›‹/FONT› tags affect everything enclosed within them and can be used to cover a whole page or a single character. Some Web sites use a large number of font size changes to get an effect such as that in figure 28.

The HTML used to produce Figure 28 is enough to put most people off varying the type size from word to word, or letter to letter:

```
‹HTML›
‹HEAD›
‹TITLE›Font Size changes in Netscape‹/TITLE›
‹/HEAD›
‹BODY›
‹BASEFONT SIZE=1›
‹P›
‹FONT SIZE=+1›C‹/FONT›‹FONT SIZE=+2›h‹/FONT›‹FONT SIZE=+3›a‹/FONT›
‹FONT SIZE=+4›n‹/FONT›‹FONT SIZE=+5›g‹/FONT›‹FONT SIZE=+6›i‹/FONT›
‹FONT SIZE=+7›n‹/FONT›‹FONT SIZE=+6›g‹/FONT› ‹FONT SIZE=+5›the‹/FONT›
‹FONT SIZE=+4›font‹/FONT› ‹FONT SIZE=+3›size‹/FONT›
‹FONT SIZE=+2›too‹/FONT› ‹FONT SIZE=+1›often‹/FONT›
‹FONT SIZE=+2›is a mistake‹/FONT› ‹FONT SIZE=+1›on‹/FONT›
‹FONT SIZE=+4›the ‹/FONT› ‹FONT SIZE=+6›Web‹/FONT› ‹FONT
SIZE=+2›just‹/FONT› ‹FONT SIZE=+5›as‹/FONT› ‹FONT SIZE=+2›it is‹/FONT›
‹FONT SIZE=+4›in ‹/FONT› ‹FONT SIZE=+7›print,‹/FONT›
‹FONT SIZE=+5›although‹/FONT› ‹FONT SIZE=+2›you can get‹/FONT›
‹FONT SIZE=+5›some‹/FONT› ‹FONT SIZE=+3›very‹/FONT›
‹FONT SIZE=+7›effective‹/FONT› ‹FONT SIZE=+1›results‹/FONT›
‹FONT SIZE=+7›.‹/FONT›
‹/P›
‹/BODY›
‹/HTML›
```

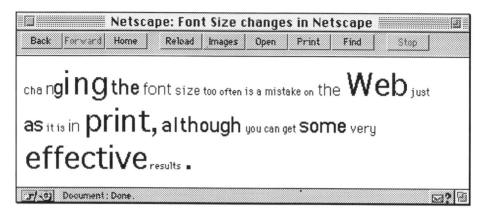

Figure 28: Way too many font size changes in one page

The ‹FONT› tag can be used to approximate a drop cap at the start of a paragraph or page, but it causes havoc with line spacing. The amount of space under the initial line will differ from that under subsequent lines. If the opening word is also a hot link, there will be a break in the underline where the font changes size. It you want to use drop caps in earnest, it may be worth considering using small images instead.

NO BREAK AND WORD BREAK

The Netscape extensions ‹NOBR› and ‹WBR› can be very useful if you have a string of characters that should not be split across two or more lines. Text enclosed within the ‹NOBR›‹/NOBR› tags cannot be broken. If this is used on a long string of text it can look very peculiar. Word break, ‹WBR›, can be used to mark a point with a no break section where Netscape can break the line if necessary. It does not force a break—you would need to use ‹BR› to do that—but allows one at a particular point that you have specified.

LISTS

The Netscape extensions allow a little more control over the display of lists. The bullets and the numbering systems on lists can be controlled with the additional elements introduced by Netscape. With an unordered list, the type of bullet used for each item can be specified with the TYPE attribute. The bullets can be set as either discs, circles or squares. This can be very useful if you want to control the appearance of nested lists.

To set the whole list to appear with square bullets, you would need to use to following tags:

‹UL TYPE=SQUARE›‹/UL›

Figure 29 shows square bulletted lists nested within a circle bulletted list.

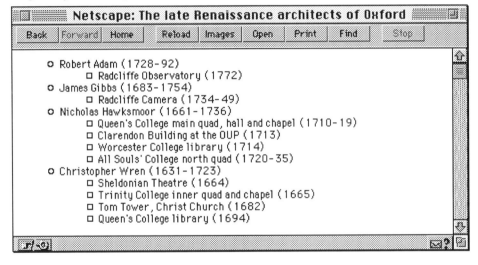

Figure 29: Netscape variations on the unordered list

This was set up with the following HTML file:

‹HTML›
‹HEAD›
‹TITLE›The late Renaissance architects of Oxford‹/TITLE›

```
</HEAD>
<BODY>
<UL TYPE=CIRCLE>
<LI>Robert Adam (1728-92)
<UL TYPE=SQUARE>
<LI>Radcliffe Observatory (1772)
</UL>
<LI>James Gibbs (1683-1754)
<UL TYPE=SQUARE>
<LI>Radcliffe Camera (1734-49)
</UL>
<LI>Nicholas Hawksmoor (1661-1736)
<UL TYPE=SQUARE>
<LI>Queen's College main quad, hall and chapel (1710-19)
<LI>Clarendon Building at the OUP (1713)
<LI>Worcester College library (1714)
<LI>All Souls' College north quad (1720-35)
</UL>
<LI>Christopher Wren (1631-1723)
<UL TYPE=SQUARE>
<LI>Sheldonian Theatre (1664)
<LI>Trinity College inner quad and chapel (1665)
<LI>Tom Tower, Christ Church (1682)
<LI>Queen's College library (1694)
</UL>
</UL>
</BODY>
</HTML>
```

The TYPE attribute can also be added to the <LI> tag, so that it affects that particular list item, and any subsequent items.

It is also possible to specify how ordered list items are counted. The default setting for ordered lists is arabic numbers. With the Netscape extensions, however, you can choose to order your lists with capital letters (TYPE=A), lower case letters (TYPE=a), large roman numerals (TYPE=I), small roman numerals (TYPE=i) or the default arabic numerals (TYPE=1). These settings can be applied to the whole list, by adding one of them to the ‹UL› tag, or to individual list items by adding one to the ‹LI› tag.

The starting value of the whole list, or from a particular item, can be changed by adding a START attribute. Whether the list is set to display with roman numerals or letters, the starting value should be set in arabic numbers. To set up an ordered list with large roman numerals, starting from "X", you would need to use the following tags

‹OL TYPE=I START=10›‹/OL›

The following example (see figure 30) shows the main list ordered with uppercase letters, and the sub lists with small roman numerals. The start value of the main list is set to "D".

‹HTML›
‹HEAD›
‹TITLE›The late Renaissance architects of Oxford‹/TITLE›
‹/HEAD›
‹BODY›
‹OL TYPE=A START=4›
‹LI›Nicholas Hawksmoor (1661-1736)
‹OL TYPE=i›
‹LI›Queen's College main quad, hall and chapel (1710-19)
‹LI›Clarendon Building at the OUP (1713)
‹LI›Worcester College library (1714)
‹LI›All Souls' College north quad (1720-35)
‹/OL›
‹LI›Christopher Wren (1631-1723)
‹OL TYPE=i›

```
<LI>Sheldonian Theatre (1664)
<LI>Trinity College inner quad and chapel (1665)
<LI>Tom Tower, Christ Church (1682)
<LI>Queen's College library (1694)
</OL>
</OL>
</BODY>
</HTML>
```

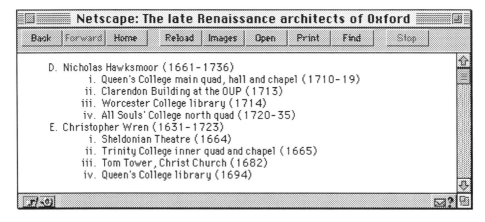

Figure 30: Netscape extensions to the ordered list

DYNAMIC DOCUMENTS: PUSH AND PULL

Netscape 1.1 introduced server push and client pull. Rather than waiting for input from the reader, where a click on a link brings down a new page, the server automatically sends another page, or adds something to the existing page. Push and pull have similar effects but work in different ways. With client pull, the original page is sent from the server. That page contains instructions to reload the page, or fetch another page after a certain amount of time. After the time has elapsed, a new connection is opened, and the relevant page is pulled down by the reader's browser. With client pull, a connection to the server is opened for each new page, and closed when that page has downloaded. This is used all over the Web, with streams of pages appearing even if the reader just sits back and watches.

With server push, the original page is downloaded, but the connection to the server is not broken. The server continues to send or push chunks of data to the client. This is displayed as it arrives. This involves a single Web page that changes, rather than a sequence of different pages that arrive. This method is usually used for small animations, or for updated information that changes over time—an image from a video camera, or a price from the Stock Exchange. The connection stays open indefinitely—until the reader interrupts it by leaving the page or until the server knows it has finished sending new data and sends a terminator.

Client pull is very simple and does not require any scripting. A new tag is added to the head section of an HTML document that contains the instructions to fetch a new document, or refresh the current one by reloading it.

```
<HTML>
<HEAD>
<META HTTP-EQUIV="Refresh" CONTENT=2>
<TITLE>A document that reloads itself</TITLE>
</HEAD>
<BODY>
<P>
A reloading document
</P>
</BODY>
</HTML>
```

Type in the above example, and save it as something like refresh.html. Open it up with Netscape 1.1 or later. This works locally and does not need to be running on a server. Every two seconds the page will reload. If you wanted it to reload every 1 second use CONTENT=1, or CONTENT=60 if you wanted it to refresh once a minute. It will continue to refresh itself until interrupted. The instruction is once only—each refresh works only once—but the reloaded version also contains the instruction to refresh.

To escape a page that refreshes itself on a looping cycle, readers will need to use the back button, close the browser window, or follow a link that provides an escape from the page.

A more interesting variation on this is the ability to load different pages. The tag is very similar to that used for reloading a second page, but with the addition of a target URL. It is important to use a complete absolute URL, including protocol, rather than a relative URL. The following example switches backwards and forwards between two pages (page1.html and page2.html) on a five second interval:

```
<HTML>
<HEAD>
<META HTTP-EQUIV="Refresh" CONTENT="5;
URL=http://www.question.co.uk/test/page2.html">
<TITLE>Page One</TITLE>
</HEAD>
<BODY>
<!--this document is saved as page1.html-->
<P>
This is page one. In five seconds page two will download.
</P>
</BODY>
</HTML>

<HTML>
<HEAD>
<META HTTP-EQUIV="Refresh" CONTENT="5;
URL=http://www.question.co.uk/test/page1.html">
<TITLE>Page Two</TITLE>
</HEAD>
<BODY>
<!--this document is saved as page2.html-->
<P>
This is page two. In five seconds page one will download.
```

```
</P>
<P>
<A HREF="page3.html">Let me out of here!</A>
</P>
</BODY>
</HTML>
```

Once you load up the initial page in Netscape, five seconds later it will reconnect with the server to fetch the second page. After another five seconds, it will load up the first page, and so on until you close the window or interrupt the loading. An easier way of building a route out of the loop is to add a link to the document that lets the reader escape to another page, as in the preceding example.

If you are unsure of the time it will take for the next page to download, you can set the interval to zero. The next page will then be fetched as soon as the original page has finished loading. This prevents half loaded pages being interrupted.

The data retrieved can be another Web page, an image, an audio clip or other type of file format. You can therefore have a continuously updating stream of images acting as frame by frame animation.

The most obvious use of client pull is to build a walk through for some of your Web site. Readers can sit back and watch as pages are automatically downloaded. This can be a good introduction to your site, or can be used to attract passers by at a demo. Overuse of client pull can be frustrating for a reader who wants to explore your site in their own time, and you should make sure that there are plenty of links out of the stream that let readers take control of their own route. Web sites and presentations are very different creatures.

Server push works by keeping the connection open between the client and the server. This can have serious adverse effects on the operation of your server particularly if there are several people using pages that take advantage of server push all at the same time. Whilst someone has a connection open, the connection remains open even if no data is being transmitted. The server must be willing to accept a dedicated allocation of a connection channel (a TCP/IP port) for the duration of each server push connection. Server push can, however, be far faster for the reader, as there is no delay as new connections are opened for each refreshed or downloaded document.

Server push can be used to push whole pages or individual images to the reader.

This can be used to produce simple animations on the page, or to push a sequence or individual frames from a video. Unfortunately, it requires scripting to achieve the stream of images being pushed to the reader. The script that produces the server push is referenced with SRC, in the way that a single still image is referenced:

<IMG SRC="http://www.question.co.uk/cgi-bin/logo.cgi">

You will need to produce the set of images yourself, although there are many ready-made server push scripts available on the Web. There is more information about the scripts needed at the Netscape site, "An exploration of dynamic documents". This URL and other resources are in the appendices.

A FEW NETSCAPE 2.0 TAGS

Netscape introduced another batch of new tags with version 2.0 of the browser. These will not be displayed by earlier versions of Netscape, or by other browsers. Some of these tags are in line with the proposed version of HTML 3.0, some are not. Netscape will be proposing them to the Internet Engineering Task Force and the World Wide Web consortium for inclusion as part of HTML. These new tags are covered in more detail in Chapter 19 "Netscape 2.0 Frames, Maps, Applets and Live Objects".

The first set of tags, which are part of HTML 3.0, control the size and position of type on the page. <BIG></BIG> sets the enclosed type to be displayed, where possible, with a larger font. This is relative to the size of the current font, rather than an absolute size. <SMALL></SMALL> sets the text to a smaller size, behaving in the same ways as the <BIG> tag.

The and tags set the enclosed type to a smaller typeface where possible, and displays it as subscript or superscript respectively. In combination with the HTML 3.0 MATH element, these can be aligned more precisely.

THE HORRID PULSING GREY SLAB OTHERWISE KNOWN AS BLINK

There is absolutely no question about using the Netscape blink tag. Don't do it. It's horrible. ‹BLINK›×/BLINK› does not make the text blink on and off. It adds a dark grey slab of "highlight" that blinks on and off over the text. If the tags include any spaces, they cannot clean up after themselves—even when it blinks off it will leave a thin slice of grey on the page. There is absolutely no excuse for using this tag. Except as satire.

WHY THE NETSCAPE EXTENSIONS AREN'T NECESSARILY A GOOD THING

The Netscape extensions offer a Web designer a wider range of tools than the "standard" version of HTML, but they also cause some difficulties. The idea of adding browser specific tags to a mark up language designed to be completely open is a problematic one.

The decision whether to work with the extensions should be taken seriously. If you rely on the appearance of your web site to convey the information, a large number of possible readers may be excluded. Poor appearance may also exclude a large number of readers who have come to expect and appreciate good design.

Work with the best layout and design possible, but do not ignore the underlying structure and the need for strong information design. The appearance of the page and the structure of the information are obviously bound closely together. Neither should be sacrificed for the other.

Some of the extension tags appear to have been added in haste, and may not last. The "official" versions of HTML may take longer to finalise, but they are almost certainly more stable. The Netscape tags are available, and they can be effective, but they are not infallible. Netscape is the most widely used browser on the Web, but popularity does not necessarily correspond with the highest quality product.

Working with the Netscape tags in addition to the standard tags can be very useful, but you should always be aware of the difference between the two. Be very wary of losing sight of the cross platform publishing ideal that lies at the heart of the Web, but do not abandon good design.

CHAPTER 17

Creating tables

Tables have many uses. Not only can they be used to arrange data coherently, they can also be used to lay out a page. Although this may not conform to the general ethos of HTML, tables are a useful tool for controlling the placement of elements on the page. This chapter explains how to build tables, step by step, and includes details about how to use the Netscape extensions to tables.

The alignment and control built into HTML tables enable the designer to exert a great deal of control over the appearance of the page. If you choose to use tables to control the layout of visual elements on the page, and you are using HTML that is "correct" there should be little problem. HTML may have been designed to control the structure of the document rather than the appearance, but if it provides the tools to control the appearance you should use them as much as you can. The HTML code used to construct tables may have been added to handle technical data and mathematics, but there is no reason why it can't be used for non-technical content. There are more details about controlling the layout of the page at the end of the section on tables.

Other HTML tags can be included within tables, including images and links. Tables can also be nested, with any number of tables being built inside another.

Are tables supported?

Although tables are part of the proposed changes to HTML some browsers already support them. Netscape, predictably, has added their own extensions to the table, but the tags used to build a basic table are not changed. Currently, not all browsers can display them, and using tables throughout a site can cause some problems. Browsers that do not support tables do not have the correct information to lay the text out on the page, and the resulting jumble can be impossible to read. Until the majority of browsers support tables, it might be a good idea to provide a text only version of the pages that contain tables. Basic table layouts can be achieved with preformatted text, but you are then restricted to monospaced type.

In this section, the standard HTML 3.0 table tags are covered first, and the Netscape extensions to tables follow.

Building a table

Building a table in HTML is a rather laborious process. The table is specified row by row and cell by cell, and the code can get very involved. Tables are designed to be constructed by computer rather than by hand. Until there are filters and converters that can convert tables from word-processing documents, it will be necessary to build them yourself. It is useful to know how tables are put together, even if you are producing them with the assistance of a filter. Don't be put off by this—tables may be laborious to produce but they can be very effective on the page.

If you are planning to build tables, it helps to sketch them on paper first. This can help you keep track of the position of each cell, which is very useful when you have a large or irregular table. The most important thing to remember is that tables are constructed row by row.

‹TABLE›

The start and finish of the table needs to be tagged with ‹TABLE›‹/TABLE›, and needs to be within the body section of an HTML file. The table is specified row by row, from top to bottom. Within the rows, each cell of the table is added from left to right.

TABLE ROWS AND TABLE DATA

Each row is tagged at start and finish, opening and closing the row with ‹TR›‹/TR›. Everything contained within those tags is added to a single row. The cells within that row are added as table data, each cell being tagged with ‹TD›‹/TD›. Table data tags can only be used within table rows. Everything contained within the table data tags is displayed within that cell of the table. You can leave a cell empty, but you still need to include the ‹TD›‹/TD› tags. If you do not balance your table with matching numbers of cells from row to row, you can get some very peculiar results.

The table will adjust itself on the page to find the best fit, and wrap the text within the cells if necessary. You can ensure that your text in a particular cell does not flow around to fit by adding the NOWRAP element to the ‹TD› tag. This prevents any line breaks within that cell. If you are using very long lines, however, you can get some rather strange results, and some very wide tables that cannot be viewed within a browser window without scrolling from side to side. The specific size of the table can be controlled only with the Netscape tags.

Using the table, the table row and the table data tags only, you can set up a basic table, as in figure 31. This table has two rows and two columns.

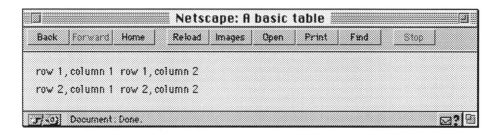

Figure 31: A basic table with two rows and two columns, but no border

```
<HTML>
<HEAD>
<TITLE>A basic table</TITLE>
</HEAD>
<BODY>
```

```
<TABLE>
<TR>
<TD>row 1, column 1</TD>
<TD>row 1, column 2</TD>
</TR>
<TR>
<TD>row 2, column 1</TD>
<TD>row 2, column 2</TD>
</TR>
</TABLE>
</BODY>
</HTML>
```

ADDING A BORDER

The table in figure 31 has no border. With the HTML 3.0 table tags, the border is set as either on or off. By adding the element BORDER to the opening ‹TABLE› tag, a thin border is drawn onto the table, with dividers between the cells. See figure 32 for the same table as above with the addition of a border. The only change is that the initial table tag is set with ‹TABLE BORDER›.

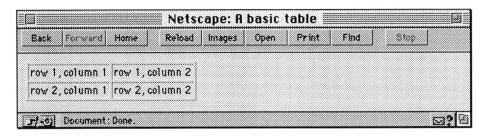

Figure 32: A basic two row, two column table with a border

ALIGNING THE ROWS OF THE TABLE

The alignment of all the content of the table can be controlled, by adding the ALIGN element to the table row or to the table cells. Starting with setting the alignment of the text row by row, it is possible to set the horizontal alignment to the LEFT, the RIGHT or the CENTER. The default setting is left. This example aligns the first row to the left and the second to the right. This table has two rows and three columns. The third column is added by including an extra cell on each row. See figure 33 for the appearance of the table.

```
<HTML>
<HEAD>
<TITLE>A basic table with aligned rows</TITLE>
</HEAD>
<BODY>
<TABLE BORDER>
<TR ALIGN=LEFT>
<TD>1.1</TD>
<TD>row 1, column 2</TD>
<TD>row 1, column 3</TD>
</TR>
<TR ALIGN=RIGHT>
<TD>row 2, column 1</TD>
<TD>2.2</TD>
<TD>r2, c3</TD>
</TR>
</TABLE>
</BODY>
</HTML>
```

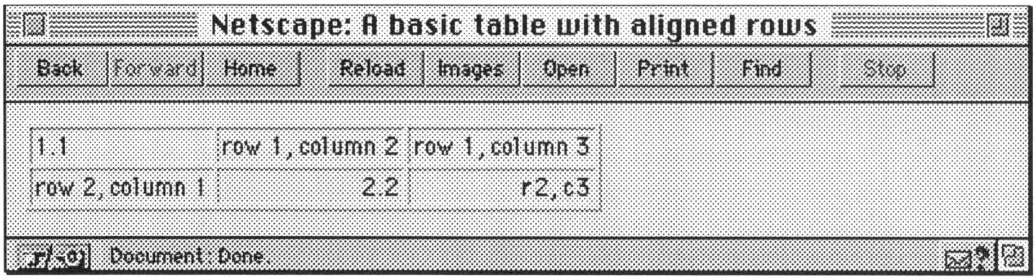

Back | Forward | Home | Reload | Images | Open | Print | Find | Stop

| 1.1 | row 1, column 2 | row 1, column 3 |
| row 2, column 1 | 2.2 | r2, c3 |

Document: Done.

Figure 33: A basic table with the rows aligned to left and right

The vertical alignment of the rows and cells can also be controlled, with the addition of the VALIGN element to the row or data tag. The content of the row can be aligned to the TOP, the MIDDLE or the BOTTOM of the cell. The default setting is in the MIDDLE. The next example, as seen in figure 34, varies the horizontal and vertical alignment from row to row. Note that the text is controlled with the use of line breaks, to force the length of the lines. These could be allowed to flow to fit, but by breaking them you can be sure of the shape of the resulting table cells. This is a three row, two column table.

```
<HTML>
<HEAD>
<TITLE>A basic table with aligned rows</TITLE>
</HEAD>
·<BODY>
<TABLE BORDER>
<TR ALIGN=LEFT VALIGN=TOP>
<TD>this row is left aligned<BR>
and aligned vertically to the top</TD>
<TD>left, top</TD>
</TR>
<TR ALIGN=CENTER VALIGN=MIDDLE>
<TD>this row is aligned<BR>
to the centre and the middle</TD>
<TD>centre, middle</TD>
</TR>
```

```
<TR ALIGN=RIGHT VALIGN=BOTTOM>
<TD>this row is right aligned<BR>
and aligned vertically to the<BR>
bottom</TD>
<TD>right, bottom</TD>
</TR>
</TABLE>
</BODY>
</HTML>
```

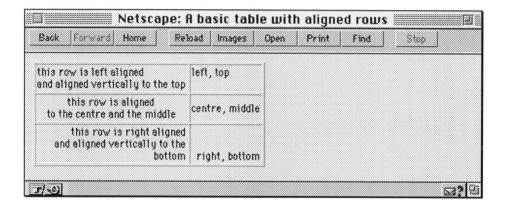

Figure 34: A table with horizontal and vertical alignment of rows

ALIGNING THE CELLS OF A TABLE

The alignment within a table can be controlled from cell to cell as well as from row to row. The alignment within table cells is specified in the same way as it is with table rows, by adding the ALIGN and VALIGN elements to the initial tag. Any tag which does not contain these elements will be set with the default of top left. You can set the alignment of one row by setting the whole row, and another row by setting each cell individually. This example shows a four cell table with each cell aligned separately. No vertical alignment is set in this example, as you can see in figure 35.

```
<HTML>
<HEAD>
<TITLE>A basic table with aligned cells</TITLE>
</HEAD>
<BODY>
<TABLE BORDER>
<TR>
<TD ALIGN=LEFT>this cell is aligned to the left</TD>
<TD ALIGN=RIGHT>this cell to the right</TD>
</TR>
<TR>
<TD ALIGN=RIGHT>this row is right</TD>
<TD ALIGN=LEFT>left</TD>
</TR>
</TABLE>
```

The vertical alignment of the cells can be controlled by adding the VALIGN element to the <TD> tag.

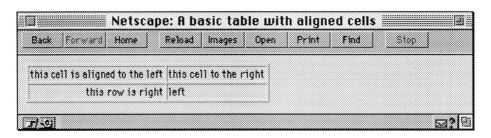

Figure 35: A four cell table, where each cell's alignment is specified individually

IRREGULAR CELL SIZES: COLUMN SPAN AND ROW SPAN

Sometimes you will want to be have cells that are multiple columns wide, or multiple rows tall. This can be controlled by adding the COLSPAN and ROWSPAN elements to the ‹TD› tag. Once you start stretching individual cells, you will find it useful to sketch out the final table before you start. This will help you keep track of the number of cells you need to specify.

The following example shows a two row, four column table, with one cell stretched over three columns (illustrated in figure 36). Because the cell is three cells wide, only the fourth cell on the row needs adding. The others are already specified with the COLSPAN element. Cells are specified from their top left corners. A stretched cell should be specified only once, from the top left corner where it first appears.

```
‹HTML›
‹HEAD›
‹TITLE›A basic table with column span‹/TITLE›
‹/HEAD›
‹BODY›
‹TABLE BORDER›
‹TR›
‹TD›column 1‹/TD›
‹TD›column 2‹/TD›
‹TD›column 3‹/TD›
‹TD›column 4‹/TD›
‹/TR›
‹TR›
‹TD COLSPAN=3 ALIGN=RIGHT›this cell spans 3 columns‹/TD›
‹TD›column 4‹/TD›
‹/TR›
‹/TABLE›
‹/BODY›
‹/HTML›
```

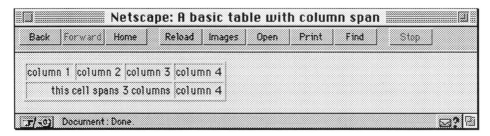

Figure 36: COLSPAN used to stretch a cell over three columns

These elements can be used in conjunction with the ALIGN and VALIGN elements either on the rows or the cells.

Cells can also be stretched over multiple rows. Use a sketch to check how many cells you will need to specify if a single cell takes up several rows. For each row that a stretched cell covers, you will need to remove a cell from that row. This example (figure 37) is two columns wide and four rows high and has one cell that spans all four rows.

```
<HTML>
<HEAD>
<TITLE>A basic table with row span</TITLE>
</HEAD>
<BODY>
<TABLE BORDER>
<TR>
<TD ROWSPAN=4>cell 1,1</TD>
<TD>cell 1,2</TD>
</TR>
<TR>
<TD>2,2</TD>
</TR>
<TR>
<TD>3,2</TD>
</TR>
```

```
<TR>
<TD>4,2</TD>
</TR>
</TABLE>
</BODY>
</HTML>
```

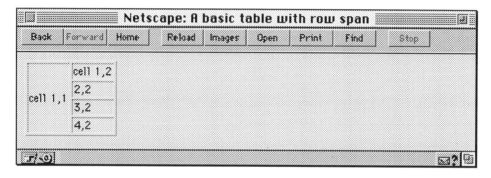

Figure 37: Using ROWSPAN to stretch a cell across multiple rows

COLSPAN and ROWSPAN can be used within the same table and within the same cell. The following example has one cell that stretches across four rows, one cell that stretches across two columns, another across four columns and one that covers two rows and two columns. See figure 38 to see how this fits together. Be careful to check that you are adding the number of table cells that you need to balance the rows and columns. Work through row by row, and count them off against your sketch. Remember that cells are included from their top left corner. You will notice that row three needs only one cell. The other cells that display as part of row three have already been specified in row one and row two.

You can choose to leave a cell empty, but you still need to specify the cell itself with ‹TD›‹/TD›.

```
<HTML>
<HEAD>
<TITLE>A table with row span and column span</TITLE>
</HEAD>
```

```
<BODY>
<TABLE BORDER>
<TR>
<TD ROWSPAN=4>rowspan 4</TD>
<TD COLSPAN=4>colspan4</TD>
</TR>
<TR>
<TD>single cell</TD>
<TD>single cell</TD>
<TD ROWSPAN=2 COLSPAN=2>rowspan 2</BR>
colspan2</TD>
</TR>
<TR>
<TD COLSPAN=2>colspan2</TD>
</TR>
<TR>
<TD>single cell</TD>
<TD>single cell</TD>
<TD>single cell</TD>
<TD>single cell</TD>
</TR>
</TABLE>
</BODY>
</HTML>
```

When you are constructing a table with irregular cell sizes, take your time and type carefully. If you have added any cell by cell alignment, or any other HTML tags, the code can become very long and complicated. You may find it helpful to add comments to mark off each row. Comments will not be displayed on the page, but can be useful when you are working on the HTML.

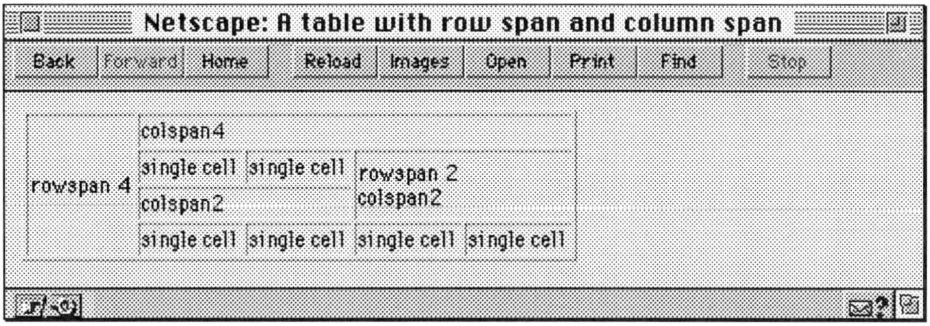

Figure 38: A table with irregular column span and row span

TABLE HEADINGS

You can add headings to your tables by using the ‹TH›‹/TH› tags. By default, headings are bold and centred, although you can change the alignment of your headings with ALIGN and VALIGN. The headings can be set to single cell width, or stretched across multiple columns. Headings can also be stretched across multiple rows. In general, they behave like any other cells, but the default setting of the text is bold and centrally aligned. The NOWRAP element can also be added to the ‹TH› tag, to prevent line breaks within that heading cell. The following example is based on the previous example, but with a table heading added that spans all five columns (see figure 39). The alignment of the header text has been changed so that it sits on the left of the cell.

```
<HTML>
<HEAD>
<TITLE>A table with row span and column span</TITLE>
</HEAD>
<BODY>
<TABLE>
<TR>
<TH COLSPAN=5 ALIGN=LEFT>table header (left)</TH>
</TR>
<TR>
```

```
<TD ROWSPAN=4>rowspan 4</TD>
<TD COLSPAN=4>colspan4</TD>
</TR>
<TR>
<TD>single cell</TD>
<TD>single cell</TD>
<TD ROWSPAN=2 COLSPAN=2>rowspan 2</BR>
colspan2</TD>
</TR>
<TR>
<TD COLSPAN=2>colspan2</TD>
</TR>
<TR>
<TD>single cell</TD>
<TD>single cell</TD>
<TD>single cell</TD>
<TD>single cell</TD>
</TR>
</TABLE>
</BODY>
</HTML>
```

Headers can be added cell by cell. In the next example, there are headers along the top row, and in the far left column. Remember to leave an empty cell in the top left if you want your table to look like the one in figure 40. The top row of header cells is added in a row of its own. The header cells on the left are set up by adding a header cell to each subsequent row.

```
<HTML>
<HEAD>
<TITLE>Adding headers to your table</TITLE>
</HEAD>
<BODY>
<TABLE BORDER>
<TR>
<TH></TH>
<TH>column 1</TH>
<TH>column 2</TH>
<TH>column 3</TH>
<TH>column 4</TH>
</TR>
<TR>
<TH>row 1</TH>
<TD>column 1</TD>
<TD>column 2</TD>
<TD>column 3</TD>
<TD>column 4</TD>
</TR>
<TR>
<TH>row 2</TH>
<TD>column 1</TD>
<TD>column 2</TD>
<TD>column 3</TD>
<TD>column 4</TD>
</TR>
</TABLE>
</BODY>
</HTML>
```

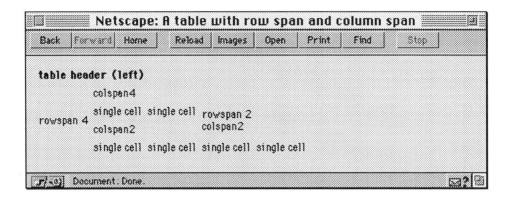

Figure 39: Adding a header to your table

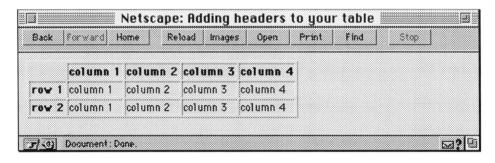

Figure 40: Headers to the top and left of a table

CAPTIONS

A caption can be added to the top or the bottom of the table. This is specified with <CAPTION ALIGN=TOP×/CAPTION> or <CAPTION ALIGN=BOTTOM×/CAPTION>. This example table (figure 41) has a caption aligned at the bottom. The caption is centred. If you want to align your caption to the left or right you may have to add it to a cell of the table instead. The caption can only be aligned to top or bottom, and you cannot use ALIGN and VALIGN in combination to control the precise setting.

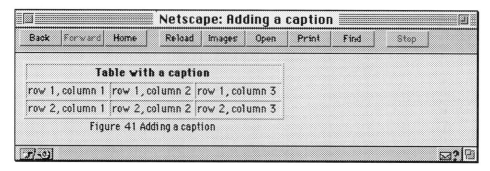

Figure 41: Table with heading and caption

<HTML>
<HEAD>
<TITLE>Adding a caption</TITLE>
</HEAD>
<BODY>
<TABLE BORDER>
<TR>
<TH COLSPAN=3>Table with a caption</TH>
</TR>
<TR>
<TD>row 1, column 1</TD>
<TD>row 1, column 2</TD>
<TD>row 1, column 3</TD>

```
</TR>
<TR ALIGN=RIGHT>
<TD>row 2, column 1</TD>
<TD>row 2, column 2</TD>
<TD>row 2, column 3
</TR>
<CAPTION ALIGN=BOTTOM>Figure 41 Adding a caption</CAPTION>
</TABLE>
</BODY>
</HTML>
```

LAYING OUT A TABLE

Have a look at the table in figure 42. Look at each row, and each column. Without reading through the HTML file that follows, try to build this table for yourself. All the HTML used has been covered in this section.

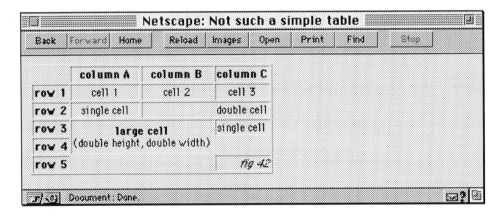

Figure 42: Practise table layout

If you are unsure of where to start, read through the previous examples again, and compare them to the browser displays. Look again at figure 42. Draw a grid over the table and work out where each cell needs to be specified. Remember that a cell is included from its top left corner. The default settings for headings are bold, centre and middle. The default settings for text are left and middle.

As you work on this example, keep saving and checking your work in a browser. Remember to use a browser that supports tables. Each time you alter the HTML file, save your changes and reload the page into the browser to view your changes.

The HTML used to build the table in figure 42 follows.

```
<HTML>
<HEAD>
<TITLE>Not such a simple table</TITLE>
</HEAD>
<BODY>
<TABLE BORDER>
<!--row one--header row-->
<TR>
<TH></TH>
<TH>column A</TH>
<TH>column B</TH>
<TH>column C</TH>
</TR>
<!--row two-->
<TR>
<TH>row 1</TH>
<TD ALIGN=CENTER>cell 1</TD>
<TD ALIGN=CENTER>cell 2</TD>
<TD ALIGN=CENTER>cell 3</TD>
</TR>
<!--row three-->
<TR>
<TH>row 2</TH>
```

```
<TD ALIGN=CENTER>single cell</TD>
<TD COLSPAN=2 ALIGN=RIGHT>double cell</TD>
</TR>
<!--row four-->
<TR>
<TH>row 3</TH>
<TD COLSPAN=2 ROWSPAN=2 ALIGN=CENTER><B>large cell</B><BR>
(double height, double width)</TD>
<TD>single cell</TD>
</TR>
<!--row five-->
<TR>
<TH>row 4</TH>
<TD></TD>
</TR>
<!--row six-->
<TR>
<TH>row 5</TH>
<TD COLSPAN=2></TD>
<TD ALIGN=RIGHT VALIGN=BOTTOM><I>fig 42</I></TD>
</TR>
</TABLE>
</BODY>
</HTML>
```

USING OTHER HTML TAGS WITHIN TABLES

You can use any other HTML tags within tables. All the tags will behave in the normal ways. One exception to this is the use of <A NAME> within a table. Netscape cannot find this tag within a table. Hopefully this will be fixed in future versions of the browser.

You have control over the alignment of the contents of each cell, and therefore a great deal of control over the appearance of the page.

You can add hyperlinks to text or images within a table, and any hard or soft formatting tags to the text. The table is a very good way of laying out a combination of images and text on the page. On a very basic level, you can use tables to achieve a simple column layout on the page. This can be extended into a full grid design. If you are using tables to lay out the elements of the page, work with the border turned on so that you can keep track of the position and shape of each cell. You can remove the border with a very simple edit once you are satisfied with the table.

NETSCAPE EXTENSIONS TO TABLES

All the table tags previously covered are part of the proposed HTML 3.0 code. There are some Netscape specific extensions to these tags which provide more specific controls over the size of the table, the cells and the space between them. The regular table settings are fairly fluid, and the table will change shape and size depending partly on the contents and partly on the size of the browser window. The Netscape tags allow you to fix the sizes.

Unlike the HTML 3.0 table tags, the Netscape extensions allow you to control the amount of spacing between the cells and within the cells. If you use the Netscape tags, the results will only be seen by readers who use Netscape themselves. If you are relying on fixed table widths to set the appearance of a page, make sure that you check the page in question in at least one other browser. Check the site with different type settings and with varying widths of browser window. The more you specify the appearance of the page, the harder you will have to test it.

TABLE WIDTH

The width of the table can be specified absolutely, in pixels, or relatively, as a percentage of the width of the page. This can be done by adding the WIDTH element to the initial ‹TABLE› tag. If the table is set to a width of 400 pixels, for example, the table will be 400 pixels wide regardless of the contents of the cells, or the number of columns. The following example shows the different effect you can get by specifying the width of a table. (figure 43)

```
<HTML>
<HEAD>
<TITLE>specifying the width of a table</TITLE>
</HEAD>
<BODY>
<PRE>
</PRE>
<TABLE BORDER>
<TR>
<TD>row 1, column 1</TD>
<TD>row 1, column 2</TD>
</TR>
<TR>
<TD>row 2, column 1</TD>
<TD>row 2, column 2</TD>
</TR>
</TABLE>
<PRE>
</PRE>
<TABLE BORDER WIDTH=500>
<TR>
<TD>row 1, column 1</TD>
<TD>row 1, column 2</TD>
</TR>
<TR>
<TD>row 2, column 1</TD>
<TD>row 2, column 2</TD>
</TR>
</TABLE>
```

‹/BODY›

‹/HTML›

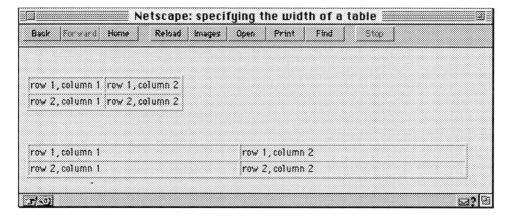

Figure 43: Setting the width of a table

If you set your table too wide, readers may have trouble viewing the table and will have to scroll from side to side. This can reduce the visual impact of an otherwise well formed table and attractive page.

COLUMN WIDTH

Within the table, the width of each cell can be set individually. This should not be used to replace COLSPAN, but to control the specific width of cells within the table structure. Adding a WIDTH to the example in figure 43, you can control the width of the cells regardless of the size of their content. In the following example, the width of the table is set to 500 pixels, the first cell to 100 pixels and the second to 400. Subsequent cells in the same columns take on the same size, and you do not need to specify the width for the cells in each row. (See figure 44).

‹HTML›

‹HEAD›

‹TITLE›specifying the width of table cells‹/TITLE›

```
</HEAD>
<BODY>
<PRE>
</PRE>
<TABLE BORDER WIDTH=500>
<TR>
<TD WIDTH=100>row 1, column 1</TD>
<TD WIDTH=400>row 1, column 2</TD>
</TR>
<TR>
<TD>row 2, column 1</TD>
<TD>row 2, column 2</TD>
</TR>
</TABLE>
</BODY>
</HTML>
```

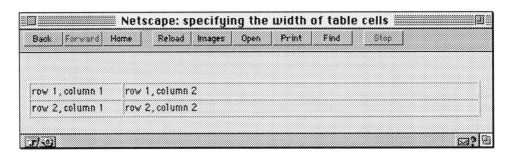

Figure 44: Setting the width of table cells

The cell width can be set as an absolute measurement in pixels, or as a percentage of the width of the table. The width of table headers can be set in the same way— by adding WIDTH to the <TH> tag. Again, the width can be set as a measurement in pixels, or as a percentage of the width of the table. If you set the width of the header cells, all the subsequent cells in the same columns will match this width. You cannot set a header cell to 400 pixels, for example, and the following cell below it to 100.

BORDER WIDTH

In HTML 3.0 the BORDER is a single on or off option. Adding the element to the initial ‹TABLE› tag adds lines around the table and between the cells. The Netscape extensions allow you to set a value for the border. The following examples show the border set at 1, at 4 and at 10 (see figure 45). The BORDER element controls the external border only, and not the lines between the cells.

```
‹HTML›
‹HEAD›
‹TITLE›specifying the border of a table‹/TITLE›
‹/HEAD›
‹BODY›
‹TABLE BORDER=1›
‹TR›
‹TD›border=1‹/TD›
‹TD›row 1, column 2‹/TD›
‹/TR›
‹TR›
‹TD›row 2, column 1‹/TD›
‹TD›‹/TD›
‹/TR›
‹/TABLE›
‹TABLE BORDER=4›
‹TR›
‹TD›border=4‹/TD›
‹TD›row 1, column 2‹/TD›
‹/TR›
‹TR›
‹TD›row 2, column 1‹/TD›
‹TD›‹/TD›
```

```
</TR>
</TABLE>
<TABLE BORDER=10>
<TR>
<TD>border=10</TD>
<TD>row 1, column 2</TD>
</TR>
<TR>
<TD>row 2, column 1</TD>
<TD></TD>
</TR>
</TABLE>
</BODY>
</HTML>
```

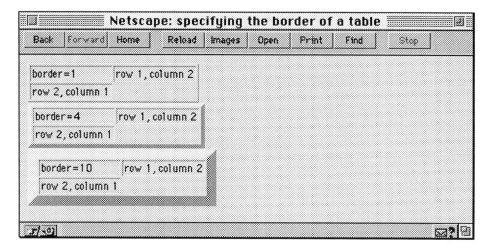

Figure 45: Changing the size of the border

Cell spacing

The lines within the table are controlled by adding a CELLSPACING element to the ‹TABLE› tag. This adds extra width to the lines that divide the cells. It does not affect the size of the cells, or of the border. This example (figure 46) includes three table with various BORDER and CELLSPACING settings.

```
‹HTML›
‹HEAD›
‹TITLE›specifying cell border and cell spacing‹/TITLE›
‹/HEAD›
‹BODY›
‹TABLE BORDER=1 CELLSPACING=1›
‹TR›
‹TD›border=1‹/TD›
‹TD›cellspacing=1‹/TD›
‹/TR›
‹TR›
‹TD›row 2, column 1‹/TD›
‹TD›‹/TD›
‹/TR›
‹/TABLE›
‹TABLE BORDER=1 CELLSPACING=3›
‹TR›
‹TD›border=1‹/TD›
‹TD›cellspacing=3‹/TD›
‹/TR›
‹TR›
‹TD›row 2, column 1‹/TD›
‹TD›‹/TD›
‹/TR›
```

```
</TABLE>
<TABLE BORDER=2 CELLSPACING=10>
<TR>
<TD>border=2</TD>
<TD>cellspacing=10</TD>
</TR>
<TR>
<TD>row 2, column 1</TD>
<TD></TD>
</TR>
</TABLE>
</BODY>
</HTML>
```

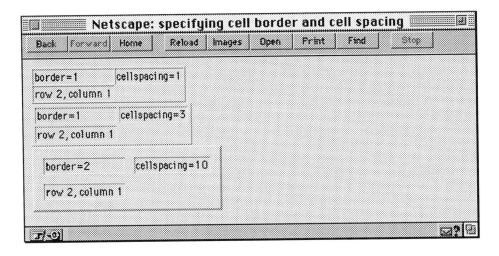

Figure 46: Cell border and cell spacing

CELL PADDING

By adding a CELLPADDING element to the ‹TABLE› tag you can set a shoulder of space within the cell itself. CELLPADDING, used in combination with CELLSPACING and BOR-DER, allows a high level of control over the spacing of the cells and the content of the cells. The default padding is zero. HTML 3.0 tables set the content of the cell very tightly against the internal cell borders.

Used without a border and without any spacing, the cell padding element gives you the means of setting a gutter between columns if you choose to use tables to lay out a page on a grid based design. The example in figure 47 shows different combinations of border, spacing and padding. This example also contains tables within tables. A parent table, without a border and without cell spacing, is used to lay out the four examples of cell padding. If you are working with layers of tables, you will need to check that each row and each cell is properly tagged at both ends throughout the parent table and all the child tables. The simplest way of doing this is to set up and test each child table and then drop them into the parent table.

```
‹HTML›
‹HEAD›
‹TITLE›cell padding and a table of tables‹/TITLE›
‹/HEAD›
‹BODY›
‹TABLE BORDER=0 CELLPADDING=15›
‹TR ALIGN=CENTER VALIGN=MIDDLE›
‹TD›

‹TABLE BORDER=1 CELLSPACING=1 CELLPADDING=1›
‹TR›
‹TD›border=1‹/TD›
‹TD›cellspacing=1‹/TD›
‹/TR›
‹TR›
```

```
<TD>cellpadding=1</TD>
<TD></TD>
</TR>
</TABLE>

</TD>

<TD>

<TABLE BORDER=1 CELLSPACING=1 CELLPADDING=10>
<TR>
<TD>border=1</TD>
<TD>cellspacing=1</TD>
</TR>
<TR>
<TD>cellpadding=10</TD>
<TD></TD>
</TR>
</TABLE>

</TD>
</TR>

<TR ALIGN=CENTER VALIGN=MIDDLE>
<TD>

<TABLE BORDER=1 CELLSPACING=3 CELLPADDING=5>
<TR>
<TD>border=1</TD>
<TD>cellspacing=3</TD>
</TR>
```

```
<TR>
<TD>cellpadding=5</TD>
<TD></TD>
</TR>
</TABLE>

</TD>

<TD>

<TABLE BORDER=2 CELLSPACING=10 CELLPADDING=5>
<TR>
<TD>border=2</TD>
<TD>cellspacing=10</TD>
</TR>
<TR>
<TD>cellpadding=5</TD>
<TD></TD>
</TR>
</TABLE>

</TD>
</TR>
</TABLE>
</BODY>
</HTML>
```

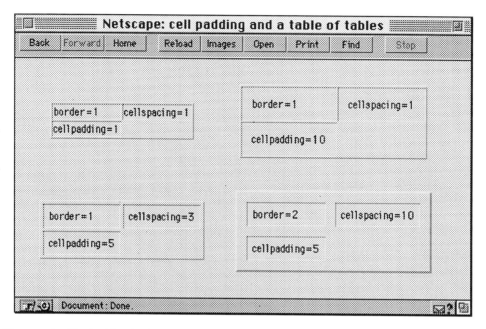

Figure 47: A table of tables showing examples of padding, spacing and border

Tables require time and concentration, but can be used to great effect. The HTML 3.0 tags are very flexible and offer a high degree of control over the structure and the appearance of your page. The Netscape additions allow more cosmetic tweaking of the look of the tables, and although they can be very useful, you may not find them necessary. If you do use the Netscape extensions, remember that their effects will only be seen when viewed with the Netscape browser.

HTML will continue to grow. The possibilities of working with the medium will expand. The greater your understanding of the mechanism, the more you will be able to explore the medium. HTML is very young, and liable to change. This is only a starting point.

CHAPTER 18

Taking control of the page with the Netscape extensions

The chapter on design, in the first section of this book, covered some of the possibilities of taking more control over the appearance of the page. This chapter covers these ideas in more detail, with examples of the HTML that you can use. Most of these methods require the Netscape extensions or some rather unconventional use of standard HTML. The next chapter introduces further controls and developments that have been made possible, largely with the release of Netscape 2.

SETTING YOUR COLOURS

If you want to avoid the dull grey background of the standard browser window you have two options. You can add a background image that is tiled to fill the window, or set the background to a single colour. The advantage of setting the background with the BGCOLOR tag is that there is no waiting while an image is downloaded. There is, however, some doubt as to whether this tag will be supported in the future.

If you want to use a GIF as your background, create the image in the normal way. Make sure that it is as small as possible in file size, and put it in a useful place. In this example, the page will be filled with paper.gif which is a plain white tile.

```
<HTML>
<HEAD>
<TITLE>Setting your background image</TITLE>
</HEAD>
<BODY BACKGROUND="paper.gif">
</BODY>
</HTML>
```

To set a white background as a colour rather than as a tiled image, the HTML is:

```
<HTML>
<HEAD>
<TITLE>Setting your background colour</TITLE>
</HEAD>
<BODY BGCOLOR="#FFFFFF">
</BODY>
</HTML>
```

Once you have your background set as a useful colour, you might want to think about adjusting the colours of the text and the links. Black text on a white page is the easiest combination to read, so you could leave the text at the default setting. For a particular effect, you might want to set the text to a very dark navy blue, or a very deep grey. Making the body text a bright colour can have a peculiar effect on readers' perceptions of the text. Solid red text will be assimilated very differently from pale blue text. It would be a good idea to read up on colour and perception before delving too deeply into vivid colours.

Link text is a different issue. The default settings for the link colours—blue for hotlinks, red or purple for visited links—are not the best. Experiment with different colours and shades, but you might consider using a red as the colour for your hot links. Visited links should be a much cooler colour. They should not jump out of the body of the text so much as the new links. A dark blue or green can be very effective.

Check your colours with different monitors and different computers, because the appearance of the colours will vary.

Some possibilities for your body text are black (TEXT="#000000"), deep blue (TEXT="#000022") or dark grey (TEXT="#111111"). The main link colour needs to attract the eye without destroying the page. A very bright pink, something like LINK="#E4136E" might be too strong. A shade of red such as AA0000 or CC0000 could be more effective. Visited links need to be recognisably different from the body text, particularly for people who switch off underlining. If you are reading a page, under-lined text can be distracting or unsightly, particularly if there are a large number of links on a single page. A shade of green like 002200 may work well, or you might find it too close to the body text colour. Something like 073F16 might stand out enough without dominating the page. A blue-green like 003333 gives you a cool colour that will not confuse people who are accustomed to looking for blue links. Using a brighter blue may confuse readers too much. If you avoid using blue links of any sort, readers will realise immediately that they need to re-establish their perception of link colours. If you make the link colour warmer and brighter than the visited link colour they will have very little trouble understanding which links to follow.

The ALINK tag is less crucial. The colour is displayed only when a reader clicks on the link. It is useful to provide the reader with some feedback so it is worth setting the ALINK colour to a brighter shade of the main link colour.

```
<BODY BGCOLOR="#FFFFFF" TEXT="#000000" LINK="#CC0000"
VLINK="#003333" ALINK="#FF0000">
```

or

```
<BODY BGCOLOR="#FFFFFF" TEXT="#000000" LINK="#BB0000"
VLINK="#004400" ALINK="#FF0000">
```

are suggested starting points.

Working with a dark background can be more difficult, but you can get some very striking results. Make sure that you check how your images look before fixing on a background, and make sure that any anti-aliasing you do is with the background colour you plan to use. If you decide to change your background, you will need to rework your graphics. If you choose to work with a dark background, you will need to ensure that your text and link colours are bright enough to be legible even at small sizes.

White or bright yellow text can work very well against a dark blue or a black background. It is not easy to read a great deal of text like this. It may look terrific when you first see it, but try reading through a few pages. If you are using light text on a dark background, it is worth increasing the size of the type with the ‹FONT SIZE=x› tags to increase the level of legibility.

‹BODY BGCOLOR="#000044" TEXT="#FFFF00" LINK="#DD0000"›

would set your page with a deep blue background, bright yellow text and red links. The difficulty is choosing a suitable colour for the visited links. When you need to work with brighter colours for legibility, it is difficult to find a fourth colour. The VLINK colour needs to be different, but not too prominent. Something like CC9900, a dull orange may work—it is duller than the main text and the link text but is in the same colour range:

‹BODY BGCOLOR="#000044" TEXT="#FFFF00" LINK="#DD0000"
VLINK="#CC9900"›

Working with a black background, yellow can be a useful colour for the link text. If you use white for the main body text, the same orange as above can be used for the VLINK colour:

‹BODY BGCOLOR="#000000" TEXT="#FFFFFF" LINK="#FFFF00"
VLINK="#CC9900"›

You could put together far more striking combinations than this, but you have to consider the effect on sustained reading, and the choice of link colours.

‹BODY BGCOLOR="#000000" TEXT="#FFFFFF" LINK="#EE0000"
VLINK="#FF3333"›

sets the background to black, the text to white, the links to red and the visited links to a salmon pink.

Netscape 2.0 introduces an extension to the ability to change the colours of your text. Rather than setting the colour of the whole page, you can change the colour of individual blocks of text. This works in a similar way to changing the size of type, with the ‹FONT› tag. Any block of text enclosed by ‹FONT COLOR="#RRGGBB"›‹/FONT› will be affected by the colour change. It would be a good idea to use this sparingly, as a large number of different colours on the page may confuse readers. Readers have become accustomed to recognising a change in colour as link text. If you vary the colours too much, readers may not be able to recognise which colours should be seen as regular text, and which as link text. Some very effective pages can be created with good use of colour, but poor colour choices will decrease legibility.

Experiment with colours but make sure that you check them repeatedly. Check them on heavy text pages as well as light text pages. Ask someone else to have a look, and check that they find it obvious which links they should follow. Check your images in combination with your background colour.

If you are setting up a site that requires careful or sustained reading, avoid difficult colour combinations. Black text on a white page is by far the easiest to read.

CONTROLLING THE LAYOUT OF THE PAGE

You do not have absolute control over the layout of the page. Without the ability to set the typeface and the precise type size, control is rather limited. There are, however, ways of reducing the amount of variation.

The first demand is probably the ability to set a margin on the page. Without forcing a margin on the page, text will flow from edge to edge of the window. This leads to unpredictable behaviour with aligned images, and uncomfortable line length for reading. The easiest way to indent your text on either side is to use the blockquote command. This does not set a maximum line length, but does build some white space around the edges of the page. Vertical white space at the top and the bottom can be added with a couple of blank lines of preformatted text.

Figures 48 and 49 show the effects of blockquoted text, with the browser window set at different widths. The margin size is fixed, but the line lengths are relative to the width of the window.

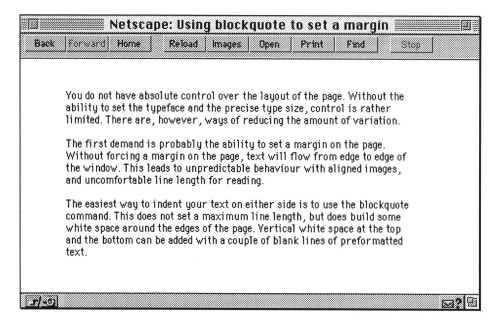

Figure 48: Blockquoted text

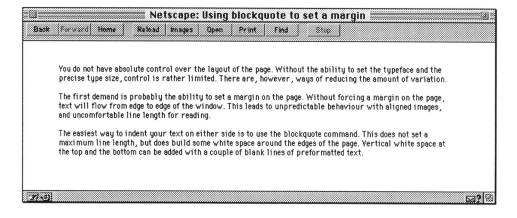

Figure 49: Blockquoted text in a wide browser window

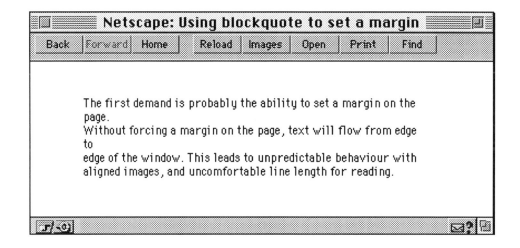

Figure 50: Line breaks that break the flow

You could set ‹BR› tags at each point where you wanted a line break, but this will work only if readers do not set their windows narrower than the intended length of your lines. As you can see from figure 50, this leads to unpleasant results that are very difficult to read.

Preformatting your text will give you more control, but you are limited to a mono-spaced font. Another problem arises when you want to change your page. You will need to tweak and re-space significant amounts of the text every time you need to change to content. This can get very annoying.

Tables give you the greatest amount of control over the flow of the text, and the Netscape extensions allow you to fix the width of each column. You cannot control the size of the type, but you can control how far each line runs. If you do not set the width, however, you will still have problems that arise from not being able to antici-pate the length of a line of text. Tables resize themselves according to the width of the browser window. As the cells of the table are resized, the contents of the cells are reflowed to fit. There is still the possibility of extremely long lines of text.

To take control of line length, you need to use the Netscape extensions. If you are controlling the appearance of your pages, you really need to use the extensions. You can use standard HTML in such a way that you can improve the appearance of your site, but there is little precision.

The following example sets up a three column table. The first and last columns are left empty, to act as fifty pixel wide margins. The centre column, the text column, is set to a width of 350. Even if the browser window is stretched to a width of 600 pixels, the lines will run no longer than the 350 wide column that contains them. Adding the NOWRAP tag will prevent the lines from running shorter than you expect.

```
<HTML>
<HEAD>
<TITLE>An Apology for Poetry</TITLE>
</HEAD>
<BODY BGCOLOR="#FFFFFF">
<PRE>
</PRE>
<B>from An Apology for Poetry</B><BR>
<I>Sir Philip Sidney</I>
<!--three column, one row table. 50.350.50-->
<TABLE>
<TR>
<TD WIDTH=50>
</TD>
 <TD WIDTH=350 ALIGN=LEFT VALIGN=TOP NOWRAP>
```

For as in outward things, to a man that had never seen an elephant or a rhinoceros, who should tell him most exquisitely all their shapes, colour, bigness and particular marks; or of a gorgeous palace, the architecture, with declaring the full beauties might well make the hearer able to repeat, as it were by rote, all he had heard, yet he should never satisfy his inward conceits with being witness to itself of a true lively knowledge; but the same man, as soon as he might see those beasts well painted, or the house well in model, should straightways grow, without need of any description, to a judicial comprehending of them: so no doubt the philosopher with his learned definition—be it of virtue, vices, matters of public policy or private government—replenisheth the memory with many infallible grounds of wisdom, which, not withstanding, lie dark before the imaginative and judging power, if they be not illuminated or figured forth by the speaking picture of poesy.

‹/TD›

‹TD WIDTH=50›

‹/TD›

‹/TR›

‹/TABLE›

‹/BODY›

‹/HTML›

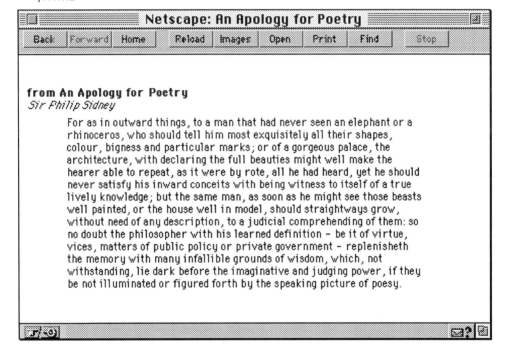

Figure 51 using a table to control line length

You may choose to let the table sit to the left of the page, as is the default. In this case, however wide the window is, all the additional white space will be to the right. This may encourage readers to resize their browser window to balance the page. Centring the table, or the whole page, is more liable to variation.

The heading above the block of text is outside the table. It could be set within the table, but putting it outside lets it sit to the left margin. Netscape cannot see ‹A NAME› within a table. If you are planning to have internal links based on headings, it would be wise to create a new table for each block of text, and leave the headings outside them.

The control that tables give you allow you to set text with some degree of precision in multiple columns. You could use the first column, or an additional one, for setting notes of headers to the side of the main text. You will probably need to set up multiple rows, use line breaks and NOWRAP to guard against confusion if readers set their text very large or very small. This will allow you, for example, to use poetry without worrying about incorrect line breaks.

The example in figure 52 has a single column, but the whole table is blockquoted to provide a margin. The combination of NOWRAP and BR allows you to set the precise line breaks regardless of the browser settings.

```
<HTML›
‹HEAD›
‹TITLE›Elegie: His Picture‹/TITLE›
‹/HEAD›
‹BODY BGCOLOR="#FFFFFF"›
‹PRE›
‹/PRE›
‹B›Elegie: His Picture‹/B›‹BR›
‹I›John Donne‹/I›
‹BLOCKQUOTE›
‹!--three column, one row table. 50.350.50--›
‹TABLE›
‹TR›
‹TD WIDTH=350 ALIGN=LEFT VALIGN=TOP NOWRAP›
Here take my Picture; though I bid farewell,‹BR›
```

Thine, in my heart, where my soule dwels, shall dwell.‹BR›
'Tis like me now, but I dead, 'twill be more‹BR›
When we are shadowes both, than 'twas before.‹BR›
When weather-beaten I come back; my hand,‹BR›
Perhaps with rude oares torne, or Sun beams tann'd,‹BR›
My face and brest of hairecloth, and my head‹BR›
With cares rash sodaine hoariness o'rspread,‹BR›
My body'a sack of bones, broken within,‹BR›
And powders blew staines scatter'd on my skinne;‹BR›
If rivall fooles taxe thee to have lov'd a man,‹BR›
So foule, and coarse, as, Oh I may seeme then,‹BR›
This shall say what I was: and thou shalt say,‹BR›
Doe his hurts reach mee? doth my word decay?‹BR›
Or doe they reach his judging minde, that hee‹BR›
Should like and love lesse, what he did love to see?‹BR›
That which in him was faire and delicate,‹BR›
Was but the milke, which in loves childish state‹BR›
Did nurse it: who now is grown strong enough‹BR›
To feed on that, which to didus'd tastes seemes tough.‹/TD›
‹/TR›
‹/TABLE›
‹/BLOCKQUOTE›
‹/BODY›
‹/HTML›

You can use HTML to achieve control over the page that was never intended. Learn what all the tags do, how they make the page behave, and use them to the best advantage. If you are concerned about access, and the use of non-graphical browsers, you will need to use much stricter HTML. If, however, you want to design your pages to the highest possible level, the more you know about HTML the more freedom you will have.

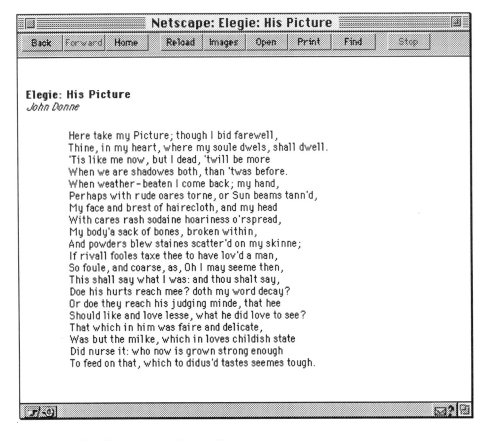

Elegie: His Picture
John Donne

Here take my Picture; though I bid farewell,
Thine, in my heart, where my soule dwels, shall dwell.
'Tis like me now, but I dead, 'twill be more
When we are shadowes both, than 'twas before.
When weather-beaten I come back; my hand,
Perhaps with rude oares torne, or Sun beams tann'd,
My face and brest of haircloth, and my head
With cares rash sodaine hoariness o'rspread,
My body'a sack of bones, broken within,
And powders blew staines scatter'd on my skinne;
If rivall fooles taxe thee to have lov'd a man,
So foule, and coarse, as, Oh I may seeme then,
This shall say what I was: and thou shalt say,
Doe his hurts reach mee? doth my word decay?
Or doe they reach his judging minde, that hee
Should like and love lesse, what he did love to see?
That which in him was faire and delicate,
Was but the milke, which in loves childish state
Did nurse it: who now is grown strong enough
To feed on that, which to didus'd tastes seemes tough.

Figure 52: Controlling line breaks and line length

CHAPTER 19

Netscape 2.0: Frames, Maps, Applets and Live Objects

Netscape 2.0 incorporates many new features that are already having a major effect on the appearance and behaviour of Web sites. The most significant additions are live objects, Java, Javascript, client side image maps and Frames. Frames in particular allow designers greater control over the layout and behaviour of Web pages. This chapter introduces live objects, such as Shockwave, and Java although their creation and implementation is covered in more detail in Section 4: Beyond HTML. Client side image maps, Javascript and Frames are covered in more detail in this chapter as they are more tightly bound to HTML.

The new tags move the Netscape extensions even further away from standard HTML. The changes and additions provide useful tools for web designers and developers, but they are breaking down the standardisation of HTML. This chapter comes before that on HTML 3.0 because the changes introduced by Netscape have already been implemented. Wherever you stand on the acceptability of additions to HTML, these new tags will be used all over the Web. They offer some useful features, and allow greater control over the page. The choice of some of the methods used may be open to argument, but the tags and the code exist.

LIVE OBJECTS

It is now possible to embed Director movies and Acrobat PDF files in Web pages. It will soon be possible to embed QuickTime movies as well. Previously, video clips and interactive elements were downloaded from a page, but had to be played outside the page with a helper application. This is no longer the case. They can now be an integral part of a Web site, adding a new element to the possibilities of a Web site. These plug-in elements can be used to add content seamlessly to the page. Plug-ins allow other objects to become part of the page. There should be no obvious disparity between the embedded objects and the main browser interface. The browser interface will remain the same, although the interface of the page and the navigation contained within a Web site will depend on the contents of that site. The player engines work behind the scenes to add functionality to the Web site, and the reader sees the elements on the page as an intrinsic part of the page. Some of the plug-ins will allow data to stream to the reader's computer, allowing the data to be seen and used as it arrives.

The incorporation of a player engine, Shockwave, for Macromedia Director movies is very exciting. A great deal of creative interactive multimedia work has already been done in Director, and the application of this experience to the Web has led to some very interesting results. Live objects are all added to the page with the ‹EMBED› tag.

‹EMBED SRC="movies/demo.dcr" WIDTH=120 HEIGHT=100›

embeds a Shockwave movie, demo.dcr, into the page. If the movie is not 120 by 100 pixels in size it will be scaled to fit the space reserved by the height and width attributes. The height and width tags are essential, rather than optional as in the case of images. If a Shockwave capable browser, like Netscape 2, loads the page containing the embedded movie, the movie will download automatically and play as part of the page. This allows Web designers to add movement, sound and interactivity to the Web in a way that was almost unthinkable a few months ago. The levels of sophistication apparent in some of the very first Shockwave movies are already changing the conception of the possible. Shockwave is covered in more detail in the next section.

There is still the bandwidth cost related to video and audio formats, and the downloading times are unlikely to be reduced significantly, but careful choice of small clips and high impact elements allow designers to implement a higher degree of activity and interactivity within the page.

The ability to include Acrobat documents within a page allows the designer full control over the appearance of type and layout within the Acrobat objects. Hyperlinks can be placed within the Acrobat documents, linking to other pages if the Acrobat document, or to any URL. The Adobe Acrobat format is covered in more detail in the next section "Beyond HTML".

There will undoubtedly be more plug-ins developed to support other formats, but this is a significant move towards highly interactive Web pages. The problems will arise, however, as developers start to overload pages with multiple high bandwidth elements. Decisions will have to be made at each step of the design process. The inclusion of large graphics already causes arguments about accessibility and the purpose of the Web. The addition of inline video and interactivity will certainly raise a few temperatures. If your audience is likely to be on a slow connection you will need to hold back on the heavy bandwidth elements. If a reader has to wait half an hour to download a page, will they bother waiting?

External video clips are nearly always seen as an optional extra, simply because they aren't an intrinsic part of the page. You can recommend that readers download a video clip, but the clip is outside the page. When the videos are built into the page, however, they will be approached in a very different way. The same decisions must be made, but they become more important. When something is being built directly into the page it ceases to be an optional extra. There are some things where video is the best way of showing your readers what they need to see but would text, audio or still images convey the message better than video? Is this the right medium for this particular message? Interactive multimedia can be highly effective, but really shouldn't be used wastefully. The bandwidth cost of multimedia is high. The possibilities have been increased, but access times have not been reduced. Readers will have to wait a significant amount of time to experience these elements — will it be worth the wait?

JAVA APPLETS

Java, a programming language developed by Sun Microsystems, allows developers to build real time interaction into Web pages. Java can be used to write small self contained programs called applets. Java is a significant addition to the Web developers' tool chest. The inclusion of Java applets in Netscape will bring the language and the possibilities it offers to the forefront of Web development. Java's main strength is that it is completely platform independent. Once an applet has been written, it can be played by any browser that supports Java, regardless of the operating system it is running under. The language itself is based on C++ and allows developers to create interactive elements on the page. Images can be changed, sounds can be played, and the page can react to the reader's input. Animated elements can be interesting, but animations that react to the user's input can be far more effective. If a button changes colour as the mouse moves over it, readers will know that the button is active. Simple feedback can be very powerful, and varying degrees of change can be built in to the response.

Ease of use will almost certainly expand the spread of Java based interactivity. The separation of design and programming can sometimes lead to the creativity being stripped out of both sides. Any tools that can help designers and programmers work together will lead to interesting collaboration.

The possibilities of Java applets are widespread—from simple animations to complex systems for creating specific pages for individual readers.There is more information in the next section about the Java language, and information about some of the resources available on the Net are in the appendices. The Java Programming Guide is recommended reading for anyone interested in working with Java.

Spinning logos are not enough. If you are planning to add live interactive elements to your Web site, stretch your imagination. The new developments in Web technology give you the chance to expand the information and entertainment value of your site. Each time there is a new development, however, the medium seems to relapse to its early stages. New media require new thinking. Adopting new techniques to achieve old goals will not always be the best way forward. "Click here to see the chairman read the annual report" really won't cut it, just as a scanned brochure does not automatically make an interesting Web site. The tools are there to do much more.

JAVASCRIPT

JavaScript is a scripting language built into Netscape 2.0. Although it shares half a name with Java, it takes a slightly different approach to adding a wide range of interactivity to the Web. JavaScript is a programming language, but is far simpler to learn and use than Java for non-programmers.

JavaScript, unlike cgi scripts, runs on the visitor's machine, rather than on the server which makes them faster and more responsive to change. The scripts are part of the HTML files, and are downloaded as text as part of the Web page that contain them. A great advantage of this, for developers, is that the scripts you write can be tested and do not need to run on a server to work. They are interpreted by the browser, so you can test you work as you go.

JavaScript can be used for many things—checking the input of forms, querying the user's browser, providing navigational feedback, generating parts of a page on the fly.

JavaScript can be used to lift information from the user's computer—like the time or the date—and react accordingly. Early examples of JavaScript have included clocks that sit on the page or the status bar, calculators, small spreadsheets, time sensitive messages and a neat tool that lets you choose background and text colours for a Web site.

The scripts can be hidden from other browsers, browsers that do not support JavaScript, by encasing them in normal HTML comments (‹!-- --›). Scripts are generally added to the HEAD of an HTML document, although small scripts can live anywhere within a page. Like HTML, the browser starts reading the page from the top, and works down. This means that JavaScripts embedded at the end of the page will not work until that part of the page has been loaded.

JavaScript is highly extendible, and can be used to create fairly complex effects, but there are some very simple tricks that can be used with very little programming. One of the nicest easy features is a link feedback, which can be added to any link to give your reader a better idea of what lies behind a link. Normally, as you move your cursor over a link, the destination URL is displayed in the status bar. Using a tiny JavaScript command, you can modify this display to add the message of your choice.

In this example, the message "send me email" would appear in the status bar if you moved the cursor over the mailto link.

```
‹A HREF="mailto:katie@question.co.uk"
onMouseOver="window.status='send me email!' ; return
true"›katie@question.co.uk‹/A›
```

One of the best uses of this feature is to explain what lies behind some of the shorter, more cryptic links you may need to use in menus. In this example, there is a short list of links, "think - focus - work - team - talk - find" which are explained more fully with the onMouseOver command.

```
‹P ALIGN=CENTER›
‹A HREF="think/index.html" onMouseOver="window.status='Think - in-depth
coverage of current issues in media' ; return true"›think‹/A› -

‹A HREF="focus/index.html" onMouseOver="window.status='Focus - join our
focus group to keep abreast of research issues' ; return true"›focus‹/A› -
```

```
<A HREF="work/index.html" onMouseOver="window.status='Work - about the
Media Business, and the work we do' ; return true">work</A> -

<A HREF="team/index.html" onMouseOver="window.status='Team - people
and departments at the Media Business' ; return true">team</A> -

<A HREF="talk/index.html" onMouseOver="window.status='Talk - contact us
by email, phone or on foot' ; return true">talk</A> -

<A HREF="find/index.html" onMouseOver="window.status='Find - delve into
our large archive of information' ; return true">find</A>
</P>
```

Obviously, JavaScript can go a great deal further than this as it can be used as a fairly fully-fledged scripting language. JavaScript can be used in combination with Java, with Shoockwave and other forms of scripting to build a higher level of interactivity into a page.

The Netscape site contains the full documentation for JavaScript, and is a very good place to start. There are plenty of other resources and tutorials online, and some of the relevant URLs are in the appendix.

FRAMES

The introduction of frames is very exciting. Frames allow Web designers to take control of the page layout to a far greater degree than any other HTML elements. Frames are similar in construction to tables, but the possibilities for their use go much further. Tables allow you to position elements on a page with a certain degree of control, but frames give each element more independence and flexibility. Frames can be used to split a page up into mulitple independent elements. Portions of the page can be frozen, to keep navigation information or other important messages on screen regardless of the reader's scrolling. This opens up a wide range of possibilities.

The main problem with frames is that other browsers will be unable to display anything contained within the frames. Netscape has added a couple of tags to allow non-compatible browsers to read part of the page, but this requires additional work for Web developers. If you have to build two sites—one for Netscape that takes advantage of frames, and one for browsers that do not handle frames—your workload is increased significantly. The non-frame alternatives can be on the same page as the frames, but this can lead to complete chaos.

THE FRAME HOLDER PAGE

The page is divided into a number of frames and each frame can itself contain a full HTML document, each with its own URL. Working with frames is slightly different from working with normal HTML. First you set up a frameholder which allocates space on the page to the different frames, and then you give instructions as to which document to place in each frame. In the initial frame holder page, the ‹FRAMESET›‹/FRAMESET› tags are used instead of the ‹BODY›‹/BODY› containers.

A frame holder page that contains a single empty frame would look like this:

```
‹HTML›
‹HEAD›
‹TITLE›A Blank Frames Page‹/TITLE›
‹/HEAD›
‹FRAMESET›
‹/FRAMESET›
‹/HTML›
```

There are no body tags. The body elements are part of the contents of the external documents that are used to fill the frames.

DIVIDING THE PAGE INTO MULTIPLE FRAMES

The layout of the frames on the page is arranged by row and column. The number of columns, and their sizes are specified with the COLS attribute.

⟨FRAMESET COLS="w, w, w"⟩

The width of each column can be set to a particular number of pixels, to a percentage of the window, or to vary according to need. Using a simple pixel value for the width is the ideal to give you the most control over the layout of the page, but the browser is able to override your settings if the reader sets the window to such a size that it is too narrow to display the columns. The total width of all the columns has to be 100% of the width of the browser window. Mixing a fixed width with a relative width may therefore be the best way of balancing the possible layouts on the page. The width of a column can be specified by percentage, or as a proportion of the available space by setting the width value with an asterisk.

⟨FRAMESET COLS="100,300,*"⟩

would produce a layout with three columns, the first 100 pixels wide, the second 300 pixels wide and the third column scaled to fit the available space.

⟨FRAMESET COLS="*, 2*, *"⟩

would set all of the widths based on the width of the browser window, but the central column would be twice the width of the outside columns.

⟨FRAMESET COLS="25%, 50%, 25%"⟩

would achieve the same balance of column widths, with the absolute sizes set by the width of the browser window.

The size and number of rows are specified in much the same way as the columns. To build a frame holder that contained two equal size rows, the HTML you would need would look like this:

```
<HTML>
<HEAD>
<TITLE>A two frame Page</TITLE>
</HEAD>

    <FRAMESET ROWS="50%, 50%">
       <FRAME SRC="top.html">
       <FRAME SRC="bottom.html">
    </FRAMESET>

</HTML>
```

alternatively,you could use the following HTML which would produce exactly the same effect. The SRC is used to reference the HTML document that is used to fill the frame. Both of these examples are shown in figure 53. In the illustration, the frames are left blank for clarity.

```
<HTML>
<HEAD>
<TITLE>A two frame Page</TITLE>
</HEAD>

    <FRAMESET ROWS="*, *">
       <FRAME SRC="top.html">
       <FRAME SRC="bottom.html">
    </FRAMESET>

</HTML>
```

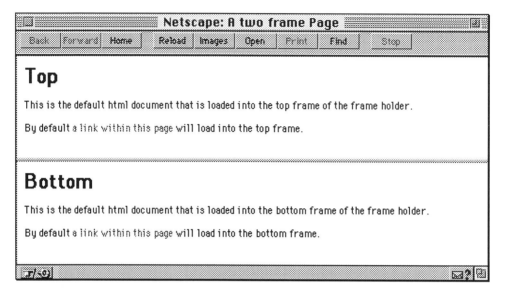

Figure 53: A two frame page

Within each set of frames, each frame and its behaviour is specified. One frameset can be nested inside another. Anywhere you can put a frame, you can put another frameset. So if your intial frameset specifies the number of columns, each column can be divided into rows on a column by column basis. If your initial frameset specifies rows, each row can be filled with a frame or a new frame set that breaks it down into any number of columns. Figure 54 shows how the following example sets up a page with two columns, and splits the first column into two rows. The block at the top left is 150 pixels wide and two-thirds of the height of the browser window.

```
<HTML>
<HEAD>
<TITLE>A two column, 3 frames Page</TITLE>
</HEAD>

<!--this is the parent frameset that divides the page into two columns-->

<FRAMESET COLS="150,*">
```

‹!--this is a nested frameset that breaks the first column into two rows--›

```
‹FRAMESET ROWS="2*, *"›
    ‹FRAME SRC="buttons.html"›
    ‹FRAME SRC="marginblock.html"›
‹/FRAMESET›
```

‹!--the second column contains a single frame--›

```
‹FRAME SRC="content.html"›
```

```
‹/FRAMESET›
```

‹!--this closes the main frameset--›

```
‹/HTML›
```

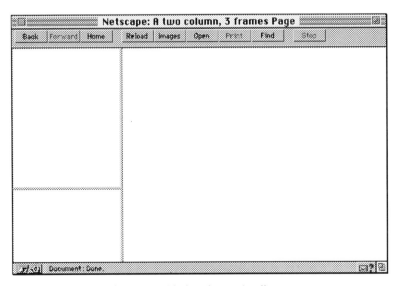

Figure 54: A two column, two row frame set,with three frames in all

The value of the SRC attribute is that of the URL of the document to be displayed in the frame. If a frame is to be left empty, no frame needs to be specified, the size of the empty frame has already been set by the FRAMESET tag.

A margin can be specified for each frame with MARGINWIDTH. MARGINHEIGHT is also set in pixels, and determines the size of the top and bottom margins for each frame. The value is specified in pixels, and cannot be less than one, although setting a margin is optional. The margins cannot be set so large that there is no room for the contents of the frame.

If you do not specify a margin, the browser will try to determine an appropriate margin. To retain control over the spacing of each frame relative to the others, however, MARGINWIDTH and MARGINHEIGHT are useful tools, particularly if the browser is able to override the sizes of the frames themselves. In early beta releases of Netscape 2, the margin controls were very unreliable.

Each frame can be scrolled independently from the page, and from the other frames. By setting the SCROLLING attribute, you can choose to suppress the scroll bars so that they are never visible with SCROLLING=NO, ensure that they are always visible with SCROLLING=YES, or let the browser decide with SCROLLING=AUTO. The scrolling is set for each frame, and the default is auto.

‹FRAME SRC="buttons.html" MARGINWIDTH=5 MARGINHEIGHT=5
SCROLLING=NO NORESIZE›

The above tag sets the contents of the frame to the document buttons.html, with a margin of five pixels all round. The size of the frame is not set in the FRAME tag, but in the FRAMESET that contains it. Scrolling is turned off so the reader will be unable to see a scroll bar on this frame. NORESIZE prevent the reader from resizing the frame by dragging the frames edge to a new position. By default all frames can be resized by the user.

Figure 55 shows the following example, again with blank frames for clarity, which forces scrollbars onto two of the three frames.

```html
<HTML>
<HEAD>
<TITLE>Frames</TITLE>
</HEAD>

<!--this is the parent frameset that divides the page into two columns-->

<FRAMESET COLS="150,*">

    <!--this is a nested frameset that breaks the first column into two rows-->

    <FRAMESET ROWS="2*, *">
        <FRAME SRC="buttons.html" SCROLLING=YES>
        <FRAME SRC="logo.html" SCROLLING=NO>
    </FRAMESET>

    <!--the second column contains a single frame-->

    <FRAME SRC="content.html" SCROLLING=YES>

</FRAMESET>

<!--this closes the main frameset-->

</HTML>
```

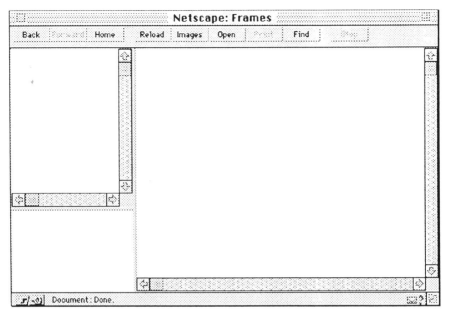

"*figure 55: frames with scrollbars*

Names and targets

Each frame can be given a NAME so that it can become a target for links from other pages, or from other frames within the same page. Names are optional, and only need to be given if you want to make a particular frame the destination of a link. They do, however, give you the control you need over the behaviour of a framed Web site. Names allow you to choose the destination for a link.

By default, clicking a link within a frame will load the destination page within the same frame. As an example, the following five html documents are set up—a frame holder and four normal pages used to load into the frames. The documents top.html and bottom.html are loaded with the frame holder, as shown in figure 56. Figure 57 shows what happens when the link in the top frame is clicked. The file toplink1.html is loaded into the top frame, and the bottom frame is unchanged. Clicking in the link in the bottom frame will load the file bottomlink1.html into the bottom frame. The documents are independent of each other but within the same page.

```
<HTML>
<HEAD>
<TITLE>A two part frame holder</TITLE>
</HEAD>

    <FRAMESET ROWS="*, *">
        <FRAME SRC="top.html" NAME="topframe">
        <FRAME SRC="bottom.html" NAME="bottomframe">
    </FRAMESET>

</HTML>

<HTML>
<HEAD>
<TITLE>default contents for topframe</TITLE>
</HEAD>
<BODY>
<H1>Top</H1>
<P>
This is the default html document that is loaded into the top frame
of the frame holder.
</P>
<P>
By default <A HREF="toplink1.html">a link within this page</A> will load into
the top frame.
</P>
</BODY>
</HTML>
```

```
<HTML>
<HEAD>
<TITLE>default contents for bottomframe</TITLE>
</HEAD>
<BODY>
<H1>Bottom</H1>
<P>
This is the default html document that is loaded into the bottom frame
of the frame holder.
</P>
<P>
By default <A HREF="bottomlink1.html">a link within this page</A> will load
into the bottom frame.
</P>
</BODY>
</HTML>

<HTML>
<HEAD>
<TITLE>contents for the link from the topframe</TITLE>
</HEAD>
<BODY>
<H1>Top Link 1</H1>
<P>
This is the document loaded by clicking on the link in the top frame.
</P>
</BODY>
</HTML>
```

```
<HTML>
<HEAD>
<TITLE>contents for the link from the bottomframe</TITLE>
</HEAD>
<BODY>
<H1>Bottom Link 1</H1>
<P>
This is the document loaded by clicking on the link in the bottom frame.
</P>
</BODY>
</HTML>
```

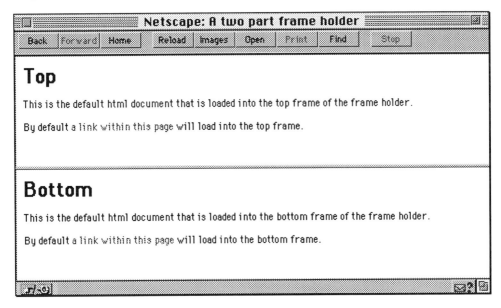

Fiigure 56: The frame holder with the default documents,top.html and bottom.html loaded.

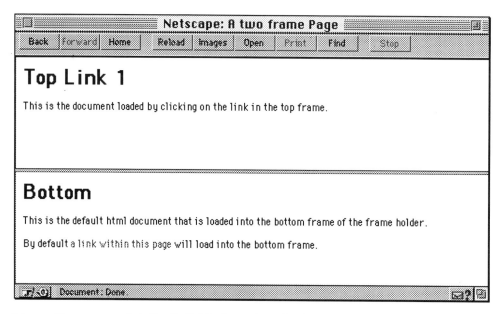

Figure 57: The same page, but after the link in the top frame has been clicked and the file toplink1.html has been loaded

If the default contents for the top frame were changed slightly, the link now behaves in a different way because the link has a named target, matching the NAME set up in the frame holder.

```
‹HTML›
‹HEAD›
‹TITLE›default contents for topframe‹/TITLE›
‹/HEAD›
‹BODY›
‹H1›Top‹/H1›
‹P›
This is the default html document that is loaded into the top frame
of the frame holder.
‹/P›
```

‹P›

By default ‹A HREF="toplink1.html"›a link within this page‹/A› will load into the top frame.

‹/P›

‹P›

By adding a target to the link it can be forced to load into another frame. ‹A HREF="toplink2.html" TARGET="bottomframe"›This link will load a document into the bottom frame.‹/A›

‹/P›

‹/BODY›

‹/HTML›

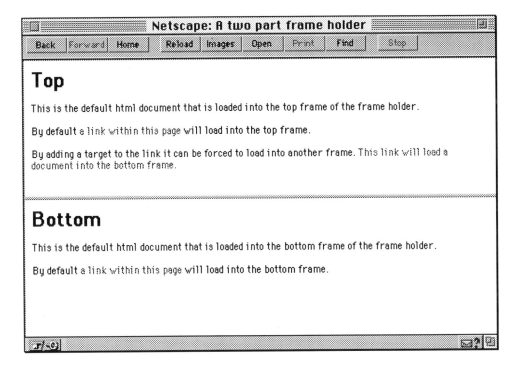

Figure 58: Shows the page after the link with the named target has been clicked

Adding a target to control the destination frame of a link is not restricted to links within your own Web site. If you are linking to an external link, you can still determine where in your frame holder the page is loaded. In the above example, you could link to the search engine Yahoo, loading the Yahoo page into the bottom frame by adding the following line to the file top.html:

```
<P>
Take a look in
<A HREF="http://www.yahoo.com" TARGET="bottomframe">Yahoo</A>
</P>
```

Unless targets have been named on the links within the Yahoo site, the links you follow will continue to load pages into the bottom frame of your frame holder.

With careful control, you can set up an entire Web site that can be navigated from a single frame holder. Loading a page into a named frame is very useful. It allows you to hold one frame for navigation—for a menu or a set of buttons. Clicking on one of the buttons will load up the relevant content into another frame. This is of great benefit to the reader who is given the navigational devices as a constant part of the page, allowing her to move more swiftly between pages, without waiting for reused graphical devices to be redrawn on each page. It allows you as the designer to leave banners, navigational devices, or logos as a fixed part of the page, unaffected by the reader's scrolling.

Sometimes you will want to escape from the existing frame holder and load up another one, perhaps with a different layout. This can be done very simply. There are a few special targets with particular effects that you can call upon. If, for example, you wanted to leave the existing frame holder and load up a new frame holder called frame4.html that contained four frames, you would use a link like this:

```
<A HREF="frame4.hmtl" TARGET="_top">
```

The underscore is an essential part of the name of the target. TARGET="_new" will open a fresh browser window and load the destination page into the new window. The underscore should not be used at the start of any target names apart from the preset ones that have a particular function.

The best way to find good uses for frames is to experiment until you find a combination of a good looking layout and a fast and effective interface. Try to take advantage of loading different pages within a single frame holder as far as you can, because this is where you will gain the most speed. There are some sites that load one frame holder after another, rather than using the flexibility of loading different pages into individual frames.

The above examples should give you a useful starting point, but look around the Web for more ambitious uses of frames. This chapter is only an introduction to the mechanisms involved. Frames give you enormous control over the behaviour of the page, and they can be used to great effect. Remember to test your site as well as you can:

- stretch the browser window into as many different sizes as possible;
- check the site on different sized monitors;

- set your browser preferences to a very different typeface and size.

Frames are more complicated than standard HTML, so it is worth spending a little more time to check that your site is totally robust before letting it go live. Test each link to make sure that each page loads into the correct frame.

DEALING WITH BROWSERS THAT DO NOT SUPPORT FRAMES

Anything contained with ‹FRAMESET›‹/FRAMESET› will be be invisible to a browser that cannot view frames. Using the ‹NOFRAMES›‹/NOFRAMES› tags, however, you can add a section to the page that will only be seen if the frames are not displayed. Regular HTML tags can be used within the NOFRAMES area, even though it is contained within the FRAMESET area of the document. You can use these tags to point other readers to a non-frames version of your site, or to the source of a browser that supports frames.

```
‹HTML›
‹HEAD›
‹TITLE›A two part frame holder with a noframes alternative‹/TITLE›
‹/HEAD›
```

```
<FRAMESET ROWS="*, *">
    <FRAME SRC="top.html" NAME="topframe">
    <FRAME SRC="bottom.html" NAME="bottomframe">
</FRAMESET>

<NOFRAMES>
<BODY>
<H1>Oops!</H1>
<P>
You have found your way into the framed section of this Web site and your
browser does not support frames. Perhaps you'd like to visit the area of this
site that has been designed for your browser?
<A HREF="plainsite/index.html">Please follow me!</A>
</P>
</BODY>
</NOFRAMES>
</HTML>
```

This example would look different depending on the browser you use to view it. If
you were using Netscape 2, you would see the framed version shown earlier. If
you were using another browser, one that did not support frames, you would only see the
warning message and the link leading you to another area of the site. If you are going
to set up any part of your Web site with frames, you must be aware of other browsers
and provide an alternative, unless you believe that all your intended audience will be
using Netscape 2.0.

CLIENT SIDE IMAGE MAPS

Image maps are a powerful but slow way of using images as a means of navigation
within a Web site. There are several problems inherent in image maps. There is no
visual feedback for a reader. As a reader moves the mouse over the image, the only

information they get is about the coordinates within the image, and nothing about their destination. Unless the image itself contains that information, a reader does not know where she is linking to when she clicks on an image map. Another problem is that when she clicks on the map, the server needs to be contacted to determine where she clicked, and there is a delay while this information is processed and the destination page is sourced. This additional delay can be significant if the server is busy or traffic is heavy. Image maps cannot be used locally, they need to run on a server, under HTTP. This server dependency can be troublesome while building and testing sites, or if the site needs to be moved from one server to another.

Within the Netscape method, there are two parts to an image map—the image and the information about the hotzones within the image and their destinations. The image is added to the page in the normal way, but with the addition of USEMAP.

‹IMG SRC="images/mediamast.gif" BORDER=0 WIDTH=487 HEIGHT=176
ALT="studies - features - help" usemap="#mediamastmap"›

This tag places the 487 by 176 pixel image mediamast.gif on the page and gives a text alternative. USEMAP="#mediamastmap" contains the instruction to use the map information named footermap contained within the same page as the image.

The map information is not contained within a separate map file, as it would be with ISMAP, but within the ‹MAP›‹/MAP› tags specified on the same page. Each hotzone within the image is specified with its own ‹AREA› tag that defines the co-ordinates of the area and its link destination. The AREA is assumed to be a rectangle, unless another shape is specified. At the moment, Netscape only supports RECT and CIRCLE. The coordinates are defined as left, top, right, bottom for each area.

‹HTML›
‹HEAD›
‹TITLE›client side image map in Netscape‹/TITLE›
‹BODY›

‹MAP NAME="mediamastmap"›

```
<AREA COORDS="107,25, 199,109"
HREF="http://www.mediabiz.co.uk/docs/mediabiz/work/studies/index.html">
<AREA COORDS="199,25, 285,109"
HREF="http://www.mediabiz.co.uk/docs/mediabiz/think/index.html">
<AREA COORDS="285,25, 370,109"
HREF="http://www.mediabiz.co.uk/docs/mediabiz/help.html">
<AREA COORDS="0,0, 435,176" NOHREF>

</MAP>

<IMG SRC="images/mediamast.gif" BORDER=0 WIDTH=487 HEIGHT=176
ALT="studies - features - help" usemap="#mediamastmap">

</BODY>
</HTML>
```

You can test client side image maps locally, without running them on a server. As you pass your cursor over the defined hotspots on the image, you will see the destination URL of the links, rather than the coordinates you see with a server side ISMAP.

This example specifies four hotzones on the image and their destination pages. The final AREA covers the whole image and has a NOHREF tag. This sets all the parts of the image that are not covered by other shapes to have no destination. This is not strictly necessary, as any region that is not covered by an AREA tag is assumed to have NOHREF.

An area, even that with NOHREF, can cover the whole image without having an effect on the hotzones. If areas overlap at all, precedence is given to the area that comes higher up in the list. If the NOHREF area above was at the top of the list, it would take precedence over all the other areas, and the image would have no active hotzones.

The map information need not be contained within the same file as the image. If you use the same image repeatedly as a map, the map information could be on a single Web page, and used all over the site.

It is possible to set up the image map so that it can be handled by local map information, or by a map file with ISMAP. This provides an image map alternative for readers who are not using Netscape. The following example would be handled by the Netscape style ‹MAP›‹/MAP› information specified with USEMAP if the reader was using the Netscape browser, or by server side image map methods if not:

‹A HREF="mediamast.map"›‹IMG SRC="images/mediamast.gif" BORDER=0 WIDTH=487 HEIGHT=176 ALT="studies - features - help" USEMAP="#mediamastmap" ISMAP›‹/A›

This is a flexible method for handling image maps, as it provides something to cover all options. The feedback and speed that client side maps offer a reader have a great advantage over server side maps. Give your readers as much feedback as possible—if you can let them know where they are going at each stage, they are more likely to make the right navigational choices and find the information they want.

The new Netscape features and extensions to HTML offer Web developers more choices. There is a higher degree of control over both the look and the behaviour of Web sites. If you do not feel that you would be excluding your main audience, you should make the best use of them you can. Expand the use of the medium, and give your readers the best site possible. It is important, however, to remember the status of the Netscape extensions and their place on the Web. Keep informed of the developments and the debates that surround the Web at all times. You will be chasing a moving target, but the more information you have the better you will be able to produce the most effective and most attractive sites.

CHAPTER 20

HTML 3.0 in more detail

HTML 3.0 is still officially "work in progress". Most of this chapter is based on information in the "HyperText Markup Language Specification Version 3.0" and the "Document Type Definition for the HyperText Markup Language" by Dave Raggett. These documents are subject to change, and redevelopment so it is well worth checking their current status at the W3 Consortium Web site. The addresses of the relevant documents are in the appendix. This chapter is an introduction to some of the changes you can expect to see with the introduction of future versions of HTML.

This section does not cover all the proposed additions and changes to HTML. I have, for example, skipped the section on mathematical layout.

This chapter may be less specific than others. That's because it is based on reading the specifications rather than on direct experience. If you are interested in trying out some of the HTML 3.0 tags, other than the ones supported by browsers like Netscape, you will have to work with the browser Arena. Arena is the W3 Consortium test browser, available from their site, which supports most of the tags as they are being developed but it runs only under Unix and X11.

STYLE SHEETS

Style sheets allow you to map HTML tags to a display that you choose. Just as in word processing or DTP packages, you can assign styles to text with a set of rules for each style. The style sheets are hierarchical, so you can specify a default style and then the exceptions, and how the styles are related. For example, once you have specified the standard body text you can specify a top level heading by saying how much bigger it is, how much space to leave above and below, that it's bold and centred. Lower level headings can be defined in terms of the higher level headings.

The addition of CLASS to HTML 3.0 allows you to map new styles to style sheets, in addition to any styles you want to apply to existing HTML tags. Almost all the tags that are allowed in the body of an HTML document can have a CLASS assigned to them. Adding CLASS to a tag indicates that it should be treated in a different way than the standard tag would be treated. If, for example, you wanted an introduction paragraph on a page to be displayed in a particular way, you could label the paragraph ‹P CLASS=INTRODUCTION› rather than just ‹P›. You can choose to be more specific than this, by adding another class to the tag like this: ‹P CLASS=INTRODUCTION.CHAPTER› or ‹P CLASS=INTRODUCTION.SECTION›. The Classes are separated with a full stop and are read left to right. Your style sheet provides the instructions to the browser about how these classes should be treated. You attach a particular style to a document with the ‹LINK› tag.

Style sheets will not provide absolute control over the appearance of Web pages but they will provide more control. You may be able to specify a typeface, or a font family and a type size but the reader will probably be able to override your decisions. You should be able to control the spacing and the alignment of elements and the colours and styles of text. For example, you might want the INTRODUCTION in the above example to have wider margins than standard body text, and the INTRODUC-TION.CHAPTER to be in italics.

The exact form that style sheets will take has not yet been decided. For the current state of the discussions you will need to check the W3 Consortium site.

‹ID› AND ‹LANG›

Like CLASS, ‹ID› and ‹LANG› can be applied to almost every tag within the body of an HTML document. ID is a replacement for NAME, and is used to mark particular parts within a document. Before HTML 3.0, the NAME was added to a point on a page like this: ‹A NAME="introduction"›‹H1›Introduction‹/H1›‹/A›. ID is slightly different: ‹H1 ID="introduction"›Introduction‹/H1›. Building a link to an ID is the same as linking to a NAME: ‹A HREF="#introduction"›.

Once HTML 3.0 is introduced, the use of ‹A NAME› will not be recommended.

‹LANG› allows you to specify the language of an element. Some punctuation, ligatures and other type elements vary from language to language. ‹LANG="en.uk"› would specify the particular variation of English as spoken in Britain if there was a need for any language specific behaviour. ‹LANG› can be added to almost all of the body tags.

DIVISIONS

The ‹DIV› tag is used in combination with ‹CLASS› to break the text into sections. Typical divisions would be chapters, sections, appendices, headers, footers or references. A footer section could be specified on the page with ‹DIV CLASS=FOOTER›‹/DIV› The treatment of each division can be handled by a style sheet for each independent section. Each division can be aligned on the page, without the need for CLASS. Everything contained within ‹DIV ALIGN=RIGHT›‹/DIV›, for example, would be aligned to the right of the page.

ALIGNMENT AND FLOW OF TEXT

‹ALIGN› has already been covered in this chapter. It can be added to paragraphs, headers or images setting them to the left, right or centre. Justify is available, but is probably not a good idea without extremely tight control over the behaviour of the type on a page.

‹CLEAR› does not behave in quite the same way as Netscape's ‹BR=CLEAR›. CLEAR=LEFT moves down past the image until the left margin is clear, CLEAR=RIGHT to the right margin and CLEAR=ALL until both margins are free. You can decide to place the next element alongside the image as long as there is enough space. You can control this by setting the minimum allowed space to 200 pixels, for example, with CLEAR="200 pixels". As you do not know exactly what size type is being displayed, you may prefer to use "en" to specify how much space is allowed. The size of an en unit is based on the type size rather than an absolute. An en is half the point size of the typeface displayed. CLEAR="36 en" would move the next element down until there were at least 36 en units free.

Text is normally allowed to flow freely depending on the width of the browser. NOWRAP prevents the text breaking except at points specified with ‹BR›.

‹P NOWRAP›

this tag prevents text from wrapping to the next line. This line would not wrap until ‹BR› was inserted.

‹/P›

If there are only a few points where the line must not break, rather than particular points where it should break, you can use a non-breaking space. The space is displayed normally, but cannot be broken across two lines.   should be used for each non-breaking space. Remember to use the ampersand and the semi-colon as with all special characters.

CHANGES TO EXISTING HTML TAGS

Most body tags have the possible additions of CLASS, ID, LAND, CLEAR and NOWRAP. Beyond this, however, there are some changes to specific tags.

Headings can be numbered or marked with bullets or special icons. Headings retain the six levels as before, but you now have the choice of adding numbers to some or all of your headings. SEQNUM lets you add a number to a header. All the headers that follow at the same level, ‹H1› or ‹H2› for example, will follow this numbering. SKIP is used to override the continuity. SKIP=1 would miss out the next number in the sequence and use the one after.

DINGBAT and SRC can also be added to headings. Using SRC you can add any image as a bullet that gets slotted in just before the heading. This simplifies the use of graphical bullets by removing the necessity of specifying and aligning them separately. Dingbats are small icons that are supplied by the browser rather than by the server. Because they are built into the browser there is no wait for them to download.

‹H1 SRC="star.gif"›Welcome‹/H1› would display the bullet star.gif before the top level heading.

Lists are expanded to include list headers. They are used in the same way as headers in a table, to indicate a label for the list. List headers are optional and can be added as the first item of a list. Headers can be used in ordered lists, unordered lists and definition lists. In this example the first item, Oxford Colleges, is the list header.

```
‹UL PLAIN›
‹LH›Oxford Colleges
‹LI›Worcester
‹LI›Wadham
‹/UL›
```

If you would rather there were no bullet before each, you can suppress them with PLAIN. As with headings, you can choose an image or a dingbat to act as a bullet. These are specified with the DINGBAT or SRC tags, one for each list item. This should be used in conjunction with PLAIN.

If you want the list to be displayed in the most compact way possible, by reducing the font size, or reducing the amount of space, you can add COMPACT to the opening list tag. The specific behaviour of compact will probably depend on the browser. If you want the list to be displayed horizontally, you can add WRAP=HORIZ so that they are ranged across the page. This can be useful for short items that could fit across a page. If the browser window is narrow, however, they could wrap around to a second line. The default WRAP is VERT, which places each list item on a new line.

Netscape allows you to control the numbering of ordered lists with START. In HTML 3.0 you can specify the initial number of an ordered list with SEQNUM, and jump the sequence with SKIP, as with headings.

The Blockquote tag is being changed to ‹BQ›‹/BQ›, and ‹CREDIT›‹/CREDIT› is added to indicate the source of the quote. The credit should be used after the quote text, before the closing ‹/BQ›. Blockquotes cannot be aligned with the ALIGN attribute.

HTML 3.0 allows you to use images in the place of plain rules. Although you can already create a rule image and add it to any page, this new kind of rule behaves as a standard horizontal rule if it is viewed with a non-graphical browser. Add the image you want to use with the SRC attribute:

```
‹HR SRC="blue2pixline.gif"›
```

Images can be aligned to left or right with ALIGN=LEFT or ALIGN=RIGHT, and the height and width can be specified. This has two advantages: an appropriately sized space can be left while the page is loading; and images can be scaled on the page. The HEIGHT and WIDTH can be specified in pixels or en units by using UNITS=PIXELS or UNITS=EN. An en unit is half the size of the point size of the text.

The use of the ‹IMG› tag for larger images is being discouraged, in favour of ‹FIG›. ‹IMG› should be used for smaller inline images and bullets or rules. ‹FIG› is more flexible and gives the designer a greater degree of control.

FORMS

There are several additions and changes to forms in HTML 3.0. Not only can ID, LANG and class be added to the forms elements, there are two new attributes that can be used with INPUT, SELECTION and TEXTAREA. DISABLED prevents the use of an input field. The field is rendered normally, but is not available for use. Text cannot be typed into an input box, check boxes cannot be checked and so on. It is fairly likely that browsers will grey the DISABLED fields out, in the way that items on a menu are greyed out when they are not available.

ERROR provides an error message if the reader's input into a form is incorrect. If the form requires at least eight characters, and the reader types in only six, the value of the ERROR could be "please choose a password of eight characters or more". The display of the error message will depend on the browser.

A TEXTAREA can be aligned on the page in the way that images are aligned, with ALIGN=LEFT or ALIGN=RIGHT. The text will then flow around the textarea as if it were a graphic. To align the textarea in relation to the baseline of the text, you will be able to use ALIGN=TOP, ALIGN=MIDDLE or ALIGN=BOTTOM. By default, the top of the textarea is aligned to baseline of the top of the text.

Images can be used for the submit and the reset button instead of text. This is added with the SRC tag. They can contain any image, but their meaning should be clear. If the button used does not suggest its purpose, readers will be unsure about how to submit their forms.

Three new input types have been added to HTML 3.0. RANGE provides a minimum and a maximum value, and the reader can choose any value within that range. The range may be controlled with a slider. VALUE can be used to set the default starting point. This example allows the reader to choose a zoom factor for an image, from a range of 1 to 10, with a starting point of 2.

‹INPUT NAME="zoom" TYPE=RANGE MIN=1 MAX=10 VALUE=2›

<INPUT TYPE=SCRIBBLE> allows the reader to draw on an image contained within the form. SRC specifies the image, and the input type is set to SCRIBBLE. There is nothing in the current specifications, however, about how scribble data is input or handled.

Graphical selection menus are a significant change to how image maps can be handled. The selection menu as a whole is an image, and zones are set up within that image to provide the selection options. The image can be aligned like other images, and is generally treated as an image. Unlike normal images, it can be handled by non-graphical browsers because there is a text value for each option. This could be a useful method for handling button bars or other graphical navigation controls.

The initial image is added to the SELECT tag with SRC. The height, width and units of measurement can be specified and the image can be aligned.

<SELECT SRC="buttons.gif" UNITS=PIXELS WIDTH=200 HEIGHT=50
ALIGN=RIGHT>

would place the 200 by 50 pixel image buttons.gif at the right margin. Each OPTION within the image is specified with SHAPE. There are several shapes available, and each one is described by its co-ordinates within the parent image. The zero points for both the x and y co-ordinates are in the upper left hand corner of the image, regardless of its alignment. If the co-ordinates are integers, they are interpreted as pixels, otherwise they will be interpreted as percentages.

SHAPE="rect x, y, w, h" sets a rectangular hot zone, with x and y as the top left co-ordinates of the area and w and h the width and height.

SHAPE="circle x, y, r" produces a circular hot zone. r is the radius of the circle measured from the centre point specified with x and y.

SHAPE="polygon x1, y1, x2, y2, x3, y3" can be used to create an irregular area. Each corner point is specified with an x and a y co-ordinate, and a line is drawn between all the points. The last point is joined to the initial point.

SHAPE="default" sets any unspecified areas within the image as an option.

The following example is a 200 by 50 pixel image that contains two circular buttons and two square ones, each 50 pixels high and 50 pixels wide:

<SELECT SRC="buttons.gif" UNITS=PIXELS WIDTH=200 HEIGHT=50
ALIGN=RIGHT>

```
<OPTION VALUE="home" SHAPE="rect 0, 0, 50, 50">Home
<OPTION VALUE="find" SHAPE="circle 75, 25, 25">Find
<OPTION VALUE="talk" SHAPE="circle 125, 25, 25">Talk
<OPTION VALUE="exit" SHAPE="rect 150, 0, 50, 50">Exit
```

NEW STYLE TAGS FOR CHARACTERS

<DFN></DFN> indicates the first definition term.

<Q></Q> can be used for short quotations within a paragraph, where blockquote might be inappropriate. This may be displayed in italics, but will usually be displayed with quotation marks. The style used for the quote marks will be dependent on any language specific needs as determined by the LANG attribute.

<AU></AU> should be used to indicate the name of an author. This may be useful for indexing or footnotes. <PERSON></PERSON> is used for the names of people within a document. Again, this may be useful for extracting names for an index.

<ACRONYM></ACRONYM> should be used to mark up acronyms, even though the tag will probably be longer than the acronym itself. Again, this will useful for automated indexing. <ABBREV></ABBREV> is used to mark any abbreviations.

<INS></INS> marks inserted text and <DEL></DEL> deleted text. These are intended for legal documents to show where text has been added or removed.

<BIG></BIG> and <SMALL></SMALL> change the size of any enclosed text in relation to the size of the surrounding text. Like and , these are supported by Netscape 2.0. <SUB> and <SUP> renders the enclosed text as subscript and super-script. If practical, a smaller font will be used.

NEW SPECIAL CHARACTERS

Five new special characters are introduced with HTML 3.0, all of which will appeal to designers who want more control over type and type spacing.

An en space can be added to the text with   and an em space with . An en is half the point size of the current font, and an em is the same size as the cur-rent font. If they are used with mono-space fonts they will be interpreted as a single space and a double space respectively.

  inserts a nonbreaking space and thus cannot be split across two lines regardless of the width of the browser window and any other text wrapping.

&endash; and &emdash; insert an en dash and an em dash respectively. En dashes are used between ranges of numbers, and em dashes between clauses. Neither should be used to hyphenate words.

As with all special characters, remember to include the ampersand and the semicolon.

FOOTNOTES

Footnotes can be added to the text with ‹FN›‹/FN›. If possible, they will be rendered as pop-ups directly from the text. The place in the text is anchored with ‹A HREF="#foot1"›text to be footnoted‹/A› and the footnote is specified with ‹FN ID="foot1"›the footnote‹/FN›. Like NAME, you can use the same ID on different pages but it must be unique within the current document. The identifier can be made up from letters, numerals and hyphens.

HORIZONTAL TABS

HTML 3.0 introduces tabs to give you more control over the horizontal position of the text. There are a couple of ways to use tabs—by setting tab stops and by specifying an indent. Indents are simple but limited in that each indent point can only be used once.

‹P›
‹TAB INDENT=4›This line would be indented by four en units, but the tab stop could not be re-used.
‹/P›

To set up named tab stops that you can use repeatedly, you will need to use ‹TAB ID="tabname"› and ‹TAB TO="tabname"›. The most useful application of this is probably that it lets you set an indent to the first line of each paragraph:

‹P›

The first‹TAB ID="indent1"› paragraph should not have an indent.‹BR›
‹TAB TO="indent1"›The first line of each subsequent paragraph can be
indented by using the tab stop set up in the initial paragraph. If this indent
is used, you may not need to rely on the addition of a blank line to indicate
a paragraph break. The blank line inserted with the paragraph tag can break
the flow of reading in a way that an indent does not.‹BR›
‹TAB TO="indent1"›Each paragraph starts with a tabbed indent and ends
with a line break.

‹/P›

ALIGN can be added to the ‹TAB› tag. The default, ALIGN=LEFT starts the text
immediately after the designated tab stop. With ALIGN=CENTER any text up to the
next tab or line break is centred on the specified tab stop. ALIGN=RIGHT will render
the following text flush right to the tab stop. If there is no tab stop designated, the
text will be set to the right margin. ALIGN=DECIMAL aligns the first decimal point in
the following text to the tab stop. The decimal point need not be a full stop and the
character to be used is specified with DP="," for example. The default is DP="."

BANNERS

The ‹BANNER›‹/BANNER› element is used to fix a section of an HTML document so that
it remains on screen at all times, regardless of how the page is scrolled. It could be
used for navigational buttons, contents information, legal messages, logos or other
essential page elements. This seems similar to frames within Netscape 2.0, although
it is used within the body of an HTML document and will not be browser specific.

BACKGROUNDS

Although later versions of HTML may specify the background with a style sheet, HTML
3.0 backgrounds are handled in the same way as Netscape background images. You

can specify a GIF to use as a background image and it will be tiled to fit the window. The background is added to the opening body tag:

```
<BODY BACKGROUND="back.gif">
```

FIGURES

HTML 3.0 discourages the use of ‹IMG› in favour of ‹FIG› a far more flexible and useful approach to images. The existing image tag should only be used for small inline graphics, bullets and dingbats. ‹FIG› is more flexible.

Any text within the ‹FIG›‹/FIG› tags is displayed if the image is not loaded, and can be formatted and contain other HTML tags. This can be more useful than ALT, because you can add any formatted text, tables, lists and links to the text that describes the image.

```
<FIG SRC="worcesterplan.gif">
a ground plan of <B>Worcester College</B>
</FIG>
```

The image itself is still specified with SRC. You can add a name to the figure with ID, specify the height, width and units of measurement. The image can be forced to a clear spot on either margin with CLEAR=LEFT, CLEAR=RIGHT or CLEAR=ALL.

The figure can be aligned with ALIGN=LEFT, or ALIGN=RIGHT. Text will flow to the side of the image if there is space. NOFLOW disables any text flow around the image. The default alignment is ALIGN=CENTER. ALIGN=JUSTIFY scales the figure to fit the width of the page, with no text allowed to flow on either side.

ALIGN=BLEEDLEFT pushes the figure flush to the left margin, rather than allowing it to align to the left of any image or table. ALIGN=BLEEDRIGHT will align the figure to the right margin.

One of the main advantage of figures is the use of overlays. If you have several different items that you want to overlay on the same image, the main graphic can be downloaded once and cached. Each time the image is reused, it will be pulled from the cache, and only the overlays need to be downloaded. An example of this could be a photograph of a city, with one overlay showing bus routes, another showing subway routes or cycle. The main graphic is reused from the cache each time it is used within a different figure:

```
<FIG ALIGN=LEFT UNITS=PIXELS WIDTH=200 HEIGHT=200
SRC="cityphoto.gif">
<OVERLAY SRC="busroutes.gif">
photo of Oxford with an overlay showing the main bus routes through the
city
</FIG>
<FIG ALIGN=LEFT UNITS=PIXELS WIDTH=200 HEIGHT=200
SRC="cityphoto.gif">
<OVERLAY SRC="cyclepaths.gif">
photo of Oxford with an overlay showing the cycle paths
<CAPTION>map provided by the City Council</CAPTION>
</FIG>
```

In this example, the same photo would be displayed twice on the page, but with different graphics acting as overlays. If the overlaid graphic was mainly transparent, the underlying graphic would show through.

You can add a credit and a caption to the figure. It will probably be displayed below the figure, although you could align it to the TOP, BOTTOM, LEFT or RIGHT. You can apply multiple overlays to a single figure.

HTML 3.0 promises some great improvements to the possibilities of controlling the layout, appearance and behaviour of Web pages. Some of the new tags are supported by existing browsers, and more and more will be adopted even before HTML 3.0 is finalised. Check the W3 Consortium's Web site for up-to-date information about the status of HTML 3.0.

4

Beyond **HTML**

CHAPTER 21

Adobe Acrobat PDF

At about the same time as the Web protocols were being developed, Adobe Inc. were developing their own portable document format. Adobe Acrobat allows designers to create and distribute documents that contain full formatting, typesetting and graphics, complete with hyperlinks and advanced searching capabilities. Acrobat documents contain the full page description and allow for print level design control. This was originally targeted at corporate and design collaborations, as it provides a flexible way of sharing documents within work groups. Generating an Acrobat file is very simple. Once the document has been prepared in any page layout application, all you need to do is print to the format.

Until very recently, Acrobat documents had a rather uncomfortable position on the Web. Documents could be accessed through the Web and downloaded, but they were unwieldy and self-contained. One major problem was that whole documents had to be downloaded, rather than page by page as they were needed. With the growth in the Web, Adobe recognised the need for a more open system. The introduction of Netscape 2.0, which allows Acrobat files to be embedded in Web pages, and Amber, a more flexible version of Acrobat, leads to a more useful system.

The concept of a link in an Acrobat document has always been an extendable one—the link can take you to another point in the same document, or to another Acrobat document, or to a point in some other kind of external file. From version 2.1 of Acrobat, this has included the ability to link out to an URL. Acrobat documents being read in a helper app can contain links to URLs which Netscape will pick up, and then act as if an HTML link has been clicked.

The problem has been that, in order to read the Acrobat text, you have needed to download the entire file and read it in the helper app. With Netscape 2.0 and the Acrobat plug-in, only the page which you are reading will load one at a time. The page can be inline in a Web page, and will load along with other elements in the page. This is achieved by having Acrobat load in the background and handle the rendering of this part of the page.

The page which is loaded on arriving at the Web page could be a table of contents, which links to sections of the complete Acrobat file. If you click a link to another page in the Acrobat document, this page will load. Even if the document is hundreds of pages long, you never load more than the page you are reading. If you click on a Web link, Netscape will take you to the URL. The problem remains, however, that even single page Acrobat documents are very large compared to an equivilant HTML file.

In some situations, it can be important to have full control over the design of hyper-media documents. In such cases you may choose to use Acrobat elements within Web sites. Replacing HTML with PDF could be a mistaken path, but the combination of the two formats can be very powerful.

CHAPTER 22

Fun with scripts

This chapter introduces the idea of scripts that operate in tendem with HTML. It does not aim to teach you how to write Perl scripts, or AppleScripts but may give you some idea of what can be done. The Web is full of ready made scripts that can be adapted or used straight off the shelf, and there is further information in the appendix about where you might start looking for these, or for a specialised tutorial if you want to learn to write them yourself.

Hypermedia is essentially an interactive process. The reader's path through a hyper-textual space requires involvement and activity. This is, however, a starting point. The addition of programmed elements that sit behind web pages can significantly increase the levels of interactivity between the reader and the site. Scripting allows readers to interact directly with the Web, even help create a Web site. Responding to information that has been input through a form, scripts can provide a reaction to the reader and change the Web site as needed.

The Web is already a fluid medium, but increasing the levels of interactivity can make it highly responsive and very flexible. Programming scripts to respond to reader's requests and to react to their presence adds a degree of personalisation. If pages can be created on the fly, reacting to the needs and interests of the reader, the reader may be drawn far deeper into the experience of hypermedia. If the site can respond to the reader, the reader will respond more to the site.

WHAT'S A SCRIPT?

A script is an automated routine, a small programme that can run other programs or operations on the system. Scripts run on the host machine, the server, rather than on the reader's machine. This means that the script is written for the server and does not need several variations for different platforms. The effects of the script can usually be seen by the reader, but the script operates on the remote machine. The script itself can be written in any language supported by the HTTP server on the host machine. Scripts are usually known as *cgi scripts* or common gateway interface scripts.

Whether you are planning to write your own scripts, work with someone who will write them for you, or use some of the ready made scripts that are available on the Web, you will need to have a clear idea of what you want to achieve. The more precise you can be about your needs and your intentions, the easier the script writing job will be.

Plan the stages of interactivity that you need, then plan your scripts around them. Think about the input and the output at each point. What information do you need from the reader and what do you want to do with that information? Talk to your programmer and ask what is possible, and work with it. Well-chosen applications of simple scripts can be more effective and encourage a higher level of interaction that some of the more complex routines that are implemented. Speed is an important issue on the Web and the simpler the script and the simpler the process, the slicker it will seem.

There are reference books that provide tutorials in scripting languages, such as Perl or AppleScript. It is worth looking at the Web itself for up to date information about the implementation of scripts on the Net. Some ready made scripts are available as freeware or shareware. These can be a very efficient way of adding simple interaction to your site. Information about some of the sources of tutorials and ready made scripts is in the appendix. This section is not a guide to writing scripts but contains some suggestions as to how they might be used.

WHAT CAN BE DONE WITH SCRIPTS: INTERACTIVITY AND COMMUNICATION

In general, you can do anything with scripts on the Web that you can do on your computer. Well-written scripts can launch all forms of applications that you can run on the remote machine. The examples covered in this chapter are not meant to be an exhaustive survey of what is possible, but to point out some of the ways in which scripts have been used on the Web.

The most common application for scripts is as a way of handling the input from forms. Scripts are used to process the input and pass the contents on to whoever should be dealing with them. Auto-response mechanisms can be set up very easily. For example, a reader may check a box to ask for more information and the script handles the automatic emailing of an information file. Information entered on a form can be sorted and responded to. Some sites use reader response forms to encourage feedback on the site itself, asking for suggestions and comments on what they might like to see. Forms can be used as a way of establishing contact with customers or potential customers. The input can be added directly to a database or passed on to a sales or marketing team. The way in which the input is handled depends on the script that you are using to process your forms.

Forms based Web pages are one of the best ways of encouraging direct communication between the readers and the authors of a site. One way of encouraging readers to provide a little information about themselves is to ask for it. General feedback forms asking for comments and basic details such as name and email address are very common.

It is also possible to set up your site in such a way that visitors will need to register and be given a password before being allowed to read through your site. You may choose to enclose the whole site with password protection, or particular areas that have a "premium" value.

Requiring visitors to register may put some people off, but not if the registration is handled with sensitivity. Are you offering the readers something in return for the information they are giving you? Is your site worth the time spent filling out a registration form? Are you asking for personal information? As long as the questions you ask are not considered too intrusive or inappropriate, most visitors will be very happy to fill out a simple information form. Asking for home addresses and information about personal computer equipment, for example, may be seen as an open encouragement for burglars. Most people will only give a mail address if you offer to send them something. Asking for a name, an email address and general demographic information should be fine. Providing instant access to the site once the form has been filled in is more welcoming than sending a password and user name by email. The data that can be collected may prove very useful for marketing or advertising, but it should not be heavy handed or it will put potential visitors off.

Once you have a little information about your readers, you can start to create personalised Web pages for them. Careful use of scripts can add the reader's names to pages, for example. The information that you have collected in the registration process can not only be added to a general database, or used for external purposes, but can be used within the Web site. The site can react to a reader by tracking her movements from page to page across time. On a return visit, a reader can be greeted by name, and provided with a list of areas that have been added since her previous visit. She can be pointed to particular areas of the site, depending on the information that she offered in the registration form. If the registration form has a section about general areas of interest, customised contents pages can be generated for each visitor.

It is fairly straightforward to generate good statistics about access to your site. You should be able to get details about the overall number of "hits", which pages are the most and least popular, how many times your video clips have been downloaded, and so on. Remember that the number of *hits* is not the same as the number of *people*. Each time a web page is requested by a reader, a request for all the images on the page is also logged. If one particular page contains 24 images, that page will register 25 hits each time it is requested. You can get far more useful information about real access, and repeat access, by asking visitors to register. Alternatively, a spot of number crunching on your raw access statistics can provide a more accurate count of the number of readers who have visited your site in any given period.

Scripting can be used to involve the reader more deeply in the Web site. Allowing the reader some participation in the site can increase the levels of enjoyment and loyalty. You could, for example, set up an area of the site where readers can leave messages for you and for each other. A guest book, where readers can leave comments on the site, or some other subject, is a fairly common appearance on the Web. Notice boards, for sale and wanted pages, and discussions are starting to appear all over the Web. Areas like these allow the reader to leave some mark on the site. Higher levels of reader involvement seem to encourage higher levels of repeat visits. Providing a social space on your site may not always be appropriate, but it can help foster a sense of community.

Web sites can provide a more accessible front end to direct communication on the Internet. Collaborative Web sites built around MUDs (Multi User Dimensions) and MOOs (Mud Object Oriented) are starting to flourish, with the site changing depending on the interactions and contributions of the participants. The ChibaMOO and the Sprawl, developed by SenseMedia, are the best known of the WOOs, or Web MOOs, and is currently standing at about one thousand rooms. With a strong overlap between the two forms of communication, participants write their space into the MOO and the Web site changes to reflect new creations and movements. Writers can create rooms, objects and characters as and when they need them, and other participants can interact with their creations through the MOO or via the Web. Some rooms are text creations, others contain graphics. A painting hung on the wall can be an inline image on the Web page, sounds and video can be embedded into spaces where they are needed. People within the WOO can meet within a room, and hold text based conversations. This can be a simple conversation, or can be an act of creation as they write new places and objects into the space. Rooms or spaces within a WOO can be private space for the creator's own enjoyment, or can be opened up to other visitors as spaces for communication on any level.

Much of the work in this area has grown out of the MUDs and MOOs and collaborative interactive fiction. Ease of creation is very important, as important as ease of use. In this it is very similar to HTML. It is very easy to create and publish a Web site into a global arena. It is also very simple to bind your site into the rest of the Web — referring to any relevant information anywhere in the world simply by building links to it. Taking this one stage further, combining forces to build a collaborative space can be made fairly easy with some careful thought and judicious programming. Your Web sites can be made open to the public, not just as readers, but as joint creators. Providing the tools for people to add and develop the site is possible, and can be made simple for users by allowing them to work with forms rather than with raw HTML.

This interaction between visitors develops the idea that a Web site is a dynamic and explorable space, rather than a collection of linked text pages, or a static *presentation.* Collaborative creation of social space is a potentially very important step in the future development of the use of the Internet. A freely developed space, created with the assistance of easy to use tools, will allow the Net to become a place of personal, educational and business communication. The growth of graphics capability and bandwidth over time will see the move from heavily text based space to graphical representation. The whole idea of shared space and fluid communication will almost certainly become central to many parts of the Net.

Telnet windows and IRC (Internet Relay Chat) allow immediate real time conversation on the Net, but they involve text only interfaces, and fairly complex commands that may confuse newcomers. Their advantage is speed and directness. The communication between individuals conversing with IRC is very powerful, but can be off-putting to people unaware of the conventions and forms of shorthand that are often used. A form of live chat can instead be built directly into a Web page, allowing readers to enter their messages into a simple form. Pages can be updated as new messages are added. This may not be as speedy as IRC, but is far easier for some people to use. This can of course, be tied in to a system that allows other changes to take place, as in the Sprawl, where the text communication affects the Web site around it.

There are also large numbers of interactive toys and games built into Web sites. Rather than providing a downloadable application, which the reader can play with later, you could build the application into a Web page. Hyperlinks and forms allow the visitor to interact with the page. Feedback can be provided by delivering changed pages, or new pages. Colouring books, puzzles and quizzes, shoot-em-ups and other games are scattered across the Web, ranging from the very simple to fairly sophisticated.

There are various developments beyond the implementation of scripting that will allow greater levels of interactivity within Web sites. The best known of these developments include the HotJava browser and the Java language developed by Sun Microsystems, Shockwave, Macromedia's project to incorporate multimedia with the Internet, and VRML (Virtual Reality Modelling Language) a three-dimensional incarnation of hypermedia. All of these are covered in more detail later in this section.

CHAPTER 23

The fusion of the Internet and CD-ROM

The most obvious restriction that hypermedia faces is the lack of bandwidth. Sending full motion, full screen, real time video over the Internet, for example, is not yet a realistic proposition. The estimates of the time it will take to implement the necessary bandwidth and compression technology vary wildly. There is, however, the very useful interim solution of hybrid products that combine the storage of CD-ROMs and the immediacy and interactivity of the Web.

CD-ROMs can hold large amounts of graphics, video, sound and text that can be accessed at far greater speeds than they can across the Net. If the bulk of static information can be stored and distributed on CD-ROM and the more fluid information on a Web site a useful solution can be achieved. A direct link to a Web site can be built into a CD-ROM. Hitting a particular button, could activate the modem, and access a particular embedded URL, bulletin board system or online service.

There are many ways in which the two can be combined. An illustrated catalogue could be distributed quarterly on CD-ROM and the availability of products can be checked daily on a linked Web site. Products could be ordered online, and new products could be previewed within the Web site. A music CD-ROM could provide a link to a related Web site that provides current tour dates for the band, news of their latest releases, and a link to a Usenet newsgroup. A CD-ROM or brochure with a six month old share price is of very little use to someone who invests on the Stock market. On the other hand, a full company history with the year's accounts and results stored on CD-ROM that has a built-in link to the current trading prices and company news online could be very useful indeed.

CD-ROMs contain fixed information whereas Web sites can be updated as and when the information needs to be changed. The information contained on a CD-ROM could be transmitted in chunks over the Net, and stored locally on the user's machine, but the time required to download such bulk and the storage required can make this impractical. CD-ROMs are relatively cheap to produce and transport.

The fusion of CD-ROM and Internet games is an interesting development. Games players are becoming accustomed to very sophisticated three dimensional graphics and rapid game play. In contrast, the majority of the games that can be played across the net look like throwbacks to the early days of video games with their clunky graphics and slow response times. Lack of speed can be a problem if the game is meant to be based around fast moving elements. Consider the amounts of information that need to be transmitted at each stage of the game playing process.

The large amounts of information required to provide complex graphical detail can be far more suited to local storage than remote, shared access systems. Some games contain detailed scenarios where most of the information is fixed—the landscape, for example. The gameplay is concerned with the players' positions within the landscape and chains of events in which they are involved. The information required to support the interaction of two players can be swapped backwards and forwards between those players' machines over the Net as the interaction is negotiated. If there is any inter-action with the scene itself or other players, those changes would be passed to all the relevant players. The bulk of the information, however, remains static. Compared to the huge amounts of data required to render the landscapes, the interactivity, the live part of the game, can be very small. The interaction of distant players can make the game far more rewarding than solitary game-play.

This same principle can be applied to the creation of shared communication space. Graphics-heavy spaces can be created and stored on local computers to provide a rich interface for communication. The live communication between multiple users can take place over the Net, or on the Web, with bandwidth-hungry elements accessed from the user's machine.

Hybrid products are starting to appear in all sectors of the media—news, shopping, education, entertainment and finance. Until bandwidth is so plentiful that it becomes an irrelevant problem, the fusion of CD-ROM and the Net is a viable prospect.

CHAPTER 24

The future of HTML and Hypermedia

The Web is essentially a collaborative medium. It relies upon the active participation of both readers and authors. The mesh of links between sites is the tie that holds the medium together. It is the cohesion of parts that shapes the Web—an individual site is not the Web, it is part of the Web. Sites cannot stand alone. Each publication on the Web needs to be tied to others to thrive. Sites are not published into a void, but onto the Web. The pieces are more connected on the Web than with any other medium. Web sites are dependent upon each other for the paths that they build, the hyperlinks that connect them. The easy movement between sites is important.

The more the Web fragments, the less it will become. This is not about the principle of "choice" or "freedom" but the need to keep the Web alive and open. Proprietary systems and closed standards may reduce the overall strength of the Web, even as they improve certain parts of them. Developments in hypermedia should aim to open up the Web rather than close areas off.

HTML is a starting point. The language itself will inevitably become richer and more flexible, and be able to incorporate more links to other protocols. The advances in technology that can make those familiar with the medium jump up and down with glee will need to prove their viability to the general audience. Good design will no longer be seen as a luxury. The growth of the Web, and the influx of more and more readers and creators will help to push the standards forward.

The addition of interactivity and multimedia is a common goal and there has been a great deal of recent progress. Most browsers are capable of handling static images and displaying them within a Web page. Video and sound, however, is treated differently. The files are downloaded and played outside the Web page, usually with the aid of helper applications. Being able to incorporate sound and video directly into a Web page would be a distinct improvement, even if they contained no interactive elements. The release of Netscape 2 allowed the inclusion of live objects, building QuickTime movies, Adobe Acrobat PDFs, Java Applets and Director movies, as well as streamed audio or animation directly into Web pages.

Combining the separate elements into a truly active and interactive Web page would be a great step forward. Currently there are two major moves in this direction: Shockwave and Java.

CHAPTER 25

Shockwave: Macromedia Director on the Internet

Macromedia Director is probably the best known of all the multimedia authoring tools. Authoring multimedia in Director allows developers to incorporate and coordinate graphics, sounds, animations and local interactivity. The interactivity is controlled by the scripting language Lingo. This can be used to control the appearance of the title and to respond to user input.

Director is a very flexible creative tool used by hundreds of thousands of multimedia authors and designers. Director has evolved not only as a tool for bringing together a wide range of different media in a time-based interactive form but more importantly as a tool that allows pure designers and pure programmers to work together effectively to produce the best end results, although there are now very few people working in this area whose skills and talents do not cross over in some way. There are very few people who have the title "interactive designer" who do not have Director expertise.

Netscape Navigator 2.0 includes a Director playback engine, or plug-in, known as Shockwave. This allows Director authored multimedia to run within Web pages. As with images and text, the Director movie downloads automatically and starts to play. The movie is an intrinsic part of the page, rather than an external window which is launched and played with a helper application. This is known as "the Stage in the page", where the Director stage window is another page element, along with any text or graphics. The player is built into Netscape itself, so no executable code will be downloaded to the user's machine, and there will be no need to download a platform specific helper. The movie will play itself and the play-back engine will be transparent to the user.

Once a movie has been authored and added to a Web page it can be played back on any platform, as long as it is viewed with a browser that contains the Director engine. The movies are cross platform because the player is part of the browser.

Movies authored on the Mac can be viewed with Windows and vice-versa. In keeping with all multimedia and Web authoring, however, everything should be tested on as many platforms as possible. It is never a good idea to assume that everything will work just fine across all platforms. Movie files are platform independent, but there are many variations in hardware and operating systems. Macromedia's advice is "Test early, test often, test on all your target machines."

The incorporation of a Director engine into Netscape is part of a non-exclusive deal signed between Macromedia and Netscape. This covers the Macintosh, PowerMac, Microsoft Windows 3.1, Windows 95 and Windows NT 3.5.1, There is no Director for UNIX, but Silicon Graphics has licensed the Director player and it will be bundled with Web Force. NaviSoft, an America Online company will also be integrating the Director player engine into their NaviPress browser. Microsoft and the Blackbird interactive environment for the Microsoft Network will also be adopting the Director player.

Other browsers will be able to support and play Director movies with a separate helper application. This will not allow the movie to be an intrinsic part of the page, as it will in Netscape, but readers will be able to view and interact with the movies.

Director is built around a theatrical metaphor with the three key components of stage, score and cast. The stage is a rectangular area which contains the entire Director movie—the area that is visible to the end user. The score is a timeline that describes and contains the state of the stage at every moment during a movie. Interactivity can be generated by jumping to different frames within the score. The cast is made up of all the media elements and scripts included in the movie. Cast members are positioned on both the stage and the score to control their behaviour through time.

The scripting language Lingo is used to generate all but the most basic behaviours of cast members—to move them around in ways that change depending on circumstances that may be triggered by user input. Lingo is now so powerful that many highly interactive Director movies are produced without ever leaving the first frame. All the interactivity and animation can be produced by code alone. Unlike many programming languages, however, Lingo is intuitive and easy to read because it has its roots in the programming language SmallTalk and in Apple's HyperTalk, and is thus very similar to AppleScript and most other scripting languages.

As a Director movie plays, it looks ahead and loads the cast members needed to go forward on the score or within a script. Pre-loading of cast members can be controlled from Lingo. This is the case whether it is playing from a hard drive, a CD-ROM or over the Internet.

Shockwave will allow the movies to stream into the user's machine. The way that Director movies can be constructed means that they can start to play as they download. Individual cast members can be loaded and activated as they arrive, and there is no need to wait for a complete download before the movie starts playing. Careful planning and specific authoring techniques can help make the movies as seamless as possible and prevent wait times and strange pauses.

Because Director is used to author the majority of multimedia CD-ROMs, there is an assumption that the movies are very large, and are necessarily CD-ROM sized. Some Director movies are very large because they include video and high-quality sound, but a great deal can be achieved with much smaller movies. Some developers are currently working to a target of a 100k maximum file size. There will be no limit imposed on the size of movie, but bandwidth is an important consideration. 100k assumes an audience with 28.8k modems who would not be prepared to wait more than half a minute to view a page. Ideal file sizes will vary depending on your target audience. As with all other media on the Web, some contexts and some content justifies the use of larger files. Assess your audience, and their access to the Web. Careful authoring and good use of Lingo can reduce the size of movies considerably.

One simple way of slimming down a movie is to reduce the size of the movie's window. The majority of CD-ROM multimedia titles work with a 640 pixels by 480 pixels screen. Reducing this to 320 by 240 will trim the size considerably.

Some multimedia developers are unhappy with the idea that their movies will play within the page. There are arguments that to achieve a really immersive experience they need to take over the whole of the user's screen, rather than being constrained within a smaller window. For the time being, however, the movies will play within the Netscape browser window as part of a Web page.

Interactivity can be built into the Director movies to add a new dimension to Web pages. The interactivity is contained within the movie and does not require further information or contact with the Web server. Because the movies are self-contained, the first release of Shockwave does not support multiple movies that can communicate with each other.

The constraints of Web bandwidth, as opposed to the luxury of the storage capability of CD-ROM, is encouraging experimentation with "low-calorie" authoring techniques. The aim of most developers aiming at Web based multimedia is to deliver the greatest "bang per byte". This stretches across the whole of Web development. Including any static images on a Web page requires a consideration of their impact versus their cost in bandwidth and delivery time.

Anybody expecting Shockwave to deliver smooth all-singing, all-dancing, full screen video will be disappointed. This is not a weakness of Director, which can deliver exactly that, but a limitation of bandwidth and delivery speeds. As with all other media transmitted across the Net, improvements in bandwidth and compression technology will have a huge impact. Macromedia has also developed a compression utility called Afterburner to post-process movies. It applies a variety of compression methods to the various media elements, all of them tuned for fast decompression.

"A key technology for cross-network operation, especially with multimedia, is compression. Director titles are composed of many different media, combined into one coherent user experience. The Internet play-back technology developed by the Shockwave project incorporates several different compression schemes, each appropriate for a different media type. By using separate compression algorithms for each category of media, the best possible compression can be achieved for that piece of content, and thus for the title as a whole. This collection of compression technologies will also evolve over time as new, more efficient, algorithms become available."

(Director-on-the-Internet Technology White Paper)

Shockwave is a very exciting addition to the possibilities of the Web. The influx of talented and experienced multimedia and interactive designers will help to expand the medium. Harry Chesley, the Shockwave team leader, has written a paper on authoring Director movies for the Web. This is reprinted with permission in the appendices. The appendix also contains URLs which will point you in the direction of detailed development information as well as good examples of Shockwave on the Web.

CHAPTER 26

The HotJava browser and the Java Language

HotJava is a Web browser that can execute programs written in the Java language. Applets, small programs written in Java, can be included in HTML pages along with other elements like text or images. Using HotJava, readers can see the applications run as animated interactive elements on the page, rather than static images and text, or external video and sound. To quote the HotJava Frequently Asked Questions, available at http://java.sun.com:

"Java is the programming language that makes HotJava possible. It is an object-oriented programming language optimized for the creation of distributed, executable applications. Because Java is compiled into machine independent bytecodes, applications written in Java can migrate transparently over the Internet accessible by anyone using the HotJava browser."

Currently Java applets can only be viewed when you use the HotJava browser or Netscape 2.0. The HotJava browser is currently available for SPARC-based Solaris machines, Microsoft Windows NT and Microsoft Windows 95, although Sun has planned to release versions for other platforms. Netscape 2.0 supports Java Applets within Web pages, and includes a simplified scripting language based on Java. This scripting language, Javascript, is covered in more detail in chapter 19. Java applets themselves are not platform specific, and do not require a particular architecture or operating system to run—only the Java code and a Java compatible browser.

Assuming that you are viewing a Web site with HotJava or Netscape 2.0, if you access a page that contains Java applets you will download a stream of executable code. Once this code has been downloaded it will run on your machine to produce animations, sounds and interactive elements, depending on the nature of the applet.

Early examples contain animated images that react as you pass your cursor over them, and looping animation clips that run until they are interrupted by the user. Unlike general scripts which operate on the server machine rather than the client machine, the applet runs on the local machine. Once the applet is downloaded, the connection to the server is broken off.

There are understandable worries about downloading executable code from a wide variety of servers. Many users fear viruses and other malicious code that can be transferred to their computer at the same time. The developers have paid attention to the security issue, and have laid great emphasis on their "virus-free, tamper-free systems". The White Paper produced by Sun attempts to addresses these fears:

"They...can be assured that the code that brings their chemistry experiment to life doesn't also contain malicious code that damages the system. Code that attempts to be malicious or which has bugs, can't breach the walls placed around it by the security and robustness feature of Java."

A great strength of HotJava is the way in which it understands different types of objects and protocols. The majority of browsers have built-in protocol handlers—for example, the ability to understand HTTP.

"HotJava is given a reference to an object (a URL). If the handler for that protocol is already loaded, it is used. If not, HotJava searches, first the local system and then the system that is the target for the URL, for the protocol needed to interact with the object." (HotJava White Paper)

This adds a great deal of flexibility to the system. As new protocols are introduced, they do not need to be added to a new version of the browser, but can be made available and accessible on the relevant servers, and can be distributed as they are needed.

The HotJava browser allows readers to see and interact easily with Java applets on Web pages. Creating the applets, however, may not be so simple. Java is an object-oriented programming language designed to be as close to C++ and Objective C as possible. There are large numbers of programmers very familiar with C and C++ for whom Java should be fairly straightforward to learn. The platform independent nature of Java might lead it into the heart of Virtual Reality development.

Java is, however, very much a programming language developed for programmers. Netscape's new development software, LiveWire, provides a scripting environment that has been derived from Java. This allows developers to produces scripts and applets using LiveWire's simplified interface that also includes a compiler to produce executable byte-code versions of scripts. Developers can therefore produce live applications for use with Netscape clients. Sun are also releasing new Java development tools early in 1996. The incorporation of Java into Netscape will obviously make Java more significant to a greater number of Web developers and users, and spread it more widely into general net development.

The Java Language White Paper, which explains the concepts and applications of Java, is reprinted in the appendices with permission from Sun Microsystems.

CHAPTER 27

Virtual Reality: the future shape of the Web?

Virtual Reality is currently a long way from reality. The familiarity of the real makes high demands on the virtual representation of reality. We spend our entire existence within a rich three dimensional space. We know what reality looks like, and brightly coloured blocky building shapes and flat green expanses of fields don't even come close. This is a starting point.

At the heart of VR is the ability to build a navigable, three dimensional space in which we can move freely. The ideal is to build a populated space in which any number of people can move, communicate and interact. The key to VR is communication and a rich experience within a shared space. Visual representation of information and space is part of that experience. The representation of what is within that space will become more sophisticated. The basic structures and techniques are already in place.

If the medium itself is a representation of reality, then the medium needs to be able to handle the ways in which we perceive reality. Text is a fundamentally different way of handling information. Text describes and explains. The burden of recreating the reality that the text represents is on the reader. We have developed methods for using text, ways in which we accept text, and what it can and what it cannot convey. VR has a more difficult task. It needs to convince us that it represents reality. The suspension of disbelief has to be nurtured, encouraged and tricked into existence. We know when things look wrong. But if they are real enough, then we can use all the sensual information that surrounds us in a virtual environment. Everything within an environment adds to the experience and to the information transmitted.

There seem to be two main approaches to VR: the creation of an approximation of reality in which we can move and communicate, and a three-dimensional representation of more abstract information. If the goal is "real" VR as opposed to a stylised visual representation of information, shared virtual space has many possible applications: for research; for gaming; for collaborative work or art; for education; for social or business interaction. The possibilities of a virtual meeting space are unlimited. Much of these depend on a higher level of reality being added to VR, particularly in the way that humans can move and communicate within the virtual space. So much of our communication is based on facial and body language rather than on speech, that an expressive representation of ourselves within any virtual space becomes essential. How real do we have to be within VR? How much reality can be achieved with minimal computing power? Would it be possible to have some parts of an environment closer to reality than others?

One of the main challenges facing VR is not the creation of "real" environments, but the distribution of the information and the mechanisms that will be used to allow full interactivity between the participants and the objects within the environments. There will be major limitations on the impact of VR if it requires massive computing power to participate. The creation of the environments requires more resources than the experience of those environments, but this is almost always so. Creating a movie takes more than watching a movie on a VCR.

How far should participation and creation be divided? If users are able to create or modify their environments rather than just look at them, the environments become far more dynamic and involving. One approach is the creation of a distributed VR world, with spaces linked to spaces across the Net, in the way that Web sites are linked to other Web sites across the world. A centralised system would not be able to evolve in the same way as a distributed one.

The advantages of VR are hard to deny. Navigating a three dimensional space is far easier than following arbitrary textual links within the Web. The ideals of hypermedia are based on shared information and exploration of textual space. Adding another dimension to the information space will bring much more into the realms of the possible. One medium rarely makes another obsolete, but the possibilities inherent in certain mediums can shift the focus towards those that offer a richer experience. Textual communication will not be destroyed by VR, but some of the things that will be possible with VR are simply not achievable in two-dimensional media.

CHAPTER 28

VRML

"The Virtual Reality Modelling Language (VRML) is a language for describing multi-participant interactive simulations — virtual worlds networked via the global Internet and hyperlinked with the World Wide Web. All aspects of virtual world display, interaction and internetworking can be specified using VRML. It is the intention of its designers that VRML become the standard language for interactive simulation within the World Wide Web." (*The VRML Version 1.0 Specification*, Gavin Bell, Anthony Parisi and Mark Pesce.)

VRML is completely cross platform, in the same way that HTML and Java are cross platform. The browser used to explore spaces created with VRML may be specific to a particular operating system, but the worlds themselves are freely accessible. VRML is not an extension to HTML. HTML was designed for handling text, not three dimensional graphics, and it would be hard to tack a flexible VR system on top of the existing system. VRML is a new approach, but one that works with the Web as it stands. You can link from the Web into VRML worlds, and from VRML worlds to the Web. Clicking on a book, for example, might take you to the HTML version of the book's text.

VRML files contain text descriptions of an environment and the objects within it, and the computer that downloads the file renders this information as fully formed three dimensional graphics. The files themselves are very small and can be passed across the Net at much higher speed than files that contain video or graphics. The hard work is done by the user's computer. Realistic VR with detailed scenery and smooth natural movement requires more processing power than most personal computers can handle. The intention is that different computers will be able to process the same files according to their ability. Extremely high powered computers will be able to render far higher levels of detail, with full texture mapping, whereas a lower end personal computer may be able to render the same scenes and objects, but with less detail. Detailed textures could be ditched in favour of graded colour.

VRML was initiated at the first annual World Wide Web Conference in the spring of 1994. The group that met to discuss the possibilities of a VR interface to the Web saw the need for a common language to specifying hyperlinks and 3D scene descriptions. Several people were already working on 3D interfaces. Mark Pesce and Tony Parisi, for example, had developed Labyrinth, a program that could move between 2 and 3D web space. Dave Raggett, who has shaped much of the platform independent 3D Web work, coined the term VRML. The M originally stood for "Markup", but was soon changed to the more appropraite "Modelling". Soon after the conference, a mailing-list was set up to discuss the specification for VRML, and the list moderator, Mark Pesce, announced the intention to prepare a draft specification in time for the next conference in the autumn. Once the requirements of the first version were decided—platform independence, extensiblity and low bandwidth operation—it was necessary to choose the appropriate technologies. The decision settled on the Open Inventor ASCII File Format from Silicon Graphics, Inc. SGI placed the file format into the public domain, and this format now forms the basis of VRML.

The draft specifications were presented in October 1994 by Tony Parisi and Gavin Bell. By April 1995, Silicon Graphics Inc. had launched a VRML browser, Web Space. Within a month there were dozens of VRML sites on the Web. People are very keen to create and use three dimensional environments, even fairly basic ones that do not allow for any interactivity beyond simple movement through the space.

VRML is only in its infancy, yet it is already possible to create three dimensional worlds with hyperlinks to other worlds, HTML documents or other media on the Web. Future plans for VRML include the possibilities of animation, naturalistic physical behaviour and real time interaction between multiple users. The interactivity, beyond hyperlinking, is not yet in place. VRML has not yet reached the levels of VR in other fields, but it does not need special equipment, gloves, headsets or heavy duty computing power to use. The huge advantage that VRML has is the Internet, and the links to the Web. A massively distributed and accessible form of VR is going to have a greater immediate impact on more people than specialised high-end VR. The more sophisticated appearance and interactivty of "normal" VR will start to be added to VRML, and the differences will begin to even out. The different forms of VR could be combined—with Apple's QuickTime VR providing detailed realistic spaces, and VRML adding the rapid interactivity and dynamism needed to make VR flourish.

Dave Raggett's paper from Spring 1994, "Extending WWW to support Platform Independent Virtual Reality", is reprinted in the appendices. This paper contains the key aims and concepts of the possibilities of VR on the Web, and points the way for the future. This chapter is only a very brief introduction to VRML, and does not go into detail about the specifics of the language. There are excellent resources for more information about VRML on the Web, and there are details of some of these in the appendices.

CHAPTER 29

QuickTime VR

Apple and Netscape signed a deal to incorporate an Apple QuickTime VR player, or plug-in, into the Netscape Navigator. As yet, there are no details about how this will be implemented, but the intention is to allow seamless VR space to be accessed directly through the Web page. It is already possible to download QuickTime VR (QTVR) files from the Web and play them with an external helper application, but this new step is very exciting.

QTVR is an extension of QuickTime that allows users to experience three-dimensional space with no specialised hardware other than a Macintosh or Windows computer. QTVR is based around 360 degree panoramic scenes that can be generated from photographic sources or computer rendered landscapes. QTVR scenes are very simple to navigate, and the perspective that is generated on each view of the scene is incredibly accurate. Unlike VRML, QTVR is recorded rather than descriptive VR.

Panoramic movies can be created that allow users to view and explore realistic or imaginary spaces. Scenes can contain a single viewpoint, so that a user can look around and up and down from a single place in the centre of a space, or multiple viewpoints so the user can move between them. Changing viewpoint or position requires only a click of a mouse. Object movies can be integrated into panoramic movies to allow users to examine and interact with them from all angles.

Further hotspots within the movies can integrate other forms of media into the QTVR landscape. Clicking on a hotspot can launch a sound clip, a video clip, text or still images. The interface is straightforward and intuitive, and movement within a landscape is user controlled. The sequence of actions—zooming in or out, looking around, moving between viewpoints—is chosen by the user rather than the author.

The image quality of QTVR can be very high, as the panoramas can be generated from 35mm film, rather than being restricted to video. Scenes generated from photographic panoramas are larger than computer rendered scenes, but are relatively small considering the amount of information that they contain. Early examples are available from Apple's QTVR Web site, and the typical size of a 360 degree panoramic movie is around 500k. This does, however, take a considerable time to download over an average modem. There are no details about how this will work within a Web page. This information will be available from Apple and from Netscape as the player engine is designed and built.

The potential uses of QTVR within the Web are widespread. Adding explorable three-dimensional space to hypermedia allows a far richer experience than text or still images alone. QTVR is not an all-immersing experience in the way that high end Virtual Reality, with head-sets and data-gloves, can be. The relatively low amounts of computer power required to author and to run QTVR, however, mean that it is can be used on a far wider basis at the moment. The main limitation at the moment is bandwidth, and we may see a wider use of QTVR on CD-ROMs than on the Web. As transfer speeds improve, however, QTVR will almost certainly have a considerable impact on the Web. Combined with VRML, it can be used to create realistic and dynamic 3D environments.

The movies generated with QTVR make it possible to move with some freedom around realistic or imaginary scenes. This is another move closer to "show" rather than "tell". The ability to examine individual objects within a scene makes QTVR far more flexible than forms of VR which do not allow any interaction beyond the movement of a viewer through a space. A series of still images and some descriptive text can never be as powerful as a three dimensional model of a sculpture that you can move around and view from any angle you want. A QTVR movie of a planned building can give you a greater idea of the space than a floor plan.

Although QTVR can be played on Macs and Windows PCs, the authoring can only be done on the Mac, using the QuickTime VR Authoring Tools Suite available from Apple. The authoring process can be broken up into four stages—planning, capturing or generating the images, digitisation and the authoring of the VR scenes themselves. QTVR authoring requires a fairly high level of multimedia production knowledge, including Lingo or HyperCard scripting as well as image processing skills.

The planning process is related to every other multimedia and hypermedia production planning. The most important questions concern the intended user experience and the intended audience for the product, and of course, the practical limitations of the technology. Very complex projects will require more production time and resources, and greater space and memory requirements for the user. If the files are to be distributed through the Web, file size is an important consideration.

When planning a Web site, the main considerations are related to the structure of the site and the reader's movement around it. QTVR also depends upon the user's movement around the space that you create. With QTVR, however, the considerations are related to the number of nodes or panoramas within a movie, the scope of navigational freedom and the number and behaviour of objects within a scene. If the movie is to be generated from photographic images, a floor plan with each node marked on it would be a useful starting point.

Panoramic photographs are based on the full 360 view from a single point within a scene. This is generated by taking an overlapping series of photos from a single point, rotating the camera on a tripod that has been set up according to the specific needs of QTVR. Any interactive objects that you want to include will also need to be photographed from all angles.

Computer generated panoramas and objects, on the other hand, can be created with a wide variety of rendering packages. Some of these packages allow you to render full 360 degree panoramas.

Once the images have been photographed they will need to be digitised in order to be manipulated into VR scenes, which are created from PICTs. The QTVR authoring software incudes a tool to "stitch" the images together to create a seamless panorama with corrected perspective. The images are blended together to create a single smooth landscape, removing any irregularities. Hotspots can then be added, so that there are interactive objects within the scene.

The movie is then compressed and "diced" into single tiles that can be played back as linear QuickTime files. The next stage allows you to set the default size of the movie window, as well as the degree to which users can zoom in and out. You can control the size and resolution of the movie, but the default of 320x240 may be best suited to the largest number of users. It is possible, however, to have full screen 640x480 QTVR movies, but these will not perform so well on low-end machines.

To create scenes which contain multiple viewpoints, you need to use the Scene Editor, a HyperCard stack that allows you to build and position the links between the viewpoints. Using the Scene Editor, you can control the possibilities of movement around the scenes and the behaviour of objects within them.

It is already possible to build both panoramic and object based QTVR movies into

Director movies that can be played on Macintosh and Windows computers. QTVR files may therefore arrive fairly quickly on the Web as part of Shockwave, although not as part of the first release of Shockwave.

CHAPTER 30

Where do you go from here?

The World Wide Web is expanding daily. New technologies and new creativity are being brought into play. This book does not provide all the answers, but I hope that it has provided you with some new questions. The more you can learn about how the medium works, the more empowerment you will experience.

This book is a starting point. It should have given you a good understanding of HTML, some ideas about structuring a Web site and working with hypermedia. The most important thing, however, is to put this into practice. Publishing on the Web is a hugely rewarding experience. I look forward to seeing your Web sites. Drop me an email with your URLs.

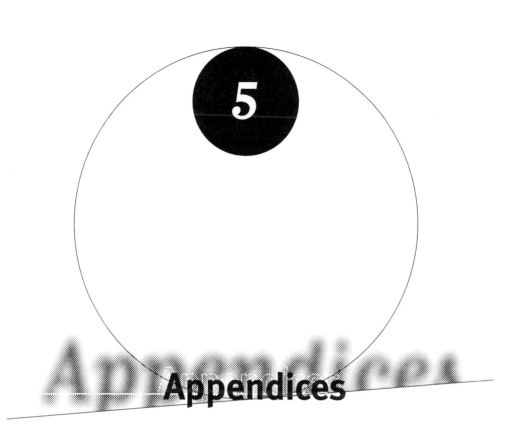

5

Appendices

APPENDIX 1

Shockwave for Director authoring

A WHITE PAPER ON PREPARING DIRECTOR MOVIES FOR OPTIMAL DISTRIBUTION OVER THE INTERNET

This document provides a guide to writing Director movies to be viewed over the Internet within a World Wide Web browser page with the Shockwave for Director player. The principal challenge that multimedia developers need to keep in mind is the speed of the Internet. Most Web users dial in with modems at 14,400 and 28,800 bits per second. At these rates, the user sees only about one to two kilobytes per second of effective throughput. If the Internet host is heavily loaded, or there is unusual network congestion, this rate can drop even lower. Multimedia developers face the task of maximising the impact of their productions while minimising the time a user must wait to see them. Using Director movies with the Shockwave player, developers can turn static pages into dynamic productions without substantially increasing the amount of time a user waits. As the speed of the Internet increases with ISDN, cable modems and private networks, multimedia developers can rely on the same Director developemt tools and the Shockwave player for multimedia production and delivery.

The rest of this document goes into more detail about what you need to know to build effective, compelling multimedia productions for the Internet. It covers the capabilities of Shockwave for Director, the differences between the Shockwave player and the Director 4.0 projector, and tips and techniques to get the most out of a multimedia production for the Internet. Because the development of multimedia for the Internet is an evolving art, you as an author can contribute to it. Please share the tips and techniques that you develop as you make and distribute Director movies.

Caveats

- This document assumes a basic knowledge of Director

- This information is preliminary and may change before the first release of Shockwave for Director. However, it is believed to be as close to the first release functionality as possible. The information provided does not represent all future functionality to be provided in subsequent Shockwave for Director releases.

Topics Covered

- Using What You Know about Director

- Adding the Internet to Director

- Challenges of Life on the Internet

- Tips & Techniques

- What the Future Holds

- Content by Channel Speed

- Definitions

Using What You Know about Director

Authoring for the internet is fundamentally the same as authoring for other types of distribution. If you're familiar with Director, you're 90% of the way to being able to create Internet titles. And, similarly, 90% of what you know will be directly applicable when working on the Internet.

To author a Shockwave title, you start with the regular Director 4.0 authoring environment on a PC or a Mac. You create and test the title on your local file system. Then you post-process the title through an application called Afterburner—this step primarily compresses the title in order to save download time. The resulting file is placed on an HTTP server for a Web browser to download to the user's machine.

In creating the title, you can use virtually all of the existing Director features, your existing Director content and all of the supporting tools that you currently use to produce media that is imported into Director. Shockwave for Director is not a new authoring environment. It's a new way to package and deliver Director interactive movies.

The Afterburner post-processing step does not change the appearance of the movie. It simply compresses it. So you don't have to worry while authoring how the post-process step will change your work.

An HTTP server is used to serve the title across the network. Director developers need not be expert in setting up and configuring HTTP servers. There are no special requirements made of HTTP servers to deliver Director movies. As with other media types, you do need to tell the server that Director movies have a MIME type of "application/x-director", but that's all. Consult your HTTP server documentataion or administrator for details.

ADDING THE INTERNET TO DIRECTOR

The new facilities available with Shockwave fall into two categories: integration with network browsers such as Netscape Navigator 2.0 and new, network-oriented Lingo commands.

NETSCAPE NAVIGATOR INTEGRATION

With the Director players installed, Web pages include Director movies just as existing browsers can include JPEG graphics. Director movies are included in the Netscape Navigator browser using the EMBED tag in the HTML source. In brief, the tag specifies a rectangle in which to display the movie and an URL specifiying the location of the movie on the network.

Documents can include more than one movie per HTML page. The HTML page containing the movie can be scrolled while the movie is playing. The user can interact with the movie by clicking on the visible portions of the movie. And the movie, using new Lingo commands can access information from the network and open new URLs.

Lingo Network Extensions

Several new commands are available for accessing the network from Director Lingo scripts. This section lists each of these new commands and functions and explains their usage.

Since the network is essentially an asynchronous place—i.e. it takes time to get things from the net, and in the meantime, Director can continue to interact with the user—most of the network commands involve starting an operation then checking to see if it has completed, then getting the results. This is different from most Lingo commands, which immediately return the result.

Three commands are available to start asynchronous operations, and one to preload into cache: Note that an URI is a more general specification than an URL, but for practical purposes they can be considered as identical.

StartGetNetText

uri

This command starts the retrieval of an HTTP item, to be read by Lingo as text. The uri parameter is a universal resource identifier which specifies the HTTP item to be retrieved. At present, only HTTP URLs are supported as valid uri parameters.

StartGetNetCast

uri

This command starts the retrieval of an HTTP item which is a Director movie, the cast of which should be added to the cast of the currently running movie. The uri parameter is a universal resource identifier which specifies the HTTP item to be retrieved. At present, only HTTP URLs are supported as valid uri parameters. This command is only available in release 1.1 and later.

StartPostNetText uri,

posttext

This command starts an HTTP POST of the text in the posttext parameter. The uri parameter is a universal resource identifier which specifies the HTTP item to be retrieved. At present, only HTTP URLs are supported as valid uri parameters. This command is only available in version 1.1 and later.

NetPreload uri

This command starts preloading an HTTP item into the local file cache. The uri parameter is a universal resource identifier which specifies the HTTP item to be retrieved.

At present, only HTTP URLs are supported as valid uri parameters.

In general, an item which has been preloaded can be accessed immediately, since it is taken from the local disk cache rather than from the network. However, it is impossible to determine when an item may be removed from the local disk cache.

Two functions allow Lingo to determine the state of the asynchronous operation:

NetDone()

This function returns true when the asynchronous network operation is finished. Until that point, it returns true.

NetError()

This function returns the empty string until the asynchronous network operation is finished. Then it returns "OK" if the operation completed successfully, or a string describing the error if it failed to complete successfully.

Once an asynchronous operation has finished, three functions are available to retrieve the results:

NetTextResult()

This function returns the text result of the operation. For a GetNetText operation, this is the text of the HTTP item.

NetMIME()

This function returns the MIME type of an HTTP item.

NetLastModDate()

This function returns the last modified date string from the HTTP header for the item.

One command can be used to abort a network operation which is in progress:

NetAbort

This command aborts a network operation without waiting for a result.

Note, however, that the NetTextResult, NetMIME, and NetLastModDate can only be called from the time NetDone or NetError report that the operation is complete until the next operation is started. Once the next operation is started, we discard the results of the previous operation in order to preserve memory space.

It is possible to have more than one operation active at a time. When the two operations are started, the Lingo script needs a way to identify them. After an operation is started, and until the next operation is begun, the following function can be called to retrieve a unique identifier for that operation:

NetOperationID()

This function returns a unique identifier for the last asynchronous operation which was started.

Each of the functions NetDone, NetError, NetTextResult, NetMIME, NetLastModDate, and NetAbort, take as an operational unique identifier returned by NetOperationID.

In addition there are two more asynchronous commands:

StartNetGoto uri

This command retrieves and goes to a new Director movie from the network. The uri parameter is a universal resource identifier which specifies the HTTP item which contains the movie. At present, only HTTP URLs are supported as valid uri parameters.

StartNetOpen uri

This command will open an arbitrary uri, whether it is a Director movie or not. Since this involves invoking the Internet browser to determine the type of item being opened and to handle it appropriately, it is a less efficient operation than NetGoto or NetPlay, which assume that the item must be a Director movie, and which therefore handles the entire operation within the Director player.

CHALLENGES OF LIFE ON THE INTERNET

Given the challenges of the Internet platform, we have tried to strike a reasonable balance in the first release among functionality, user security and timing of the Shockwave 1.0 for Director release.

Temporary Limitations

Linked media is problematical in a networked environment, since it is possible to successfully retrieve the movie, but then fail to retrieve the linked media. We are investigating a solution which would bundle the linked media with the movie, but it will not be available in the 1.0 release (indirect support through URLs is still available).

In addition, most QuickTime movies are too large to allow effective serving over the Internet. Longterm, a likely approach to video over the Internet will be a constant stream of video. These streams can be "broadcast" in real time like a television show everyone watches at a scheduled time or sent on demand point to point from a server to an individual desktop. Higher speed network technologies such as ISDN, cable modems and private networks are key for video quality.

Titles cannot use movie-in-a-window. This is difficult to do properly under Windows. We will look into how to make this available in some future version.

Titles cannot use any of the "Wait for..." options in the tempo channel. There are, however, simple Lingo-based work-arounds.

The 1.0 release also does not allow custom menus.

Safety

A set of functionality restrictions prevent arbitrary Director movies from performing unwanted operations on the user's machine. This allows users to download arbitrary movies, from Internet sites they don't necessarily trust, without threat of viruses or mischief directly from the movie. To provide this level of safety, the following facilities have been disabled in the Shockwave player:

- XObject, XCMDs, and XFCNs in the movie

- The FileIO XObject

- The SerialIO XObject

- The OrthoPlay XObject

- The MCI command

- Quit, restart and shutdown commands

- The resource and XLib commands OpenXlib, OpenResFile, CloseXLib, and CloaseResFile

- The open, openDA, and closeDA commands

- The open window and close window commands

- The saveMovie command

- The importFileInto command

- The file name and path properties and functions fileName of cast, fileName of window, getNthFileNameInFolder, moviePath, pathName, searchCurrentFolder, and searchPaths

- The printFrom command

Longer term network security solutions are emerging for Director and other application types in the Internet. For Director movies, we are looking into ways to authenticate the source of movies and allow the user to establish sources that they trust. For example, you buy a CD-ROM in a store today. If that CD deletes some files you wanted to keep, you have a publisher who is responsible for their products. Someone is held responsible for deleting your files. This kind of traceable business relationship has yet to be established on the Internet.

TIPS AND TECHNIQUES

The following are some tips and techniques we've discovered in producing Shockwave movies during development:

- Movie size is everything for fast downloading, so keep each cast member as small as possible. Use the cast info button to check size. Try resizing images on the stage to make them bigger rather than having large images in the cast. Small bandwidth movies are not supposed to make everything look perfect.

- Use Lingo! Interactive titles are much more involving than non-interactive, couch-potato ones. And Lingo can make a movie seem longer than it is by avoiding fixed, repeating sequences.

- If you have a cast member with only a few colours in it, try using the Transform Bitmap option to dither it down to 1, 2 or 4 bit depth to save space. But save your movie first because you cannot undo this; then Revert if you don't like it.

- When compared to bitmap rendered text, the text tool is almost free in terms of byte size. It doesn't look as nice as pre-processed, anti-aliased text, but you can fit a lot of text into a very small movie using this approach.

- All the tools window objects are nearly byte free, including the geometric shapes, text, buttons and tiles. Simple shapes are great for animation masks, animated shape paths and image frames. Use Ink Effects to get interesting crossover shape colours.

- Used cautiously, Ink Effects can give you multiple colours from the same cast member without having to make another one. Try these on film loops of the same cast members to get different looks without having to duplicate the cast member.

- Any one bit cast member can switch colours for film loops by using the tools window colour squares without creating new cast members. So if you had a purple and red four frame picture, 1 score with the picts on the stage, and then copy and paste them into a new film loop over and over again.

- Tiling is a good way to get backgrounds in small movies. Plan your tiles to have heights and widths of 16, 32, 64 or 128 pixels.

SMALL SOUND TRACKS

- Sound is important. Think of it as the difference between watching a silent film without sound and watching Star Wars. Don't try to keep your movies small by ignoring the need for sounds. A good rule of thumb is to save around 40k of space for sounds in a 200k movie. The impact of your animations and the general feel of your movie will be greatly enhanced if you use the sound channels wisely.

- Sounds can take up a lot of bytes unless you're smart about it. The lowest sound format you can use is 11.025 kHz (CD) since Windows will make anything less sound like the Chipmunks due to the limitations in popular sound cards. Keep the tracks short and loop. Remember, you are not cutting a gold disc audio CD, you are making a very small movie, which you can update daily, to play on the internet.

- Loop sounds for long background tracks. In Sound Edit hold down the option key when playing back to hear how the loop sounds. It will probably skip, which means you will have to pick the looping carefully to make it seamless. Use your ears to loop on drumbeats or every four beats for most pop music. The source track will determine how easy the looping will be, so use common sense when picking sounds. In the Cast Info box, check Loop.

- Get more out of your sound channels by using lots of little 4k snips with at least one or two big 15k-30k tracks spread around to break up the monotony of the loop. People also like to hear something when they click, both as feedback and reward. And remember—techno may be easy to loop but some people get a little crazy from hearing repetitive beats over and over and over and over.

SHRINKING VIDEO EFFECTS

- A small footprint alternative to digital video is to use 1 bit screen pict sequences, with say, 4 frames and loop them. Each pict takes up only 4k and you can change the colour while making loops by using the colour squares in the tools window.

- To fake video using 1 bit pict sequences, use high contrast clips. Adjust the brightness and contrast to get a cleaner 1 bit version. Try rendering your 3D animations in 1 bit too. You can also overlap these clips with ink effects and by changing the foreground and background colour squares in the tools window.

- Use small cast member 3D animation loops rendered on white backgrounds with anti-aliasing turned off to give more dimensional looks to the movement on the screen.

- Use lots of layers of different types of small size media. You could do a blue screen video of someone jumping around wearing all white then drop the pict sequence down to one bit and have an army of multicoloured jumpers in Director for 20k.

WHAT THE FUTURE HOLDS

Today multimedia, including Director movies, delivered over the Internet is limited by the transfer speed of the network and the patience of the browser user. Multimedia developers will have more satisfied users when they scale the size of their multimedia productions to the transfer speeds of the intended audience. Keep in mind that for the immediate future, most users dialing in do so at relatively slow speeds, about one to two kilobytes per second.

Over time, however, this will change. The data transfer rate over the network is constantly increasing. And it appears likely that entirely new technologies such as cable modems will arrive within the next few years to dramatically boost the speed of the network.

We expect that within the decade, the transfer rate on the Internet will be comparable to that of CD-ROMs. When that happens, the performance limits imposed by the current technology will recede. The network will have all the advantages of CD-ROM delivery, but will be arbitrarily large, dynamic, and far more interconnected.

In a sense, the route that the multimedia industry has travelled over the past decade, going from limited delivery on floppy to today's delivery on CD-ROM, will be repeated in the network arena. In a surprisingly short time, we will be back where we are today in terms of capability, and beyond, but delivering over a far more flexible channel than CD-ROM.

CONTENT BY CHANNEL SPEED

The following table gives an indication of the types of content which can be produced at different channel speeds.

COMMON MODEM THROUGHPUTS ON THE WEB TODAY

Speed	Typical Content	Size	Download Time
14.4kbps	small graphics and animation	30k	20 seconds
14.4kbps	small complete title	100/200k	1 -2 minutes
28.8kbps	small graphics and animation	30k	10 seconds
28.8kbps	small complete title	100/200k	30 - 60 seconds
28.8kbps	short video clip	500k	2 - 3 minutes

ISDN THROUGHPUT WHEN USING A SINGLE B CHANNEL

Speed	Typical Content	Size	Download Time
56kbps	small graphics and animation	30k	5 seconds
56kbps	small complete title	100/200k	15 - 30 seconds
56kbps	short video clip	500k	1 minute
56kbps	full size title	1m	2 minutes

Representative Throughput on a Shared 10.0mbps Cable Modem or Ethernet LAN

Speed	Typical Content	Size	Download Time
1.5mbps	small graphics and animation	30k	‹1 second
1.5mbps	small complete title	100 -200k	1 second
1.5mbps	short video clip	500k	3 seconds
1.5mbps	full size title	1m	6 seconds
1.5mbps	title with full video and sound	2m	12 seconds
1.5mbps	MPEG video stream	—	continuous

note: 1.5mbps is also the throughput of single-speed CD-ROM.

Definitions

Afterburner

The Shockwave post-processor which takes a Director movie and compresses it. We call Afterburned movies "fried green Director movies" and also "burned movies".

HTTP Server

The server software which delivers World Wide Web data across the Internet. HTTP stands for "HyperText Transport Protocol". In response to a request specifying a URL, the HTTP server returns a block of data, plus the type of that data. The data type is called a MIME type. In the case of a Director movie, the MIME type is "application/x-director".

MIME Type

A specification of the type of block data. MIME stands for "Multi-purpose Internet Mail Extensions". It was originally proposed and used for enriching the potential content of mail messages. In the context of the World Wide Web and HTTP in particular, MIME types specify what type of data is returned from a server. MIME types can include simple text, graphics of various types (GIF, JPEG, PNG, etc), sound, or Director movies.

A MIME type consists of two parts, the content type and the content subtype. The content type specified a major category, such as "image", "audio", or "application". The subtype specifies a particular data type within that category, such as "image/jpeg" or "application/x-director".

Shockwave for Director

The product name for the Macromedia Director-on-the-Internet project. Shockwave for Director includes three distinct pieces of functionality:

1. Afterburner is a post-processor for Director movie source files. Multimedia developers use it to prepare content for Internet distribution. Afterburner compresses movies and makes them ready for uploading to an HTTP server, from which they'll be accessed by Internet users.

2. Shockwave player plug-in for Web browsers which allows movies to be played seamlessly within the same window as the browser page.

3. Shockwave player helper application which plays movies with any browser being used, but movies appear in a separate window from the browser page.

URL

Universal Resource Locator (URL) is the location on the network of a referenced data link. It specifies which protocol from a set of established protocols, the server location, the file location, and parameters to be used in retrieving the data. An URL is one type of Universal Resource Identifier (URI). An URL specifies location, while other types of URIs specifiy name or agent. Today, URLs are the only type of URI that are widely used.

This White Paper is reprinted with permission of Macromedia. For up to date information about Shockwave, tips and techniques, and examples of movies take a look at the Macromedia Web site: http://www.macromedia.com.

The Java (tm) language: A white paper

The Java programming language and environment is designed to solve a number of problems in modern programming practice. It started as a part of a larger project to develop advanced software for consumer electronics. These devices are small, reliable, portable, distributed, real-time embedded systems. When we started the project, we intended to use C++, but we encountered a number of problems. Initially these were just compiler technology problems, but as time passed we encountered a set of problems that were best solved by changing the language.

This document contains many technical words and acronyms that may be unfamiliar. See the Glossary for help. The companion paper, The HotJava Browser: A White Paper, describes a powerful application that demonstrates the power of the Java language.

JAVA

Java: A simple, object-oriented, distributed, interpreted, robust, secure, architecture neutral, portable, high-performance, multithreaded, and dynamic language.

One way to characterize a system is with a set of buzzwords. We use a standard set of them in describing Java. The rest of this section is an explanation of what we mean by those buzzwords and the problems that we were trying to solve.

Archimedes Inc. is a fictitious software company that produces software to teach about basic physics. This software is designed to interact with the user, providing not only text and illustrations in the manner of a traditional textbook, but also providing a set of software lab benches on which experiments can be set up and their behavior simulated. For example, the most basic one allows students to put together levers and pulleys and see how they act. The italicized narrative of the trials and tribulations of the Archimedes' designers is used here to provide examples of the language concepts presented.

SIMPLE

We wanted to build a system that could be programmed easily without a lot of esoteric training and which leveraged today's standard practice. Most programmers working these days use C, and most programmers doing object-oriented programming use C++. So even though we found that C++ was unsuitable, we designed Java as closely to C++ as possible in order to make the system more comprehensible.

Java omits many rarely used, poorly understood, confusing features of C++ that in our experience bring more grief than benefit. These omitted features primarily consist of operator overloading (although the Java language does have method overloading), multiple inheritance, and extensive automatic coercions.

We added auto garbage collection thereby simplifying the task of Java programming but making the system somewhat more complicated. A good example of a common source of complexity in many C and C++ applications is storage management: the allocation and freeing of memory. By virtue of having automatic garbage collection the Java language not only makes the programming task easier, it also dramatically cuts down on bugs.

The folks at Archimedes wanted to spend their time thinking about levers and pulleys, but instead spent a lot of time on mundane programming tasks. Their central expertise was teaching, not programming. One of the most complicated of these programming tasks was figuring out where memory was being wasted across their 20K lines of code.

Another aspect of being simple is being small. One of the goals of Java is to enable the construction of software that can run stand-alone in small machines. The size of the basic interpreter and class support is about 40K bytes; adding the basic standard libraries and thread support (essentially a self-contained microkernel) adds an additional 175K.

OBJECT-ORIENTED

This is, unfortunately, one of the most overused buzzwords in the industry. But object-oriented design is very powerful because it facilitates the clean definition of interfaces and makes it possible to provide reusable "software ICs."

Simply stated, object-oriented design is a technique that focuses design on the data (=objects) and on the interfaces to it. To make an analogy with carpentry, an "object-oriented" carpenter would be mostly concerned with the chair he was building, and secondarily with the tools used to make it; a "non-object-oriented" carpenter would think primarily of his tools. Object-oriented design is also the mechanism for defining how modules "plug and play."

The object-oriented facilities of Java are essentially those of C++, with extensions from Objective C for more dynamic method resolution.

The folks at Archimedes had lots of things in their simulation, among them, ropes and elastic bands. In their initial C version of the product, they ended up with a pretty big system because they had to write separate software for describing ropes versus elastic bands. When they rewrote their application in an object-oriented style, they found they could define one basic object that represented the common aspects of ropes and elastic bands, and then ropes and elastic bands were defined as variation s (subclasses) of the basic type. When it came time to add chains, it was a snap because they could build on what had been written before, rather than writing a whole new object simulation.

DISTRIBUTED

Java has an extensive library of routines for coping easily with TCP/IP protocols like HTTP and FTP. Java applications can open and access objects across the net via URLs with the same ease that programmers are used to when accessing a local file system.

The folks at Archimedes initially built their stuff for CD ROM. But they had some ideas for interactive learning games that they wanted to try out for their next product. For example, they wanted to allow students on different computers to cooperate in building a machine to be simulated. But all the networking systems they'd seen were complicated and required esoteric software specialists. So they gave up.

ROBUST

Java is intended for writing programs that must be reliable in a variety of ways. Java puts a lot of emphasis on early checking for possible problems, later dynamic (run-time) checking, and eliminating situations that are error prone.

One of the advantages of a strongly typed language (like C++) is that it allows extensive compile-time checking so bugs can be found early. Unfortunately, C++ inherits a number of loopholes in compile-time checking from C, which is relatively lax (par-ticularly method/procedure declarations). In Java, we require declarations and do not support C-style implicit declarations.

The linker understands the type system and repeats many of the type checks done by the compiler to guard against version mismatch problems.

The single biggest difference between Java and C/C++ is that Java has a pointer model that eliminates the possibility of overwriting memory and corrupting data. Instead of pointer arithmetic, Java has true arrays. This allows subscript checking to be performed. In addition, it is not possible to turn an arbitrary integer into a pointer by casting.

The folks at Archimedes had their application basically working in C pretty quickly. But their schedule kept slipping because of all the small bugs that kept slipping through. They had lots of trouble with memory corruption, versions out-of-sync and interface mismatches. What they gained because C let them pull strange tricks in their code, they paid for in quality assurance time. They also had to reissue their software after the first release because of all the bugs that slipped through.

While Java doesn't make the QA problem go away, it does make it significantly easier.

Very dynamic languages like Lisp, TCL and Smalltalk are often used for prototyping. One of the reasons for their success at this is that they are very robust: you don't have to worry about freeing or corrupting memory. Programmers can be relatively fearless about dealing with memory because they don't have to worry about it getting corrupted. Java has this property and it has been found to be very liberating.

One reason that dynamic languages are good for prototyping is that they don't require you to pin down decisions early on. Java has exactly the opposite property; it forces you to make choices explicitly. Along with these choices come a lot of assistance: you can write method invocations and if you get something wrong, you are informed about it at compile time. You don't have to worry about method invocation error. You can also get a lot of flexibility by using interfaces instead of classes.

SECURE

Java is intended to be used in networked/distributed environments. Toward that end, a lot of emphasis has been placed on security. Java enables the construction of virus-free, tamper-free systems. The authentication techniques are based on public-key encryption.

There is a strong interplay between "robust" and "secure." For example, the changes to the semantics of pointers make it impossible for applications to forge access to data structures or to access private data in objects that they do have access to. This closes the door on most activities of viruses.

Someone wrote an interesting "patch" to the PC version of the Archimedes system. They posted this patch to one of the major bulletin boards. Since it was easily available and added some interesting features to the system, lots of people downloaded it. It hadn't been checked out by the folks at Archimedes, but it seemed to work. Until the next April 1st, when thousands of folks discovered rude pictures popping up in their children's lessons. Needless to say, even though they were in no way responsible for the incident, the folks at Archimedes still had a lot of damage to control.

ARCHITECTURE NEUTRAL

Java was designed to support applications on networks. In general, networks are composed of a variety of systems with a variety of CPU and operating system architectures. To enable a Java application to execute anywhere on the network, the compiler generates an architecture neutral object file format—the compiled code is executable on many processors, given the presence of the Java runtime system.

This is useful not only for networks but also for single system software distribution. In the present personal computer market, application writers have to produce versions of their application that are compatible with the IBM PC and with the Apple Macintosh. With the PC market (through Windows/NT) diversifying into many CPU architectures, and Apple moving off the 68000 towards the PowerPC, this makes the production of software that runs on all platforms almost impossible. With Java, the same version of the application runs on all platforms. The Java compiler does this by generating bytecode instructions which have nothing to do with a particular computer architecture. Rather, they are designed to be both easy to interpret on any machine and easily translated into native machine code on the fly.

Archimedes is a small company. They started out producing their software for the PC since that was the largest market. After a while, they were a large enough company that they could afford to do a port to the Macintosh, but it was a pretty big effort and didn't really pay off. They couldn't afford to port to the PowerPC Macintosh or MIPS NT machine. They couldn't "catch the new wave" as it was happening, and a competitor jumped in ...

PORTABLE

Being architecture neutral is a big chunk of being portable, but there's more to it than that. Unlike C and C++, there are no "implementation dependent" aspects of the specification. The sizes of the primitive data types are specified, as is the behaviour of arithmetic on them. For example, "int" always means a signed two's complement 32 bit integer, and "float" always means a 32-bit IEEE 754 floating point number. Making these choices is feasible in this day and age because essentially all interesting CPUs share these characteristics.

The libraries that are a part of the system define portable interfaces. For example, there is an abstract Window class and implementations of it for Unix, Windows and the Macintosh.

The Java system itself is quite portable. The new compiler is written in Java and the runtime is written in ANSI C with a clean portability boundary. The portability boundary is essentially POSIX.

INTERPRETED

The Java interpreter can execute Java bytecodes directly on any machine to which the interpreter has been ported. And since linking is a more incremental and lightweight process, the development process can be much more rapid and exploratory.

As a part of the bytecode stream, more compile-time information is carried over and available at runtime. This is what the linker's type checks are based on, and what the RPC protocol derivation is based on. It also makes programs more amenable to debugging.

The programmers at Archimedes spent a lot of time waiting for programs to compile and link. They also spent a lot of time tracking down senseless bugs because some changed source files didn't get compiled (despite using a fancy "make" facility), which caused version mismatches; and they had to track down procedures that were declared inconsistently in various parts of their programs. Another couple of months lost in the schedule.

HIGH PERFORMANCE

While the performance of interpreted bytecodes is usually more than adequate, there are situations where higher performance is required. The bytecodes can be translated on the fly (at runtime) into machine code for the particular CPU the application is running on. For those accustomed to the normal design of a compiler and dynamic loader, this is somewhat like putting the final machine code generator in the dynamic loader.

The bytecode format was designed with generating machine codes in mind, so the actual process of generating machine code is generally simple. Reasonably good code is produced: it does automatic register allocation and the compiler does some optimisation when it produces the bytecodes.

In interpreted code we're getting about 300,000 method calls per second on a Sun Microsystems SPARCStation 10. The performance of bytecodes converted to machine code is almost indistinguishable from native C or C++.

When Archimedes was starting up, they did a prototype in Smalltalk. This impressed the investors enough that they got funded, but it didn't really help them produce their product: in order to make their simulations fast enough and the system small enough, it had to be rewritten in C.

MULTITHREADED

There are many things going on at the same time in the world around us. Multithreading is a way of building applications with multiple threads. Unfortunately, writing programs that deal with many things happening at once can be much more difficult than writing in the conventional single-threaded C and C++ style.

Java has a sophisticated set of synchronization primitives that are based on the widely used monitor and condition variable paradigm that was introduced by C.A.R. Hoare. By integrating these concepts into the language they became much easier to use and are more robust. Much of the style of this integration came from Xerox's Cedar/Mesa system.

Other benefits of multithreading are better interactive responsiveness and real-time behaviour. This is limited, however, by the underlying platform: stand-alone Java run-time environments have good real-time behaviour. Running on top of other systems like Unix, Windows, the Macintosh, or Windows NT limits the real-time responsiveness to that of the underlying system.

Lots of things were going on at once in their simulations. Ropes were being pulled, wheels were turning, levers were rocking, and input from the user was being tracked. Because they had to write all this in a single threaded form, all the things that happen at the same time, even though they had nothing to do with each other, had to be manually intermixed. Using an "event loop" made things a little cleaner, but it was still a mess. The system became fragile and hard to understand. They were pulling in data from all over the net. But originally they were doing it one chunk at a time. This serialized network communication was very slow. When they converted to a multithreaded style, it was trivial to overlap all of their network communication.

DYNAMIC

In a number of ways, Java is a more dynamic language than C or C++. It was designed to adapt to an evolving environment.

For example, one major problem with using C++ in a production environment is a side-effect of the way that code is always implemented. If company A produces a class library (a library of plug and play components) and company B buys it and uses it in their product, then if A changes it's library and distributes a new release, B will almost certainly have to recompile and redistribute their own software. In an environment where the end user gets A and B's software independently (say A is an OS vendor and B is an application vendor) problems can result.

For example, if A distributes an upgrade to its libraries then all of the software from B will break. It is possible to avoid this problem in C++, but it is extraordinarily difficult and it effectively means not using any of the language's OO features directly.

Archimedes built their product using the object-oriented graphics library from 3DPC Inc. 3DPC released a new version of the graphics library which several computer manufacturers bundled with their new machines. Customers of Archimedes that bought these new machines discovered to their dismay that their old software no longer worked. (In real life, this only happens on Unix systems. In the PC world, 3DPC would never have released such a library: their ability to change their product and use C++'s object oriented features is severely hindered.)

By making these interconnections between modules later, Java completely avoids these problems and makes the use of the object-oriented paradigm much more straightforward. Libraries can freely add new methods and instance variables without any effect on their clients.

Java understands interfaces— a concept borrowed from Objective C which is similar to a class. An interface is simply a specification of a set of methods that an object responds to. It does not include any instance variables or implementations. Interfaces can be multiply-inherited (unlike classes) and they can be used in a more flexible way than the usual rigid class inheritance structure.

Classes have a runtime representation: there is a class named Class, instances of which contain runtime class definitions. If, in a C or C++ program, you have a pointer to an object but you don't know what type of object it is, there is no way to find out. However, in Java, finding out based on the runtime type information is straightforward. Because casts are checked at both compile-time and runtime, you can trust a cast in Java. On the other hand in C and C++, the compiler just trusts that you're doing the right thing.

It is also possible to look up the definition of a class given a string containing its name. This means that you can compute a data type name and have it easily dynamically-linked into the running system.

To expand their revenue stream, the folks at Archimedes wanted to architect their product so that new aftermarket plug-in modules could be added to extend the system. This was possible on the PC, but just barely. They had to hire a couple of new programmers because it was so complicated. This also added problems when debugging.

SUMMARY

The Java language provides a powerful addition to the tools that programmers have at their disposal. Java makes programming easier because it is object-oriented and has automatic garbage collection. In addition, because compiled Java code is architecture-neutral, Java applications are ideal for a diverse environment like the Internet. For more information send mail to java@java.sun.com.

The Java White Paper is reprinted herein with permission from Sun Microsystems. Copyright 1995 Sun Microsystems Inc. All rights reserved.
   Recommended follow up reading: The Java Language Environment: A White Paper URL: http://www.javasoft.com/whitePaper/javawhitepaper1.html

Extending WWW to support platform independent virtual reality

DAVID RAGGETT, HEWLETT PACKARD LABORATORIES

This is a proposal to allow VR environments to be incorporated into the World Wide Web, thereby allowing users to "walk" around and push through doors to follow hyperlinks to other parts of the Web. VRML is proposed as a logical markup format for non-proprietary platform independent VR. The format describes VR environments as compositions of logical elements. Additional details are specified using a universal resource naming scheme supporting retrieval of shared resources over the network. The paper closes with ideas for how to extend this to support virtual presence teleconferencing.

INTRODUCTION

This paper describes preliminary ideas for extending the World Wide Web to incorporate virtual reality (VR). By the end of this decade, the continuing advances in price/performance will allow affordable desktop systems to run highly realistic virtual reality models. VR will become an increasingly important medium, and the time is now ripe to develop the mechanisms for people to share VR models on a global basis. The author invites help in building a proof of concept demo and can be contacted at the email address given above.

VR systems at the low end of the price range show a 3D view into the VR environment together with a means of moving around and interacting with that environment. At the minimum you could use the cursor keys for moving forward and backwards, and turning left and right. Other keys would allow you to pick things up and put them down. A mouse improves the ease of control, but the "realism" is primarily determined by the latency of the feedback loop from control to changes in the display. Joysticks and SpaceBalls improve control, but cannot compete with the total immersion offered by head mounted displays (HMDs). High end systems use magnetic tracking of the user's head and limbs, together with devices like 3D mice and datagloves to yet further improve the illusion.

Sound can be just as important to the illusion as the visual simulation: the sound of a clock gets stronger as you approach it. An aeroplane roars overhead crossing from one horizon to the next. High end systems allow for tracking of multiple moving sources of sound. Distancing is the technique where you get to see and hear more detail as you approach an object. The VR environment can include objects with complex behaviour, just like their physical analogues in the real world, e.g. drawers in an office desk, telephones, calculators, and cars. The simulation of behaviour is frequently more demanding computationally than updating the visual and aural displays.

The Virtual environment may impose the same restrictions as in the real world, e.g. gravity and restricting motion to walking, climbing up/down stairs, and picking up or putting down objects. Alternatively, users can adopt superpowers and fly through the air with ease, or even through walls! When using a simple interface, e.g. a mouse, it may be easier to learn if the range of actions at any time is limited to a small set of possibilities, e.g. moving forwards towards a staircase causes you to climb the stairs. A separate action is unnecessary, as the VR environment builds in assumptions about how people move around. Avatars are used to represent the user in the VR environment. Typically these are simple disembodied hands, which allow you to grab objects. This avoids the problems in working out the positions of the user's limbs and cuts down on the computational load.

PLATFORM INDEPENDENT VR

Is it possible to define an interchange format for VR environments which can be visualised on a broad range of platforms from PCs to high-end workstations?

At first sight there is little relationship between the capabilities of systems at either extreme. In practice, many VR elements are composed from common elements, e.g. rooms have floors, walls, ceilings, doors, windows, tables and chairs. Outdoors, there are buildings, roads, cars, lawns, and trees etc. Perhaps we can draw upon experience with document conversion and the Standard Generalized Markup Language (SGML) [ref. 4] and specify VR environments at a logical level, leaving browsers to fill in the details according to the capabilities of each platform.

The basic idea is to compose VR environments from a limited set of logical elements, e.g. chair, door, and floor. The dimensions of some of these elements can be taken by default. Others, like the dimensions of a room, require lists of points, e.g. to specify the polygon defining the floor plan. Additional parameters give the colour and texture of surfaces. A picture frame hanging on a wall can be specified in terms of a bitmapped image.

These elements can be described at a richer level of detail by reference to external models. The basic chair element would have a subclassification, e.g. office chair, which references a detailed 3D model, perhaps in the DXF format. Keeping such details in separate files has several advantages:

- Simplifies the high level VR markup format

This makes it easier to create and revise VR environments than with a flat representation.

- Models can be cached for reuse in other VR environments

Keeping the definition separate from the environment makes it easy to create models in terms of existing elements, and saves resources.

- Allows for sharing models over the net

Directory services can be used to locate where to retrieve the model from. In this way, a vast collection of models can be shared across the net.

- Alternative models can be provided according to each browser's capabilities.

Authors can model objects at different levels of detail according to the capabilities of low, mid and high end machines. The appropriate choice can be made when querying the directory service, e.g. by including machine capabilities in the request. This kind of negotiation is already in place as part of the World Wide Web's HTTP protocol [ref. 3].

Limiting VR environments to compositions of known elements would be overly restrictive. To avoid this, it is necessary to provide a means of specifying novel objects, including their appearance and behaviour. The high level VR markup format should therefore be dynamically extendable. The built-in definitions are merely a short cut to avoid the need to repeat definitions for common objects.

UNIVERSAL RESOURCE LOCATORS (URLs)

The World Wide Web uses a common naming scheme to represent hypermedia links and links to shared resources. It is possible to represent nearly any file or service with a URL [ref. 2].

The first part always identifies the method of access (or protocol). The next part generally names an Internet host and is followed by path information for the resource in question. The syntax varies according to the access method given at the start. Here are some examples:

http://info.cern.ch/hypertext/WWW/TheProject.html

This is the CERN home page for the World Wide Web project. The prefix "http" implies that this resource should be obtained using the hypertext transfer protocol (HTTP).

http://cui_www.unige.ch/w3catalog
The searchable catalog of WWW resources at CUI, in Geneva. Updated daily.

news:comp.infosystems.www
The Usenet newsgroup "comp.infosystems.www".
This is accessed via the NNTP protocol.

ftp://ftp.ifi.uio.no/pub/SGML
This names an anonymous FTP server: ftp.ifi.uio.no which includes a collection of information relating to the Standard Generalized Markup Language—SGML.

APPLICATION TO VR

The URL notation can be used in a VR markup language for:

* Referencing wire frame models, image tiles and other resources

For example, a 3D model of a vehicle or an office chair. Resources may be defined intensionally, and generated by the server in response to the user's request.

* Hypermedia links to other parts of the Web.

Major museums could provide educational VR models on particular topics. Hypermedia links would allow students to easily move from one museum to another by "walking" through links between the different sites.

One drawback of URLs is that they generally depend on particular servers. Work is in progress to provide widespread support for lifetime identifiers that are location independent. This will make it possible to provide automated directory services akin to X.500 for locating the nearest copy of a resource.

MIME: MULTIPURPOSE INTERNET MAIL EXTENSIONS

MIME describes a set of mechanisms for specifying and describing the format of Internet message bodies. It is designed to allow multiple objects to be sent in a single message, to support the use of multiple fonts plus non-textual material such as images and audio fragments. Although it was conceived for use with email messages, MIME has a much wider applicability. The hypertext transfer protocol HTTP uses MIME for request and response message formats. This allows servers to use a standard notation for describing document contents, e.g. image/gif for GIF images and text/html for hypertext documents in the HTML format. When a client receives a MIME message the content type is used to invoke the appropriate viewer. The bindings are specified in the mailcaps configuration file. This makes it easy to add local support for a new format without changes to your mailer or web browser. You simply install the viewer for the new format and then add the binding into your mailcaps file.

The author anticipates the development of a public domain viewer for a new MIME content type: video/vrml. A platform independent VR markup language would allow people to freely exchange VR models either as email messages or as linked nodes in the World Wide Web.

A SKETCH OF THE PROPOSED VR MARKUP LANGUAGE (VRML)

A major distinction appears to be indoor and outdoor scenes. Indoors, the scene is constructed from a set of interconnected rooms. Outdoors, you have a landscape of plains, hills and valleys upon which you can place buildings, roads, fields, lakes and forests, etc. The following sketch is in no way comprehensive, but should give a flavour of how VRML would model VR environments. Much work remains to turn this vision into a practical reality.

INDOOR SCENES

The starting point is to specify the outlines of the rooms. Architects drawings describe each building as a set of floors, each of which is described as a set of interconnected rooms. The plan shows the position of windows, doors and staircases. Annotations define whether a door opens inwards or outwards, and whether a staircase goes up or down. VRML directly reflects this hierarchical decomposition with separate markup elements for buildings, floors, rooms, doors and staircases etc. Each element can be given a unique identifier. The markup for adjoining rooms use this identifier to name interconnecting doors. Rooms are made up from floors, walls and ceilings. Additional attributes define the appearance, e.g. the colour of the walls and ceiling, the kind of plaster coving used to join walls to the ceiling, and the style of windows. The range of elements and their permitted attributes are defined by a formal specification analogous to the SGML document type definition.

Rooms have fittings: carpets, paintings, book cases, kitchen units, tables and chairs etc. A painting is described by reference to an image stored separately (like inlined images in HTML). The browser retrieves this image and then applies a parallax transformation to position the painting at the designated location on the wall. Wallpaper can be modelled as a tiling, where each point on the wall maps to a point in an image tile for the wallpaper. This kind of texture mapping is computationally expensive, and low power systems may choose to employ a uniform shading instead. Views through windows to the outside can be approximated by mapping the line of sight to a point on an image acting as a backcloth, and effectively at infinity. Kitchen units, tables and chairs etc. are described by reference to external models. A simple hierarchical naming scheme can be used to substitute a simpler model when the more detailed one would overload a low power browser.

Hypermedia links can be represented in a variety of ways. The simple approach used in HTML documents for depicting links is almost certainly inadequate. A door metaphor makes good sense when transferring to another VR model or to a different location in the current model. If the link is to an HTML document, then an obvious metaphor is opening a book (by tapping on it with your virtual hand?). Similarly a radio or audio system makes sense for listening to a audio link, and a television for viewing an MPEG movie.

OUTDOOR SCENES

A simple way of modelling the ground into plains, hills and valleys is to attach a rubber sheet to a set of vertical pins of varying lengths and placed at irregular locations: $zi = fi(x, y)$. The sheet is single valued for any x and y, where x and y are orthogonal axes in the horizontal plane. Smooth terrain can be described by interpolating gradients specified at selected points. The process is only applied within polygons for which all vertices have explicit gradients. This makes it possible to restrict smoothing to selected regions as needed.

The next step is to add scenery onto the underlying ground surface:

- Texture wrapping—mapping an aerial photograph onto the ground surface.

This works well if the end-user is flying across a landscape at a sufficient height that parallax effects can be neglected for surface detail like trees and buildings. Realism can be further enhanced by including an atmospheric haze that obscures distant details.

- Plants—these come in two categories: point-like objects such as individual trees and area-like objects such as forests, fields, weed patches, lawns and flower beds.

A tree can be placed at a given (x, y) coordinate and scaled to a given height. A range of tree types can be used, e.g. deciduous (summer/fall), and coniferous. The actual appearance of each type of tree is specified in a separate model, so VRML only needs the class name and a means of specifying the model's parameters (in many cases defaults will suffice). Extended objects like forests can be rendered by repeating an image tile or generated as a fractal texture, using attributes to reference external definitions for the image tile or texture.

- Water—streams, rivers and water falls; ponds, lakes and the sea. The latter involves attributes for describing the nature of the beach: muddy estuary, sandy, rocky and cliffs.

- Borders—fences, hedges, walls etc. which are fundamentally line-like objects

- Roads—number of lanes, types of junctions, details for signs, traffic lights etc.

Each road can be described in terms of a sequence of points along its centre and its width. Features like road lights and crash barriers can be generated by default according to the attributes describing the kind of road. Road junctions could be specified in detail, but it seems possible to generate much of this locally on the basis of the nature of the junction and the end points of the roads it connects: freeway-exit, clover- leaf junction, 4-way stop, round-about etc. In general VRML should avoid specifying detail where this can be inferred by the browsing tool. This reduces the load on the network and allows browsers to show the scene in the detail appropriate to the power of each platform. Successive generations of kit can add more and more detail leading to progressively more realistic scenes without changes to the original VRML documents.

- Buildings—houses, skyscrapers, factories, filling stations, barns, silos, etc.

Most buildings can be specified using constructive geometry, i.e. as a set of intersecting parts each of which is defined by a rectangular base and some kind of roof. This approach describes buildings in a compact style and makes it feasible for VRML to deal with a rich variety of building types. The texture of walls and roofs, as well as the style of windows and doors can be defined by reference to external models.

- Vehicles, and other moving objects

A scene could consist of a number of parked vehicles plus a number of vehicles moving along the road. Predetermined trajectories are rather unexciting. A more interesting approach is to let the behaviour of the set of vehicles emerge from simple rules governing the motion of each vehicle. This could also apply to pedestrians moving on a side-walk. The rules would be defined in scripts associated with the model and not part of VRML itself. The opportunities for several users to meet up in a shared VR scene are discussed in the next section.

- Distant scenery, e.g. a mountain range on the horizon

This is effectively at infinity and can be represented as a backcloth hung in a cylinder around the viewer. It could be implemented using bitmap images (e.g. in GIF or JPEG formats). One issue is how to make the appearance change according to the weather/time of day.

- Weather and Sky

Outdoor scenes wouldn't be complete without a range of different weather types! Objects should gradually lose their colour and contrast as their distance increases. Haze is useful for washing out details as the browser can then ignore objects beyond a certain distance. The opacity of the haze will vary according to the weather and time of day. Fractal techniques can be used to synthesise cloud formations. The colour of the sky should vary as a function of the angle from the sun and the angle above the horizon. For VRML, the weather would be characterised as a set of predetermined weather types.

- Distancing

The illusion will be more complete if you can see progressively more detail the closer you get. Unfortunately, it is impractical to explicitly specify VR models in arbitrary detail. Another approach is to let individual models to reference more detailed models in a chain of progressively finer detail, e.g. a model that defines a lawn as a green texture can reference a model that specifies how to draw individual blades of grass.

The latter is only needed when the user zooms in on the lawn. The browser then runs the more detailed model to generate a forest of grass blades.

ACTIONS AND SCRIPTS

Simple primitive actions are part of the VRML model, for example the ability of the user to change position/orientation and to pick up/put down or "press" objects. Other behaviour is the responsibility of the various objects and lies outside the scope of VRML. Thus a virtual calculator would allow users to press keys and carry out calculations just like the real thing. This rich behaviour is specified as part of the model for the calculator object class along with details of its appearance. A scripting language is needed for this, but it will be independent of VRML, and indeed there could be a variety of different languages. The format negotiation mechanism in HTTP seems appropriate to this, as it would allow browsers to indicate which representations are supported when sending requests to servers.

ACHIEVING REALISM

Another issue, is how to provide realism without excessive computional demands. To date the computer graphics community has focused on mathematical models for realism, e.g. ray tracing with detailed models for how objects scatter or transmit light. An alternative approach could draw upon artistic metaphors for rendering scenes. Paintings are not like photographs, and artists don't try to capture all details, rather they aim to distil the essentials with a much smaller number of brush strokes. This is akin to symbolic representations of scenes. We may be able to apply this to VR. As an example consider the difficulty in modelling the folds of cloth on your shirt as you move your arm around. Modelling this computationally is going to be very expensive, perhaps a few rules can be used to draw in folds when you fold your arms.

VIRTUAL PRESENCE TELECONFERENCING

The price performance of computer systems currently doubles about every 15 months. This has happened for the last five years and industry pundits see no end in sight. It therefore makes sense to consider approaches which today are impractical, but will soon come within reach.

A world without people would be a dull place indeed! The markup language described above allows us to define shared models of VR environments, so the next step is to work out how to allow people to meet in these environments. This comes down to two parts.

- The protocols needed to ensure that each user sees an up to date view of all the other people in the same virtual location, whether this is a room or somewhere outdoors.

- A way of visualising people in the virtual environment, this in turn begs the question of how to sense each user - their expressions, speech and movements.

For people to communicate effectively, the latency for synchronising models must of order 100 milliseconds or less. You can get by with longer delays, but it gets increasingly difficult. Adopting a formal system for turn taking helps, but you lose the ability for non-verbal communication. In meetings, it is common to exchange glances with a colleague to see how he or she is reacting to what is being said. The rapid feedback involved in such exchanges calls for high resolution views of people's faces together with very low latency.

A powerful technique will be to use video cameras to build real-time 3D models of people's faces. As the skull shape is fixed, the changes are limited to the orientation of the skull and the relative position of the jaw. The fine details in facial expressions can be captured by wrapping video images onto the 3D model. This approach greatly reduces the bandwidth needed to project lifelike figures into the VR environment. The view of the back of the head and the ears etc. is essentially unchanging and can be filled in from earlier shots, or if necessary synthesised from scratch to match visible cues.

In theory, the approach needs a smaller bandwidth than conventional video images, as head movements can be compressed into a simple change of coordinates. Further gains in bandwidth could be achieved at a cost in accuracy by characterising facial gestures in terms of a composition of "identikit" stereotypes, e.g. shots of mouths which are open or closed, smiling or frowning. The face is then built up by blending the static model of the user's face and jaw with the stereotypes for the mouth, cheeks, eyes, and forehead.

Although head mounted displays offer total immersion, they also make it difficult to sense the user's facial expressions. They are also uncomfortable to wear. Virtual presence teleconferencing is therefore more likely to use conventional displays together with video cameras mounted around the user's workspace. Lightweight headsets are likely to be used in preference to stereo or quadraphonic loudspeaker systems, as they offer greater auditory realism as well as avoiding trouble when sound spills over into neighbouring work areas.

The cameras also offer the opportunity for hands free control of the user's position in the VR environment. Tracking of hands and fingers could be used for gesture control without the need for 3D mice or spaceballs etc. Another idea is to take cues from head movements, e.g. moving your head from side to side could be exaggerated in the VR environment to allow users to look from side to side without needing to look away from the display being used to visualise that environment.

WHERE NEXT?

For workstations running the X11 windowing system, the PEX library for 3D graphics is now available on most platforms. This makes it practical to start developing proof of concept platform independent VR. The proposed VRML interchange format could be used within the World Wide Web or for email messages. All users would need to do is to download a public domain VRML browser and add it to their mailcaps file. The author is interested in getting in touch with people willing to collaborate in turning this vision into a reality.

REFERENCES

1. "Hypertext Markup Language (HTML)", Tim Berners-Lee, January 1993.
   URL: ftp://info.cern.ch/pub/www/doc/html-spec.ps
   URL: http://info.cern.ch/hypertext/WWW/MarkUp/MarkUp.html
2. "Uniform Resource Locators", Tim Berners-Lee, January 1992.
   URL: ftp://info.cern.ch/pub/www/doc/url7a.ps
   URL: http://info.cern.ch/hypertext/WWW/Addressing/Addressing.html
3. "Protocol for the Retrieval and Manipulation of Texual and Hypermedia
   Information", Tim Berners-Lee, 1993.
   URL: ftp://info.cern.ch/pub/www/doc/http-spec.ps
   URL: http://info.cern.ch/hypertext/WWW/Protocols/HTTP/HTTP2.html
4. "The SGML Handbook", Charles F. GoldFarb, pub. 1990 by the Clarendon Press,
   Oxford.

This paper is reprinted with the kind permission of Dave Raggett

Online information

BACKGROUND INFORMATION

As We May Think, Vannevar Bush's 1945 article, originally published in Atlantic Monthly
URL: http://www.isg.sfu.ca/~duchier/misc/vbush/vbush.shtml

WHERE TO START LOOKING FOR MORE INFORMATION ABOUT THE WEB

The Yahoo indices of Web related information are a good starting point for finding more links to Web resources, tutorials, discussions and guides:
URL: http://www.yahoo.com/Computers_and_Internet/Internet/World_Wide_Web/
URL: http://www.yahoo.com/Computers/World_Wide_Web

The Webmaster Reference Library collects resources, articles and tutorials:
URL: http://www.webreference.com/

Web developers virtual library
URL: http://www.stars.com/

World wide Web FAQs
URL: http://www.boutell.com/faq/

HTML Writers Guild
URL: http://www.mindspring.com/guild/
The HTML Writers Guild runs several mailing lists:
hwg-news for general news about the Guild; hwg-talk is a general discussion forum; hwg-html-basics covers basic HTML and Web page design; hwg-business deals with marketing, contracts, and the ethics of Web authoring.
Check out the HTML Writers guild for more information about these lists and how you can subscribe to them.
The original mailing list is no longer active, but the archives are available at:
URL: http://ugweb.cs.ualberta.ca/~gerald/guild/archive.html

WEB DEVELOPMENT AND HTML TOOLS

There are comprehensive listings of available tools all over the Web, at Yahoo and at many other sites:
URL: http://www.yahoo.com/Computers/World_Wide_Web/HTML_Editors/

Mag's Big list of HTML Editors
URL: http://union.ncsa.uiuc.edu/HyperNews/get/www/html/editors.html

Shareware.com contains an amazing range of shareware, including dozens of Web tools
URL: http://www.shareware.com/

Falken's Maze lists browsers, authoring tools, graphics tools, cgi scripts and other resources for all platforms.
URL: http://commline.com/falken/tools.shtml

Mac Web Tools

Macintosh WWW Resources contains links to server software, script, HTML tools, and other Mac based Web information
URL: http://www.comvista.com/net/www/WWWDirectory.html

Jon Wiederspan's annotated collection of links to good Mac Web tool is available at:
URL: http://www.uwtc.washington.edu/Computing/WWW/Mac/Directory.html

WebMap for the Macintosh is an excellent shareware tool for preparing image maps. The sofware is on the disk that accompanies this book, but the Web site contains useful information and up to date versions as they are released
URL: http://www.city.net/cnx/software/webmap.html

Web tools for other platforms

The Ultimate Collection of Winsock Software (TUCOWS) is packed with internet software to download, including VRML viewers, email clients, IRC clients, and HTML editors. Each application is rated on a scale of 1 to 5 "cows"
URL: http://www.tucows.com/

Another major collection of Windows based Web authoring tools
URL: http://www.uwsp.edu/help/toybox.html

Mailing lists for Apple internet authoring

URL: http://abs.apple.com/apple-internet/
There are four mailing lists available from this site: apple-internet-announce, apple-internet-authoring, apple-internet-providers, and apple-internet-users.
The Apple-Internet-Announce list is a moderated, low-volume, no-discussion list for announcements of products and releases related to Apple Macintosh computers and the Internet. The Apple-Internet-Authoring list discusses authoring content for the

Internet using Macintosh computers. HTML, CGI programming and other appropriate topics should be placed here. The Apple-Internet-Providers list is for the discussion of the tools and techniques used in providing services. The Apple-Internet-Users list is for general discussion of the Internet using mac based tools.

TidBits web site

Adam and Tonya Engst's excellent source of information about the Mac on the Net
URL: http://www.dartmouth.edu/pages/TidBITS/TidBITS.html

The World Wide Web Consortium

The World Wide Web Consortium (W3C) is the best starting point for information about the current state of HTML, HTTP and the Web in general.
URL: http://www.w3.org/hypertext/WWW/

For an overview of HTTP and the Web protocols:
URL: http://www.w3.org/pub/WWW/Protocols/Overview.html

HTML 3.0

Document Type Definition for the HyperText Markup Language by Dave Raggett:
URL: http://www.hp.co.uk/people/dsr/html3/html3.dtd

The HTML 3.0 table Model is a thorough examination and specification of tables within HTML 3.0.
URL: http://www.w3.org/pub/WWW/MarkUp/Tables/950915_tables.html

STYLE SHEETS

The possible implementations of Style Sheets are covered at
URL: http://www.w3.org/hypertext/WWW/Style/

Style Sheets for on-line SGML and HTML
collection of articles about Style sheets, collected by Bert Bos
URL: http://grid.let.rug.nl/~bert/Stylesheets/

For information about the two main proposed forms of style sheets, read through:

Cascading Style Sheets: a draft Specification by Håkon W Lie, Bert Bos
URL: http://www.w3.org/hypertext/WWW/Style/css/draft.html

Information about DSSSL-Lite
URL: http://www.falch.no/~pepper/DSSSL-Lite/

SGML FAQs

URL: ftp://sgml1.ex.ac.uk/faq

AUDIO FORMATS FAQs

URL: http://www.cis.ohio-state.edu/hypertext/faq/usenet/audio-fmts/top.html

NETSCAPE

Netscape's home page is at
URL: http://home.netscape.com/

Current info about Netscape Navigator 2.0
URL: http://home.netscape.com/comprod/products/navigator/version_2.0/

More details about Netscape's additions to HTML and their status are at
URL: http://home.netscape.com/assist/net_sites/html_extensions_3.html

Earlier extensions to HTML, introduced in Netscape 1.1 are at
URL: http://home.netscape.com/assist/net_sites/html_extensions.html

An Exploration of Dynamic Documents
http://home.netscape.com/assist/net_sites/pushpull.html

SERVERS AND HTTP

Building Internet Servers is a major collection of information and links to resources about building Internet servers for DOS, Microsoft Windows, Microsoft Windows NT, the Macintosh, and the PowerMacintosh.
URL: http://www.charm.net/~cyber/

MacHTTP (Webstar) home page, maintained by Chuck Shotton, who wrote MacHTTP
URL: http://www.biap.com/

The commercial version, over at Starnine
URL: http://www.starnine.com/

MacHTTP FAQs
URL: http://arpp1.carleton.ca/machttp/doc/questions.html

CGI AND OTHER SCRIPTING RESOURCES

NCSA's overview of CGI
http://hoohoo.ncsa.uiuc.edu/cgi/overview.html

Yahoo index of CGI resources and tutorials
URL: http://www.yahoo.com/Computers_and_Internet/Internet/World_Wide_Web/
CGI___Common_Gateway_Interface/

The Webmaster's reference library has an index of links to cgi resources and tutorials:
URL: http://www.webreference.com/programming/cgi.html

Jon Wiederspan's excellent tutorial in writing CGI with Apple Script
URL: http://www.uwtc.washington.edu/Computing/WWW/Lessons/CGI.html

Thomas Boutell's library for writing CGI programs in C is well worth a look
http://sunsite.unc.edu/boutell/cgic/cgic.html

A good collection of links to ready made scripts for the Mac
URL: http://www.uwtc.washington.edu/Computing/WWW/Mac/CGI.html

News group about cgi authoring
URL: news//comp.infosystems.www.authoring.cgi

JAVA SCRIPT

Java Script documentation and handbook
URL: http://home.mcom.com/eng/mozilla/Gold/handbook/javascript/index.html

Netscape's index of JavaScript resources, examples and tutorials
URL: http://home.mcom.com/comprod/products/navigator/version_2.0/script/
script_info/index.html

The JavaScript index collects examples and good reference material
URL: http://www.c2.org/~andreww/javascript/

QuickTime

The QuickTime Continuum at Apple contains product information, authoring information and news
URL: http://quicktime.apple.com

The developer information is collected at
URL: http://quicktime.apple.com/develop.html

QuickTime VR

QuickTime VR Web site
URL: http://qtvr.quicktime.apple.com/

The QTVR player for the Mac, with full details about setting it up as a helper application for Netscape:
URL: http://qtvr.quicktime.apple.com/InMac.htm

The Windows version can be downloaded from:
URL: http://qtvr.quicktime.apple.com/InWin.htm

There is a good selection of QTVR samples at
URL: http://qtvr.quicktime.apple.com/Samples.htm

and there is a more comprehensive archive of other samples at
URL: http://quicktime.apple.com/archive/index.html

DIRECTOR AND SHOCKWAVE

Macromedia's Web site, contains the Director on the Internet Technology White Paper, current information about Director and Shockwave, and useful discussions and tools
URL: http://www.macromedia.com

The Director Web site contains listings of Internet Director resources, the archives of the Direct-l mailing list, examples, demos and techniques for authoring Director movies, the Director FAQs, as well as shareware and freeware.
URL: http://www.mcli.dist.maricopa.edu/director

Also of interest is Gretchen Macdowall's Web site.
URL: http://www.xensei.com/users/gcm/

The archives of earlier material are at:
URL: http://www.xensei.com/users/gcm/prevpage.html

Another set of Director FAQs is available at
URL: ftp://sharedcast.hccs.cc.tx.us

The Direct-L mailing list is busy but extremely helpful.
Subscribe by sending a message to listserv@uafsysb.uark.edu

JAVA AND HOTJAVA

The Sun site is the best place to look for Java related information and contains examples as well as Java tutorials, FAQs and other information about current developments. Try the Java home page for current information
URL: http://java.sun.com

There is comprehensive guide to programming with Java at
URL: http://java.sun.com/progGuide/index.html

Yahoo - Computers and Internet:Languages:Java:Applets
URL: http://www.yahoo.com/text/Computers_and_Internet/Languages/Java/Applets/

Yahoo - Computers and Internet:Languages:Java programming in java
URL: http://java.sun.com/progGuide/java/index.html

John December's on-line bibiography for Java
URL: http://www.rpi.edu/~decemj/works/java/bib.html

Sun Microsystems have set up several mailing lists covering Java and HotJava:
Java-announce is a strictly moderated forum for announcements about Java or HotJava
technologies. It is expected to be have very little traffic, maybe one announcement
every few weeks.
To subscribe send the word "subscribe" in the body of a message to
java-announce-request@java.sun.com

Java-interest mailing list covers the Java Programming Language, independent of the
HotJava Browser.
To subscribe send the word "subscribe" in the body of a message to
java-interest-request@java.sun.com

The hotjava-interest mailing list is concerned with Sun's WWW browser with executable
content.
To subscribe send the word "subscribe" in the body of a message to
hotjava-interest-request@java.sun.com

An interesting external mailing list covering Java is the Java User's Group, maintained
by Dimension X, Inc. http://www.dimensionx.com/
To subscribe to the Java(tm) User's Group mailing list send mail to
majordomo@dimensionx.com with the words
"subscribe jug your@email.address" in the message body.

VRML

The specifications for VRML 1.0 spec written by Gavin Bell of Silicon Graphics, Anthony Parisi of Intervista Software, and Mark Pesce, VRML List Moderator are available at URL: http://www.hyperreal.com/~mpesce/vrml/vrml.tech/vrml10-3.html

VRML Information and listings

VRML site at Wired, including the VRML Visions and futures
URL: http://vrml.wired.com
URL: http://vrml.wired.com/concepts/visions.html

The VRML Repository, with information from the www-vrml mailing lists
URL: http://www.sdsc.edu/vrml

A comprehensive collection of links to VRML resources and sites is at:
URL: http://www.well.com/user/spidaman/vrml.html

VRML World magazine by Mecklermedia—articles, interviews, events, archives, etc
URL: http://www.mecklerweb.com/vrml/current/vrml.htm

VRML FAQ
URL: http://www.oki.com/vrml/VRML_FAQ.html

There are a number of key VRML mailing lists:
vrml-modeling@sdsc.edu is a technical discussion of geometry description issues in VRML. Topics include features of current and proposed geometric primitives, import/export tools, compatibility with existing systems, implementation details, performance and cross-platform issues. To subscribe, email to listserv@sdsc.edu with "add vrml-modeling" in the message body.

vrml-behaviors@sdsc.edu is a technical discussion of describing behaviours within

VRML. Topics include how to add interaction and animation behaviours to VRML, scripting language issues, implementation details. To subscribe, email to listserv@sdsc.edu with "add vrml-behaviors" in the message body.

www-vrml@wired.com is a general discussion on VRML. To subscribe, email to majordomo@wired.com with "subscribe www-vrml your-email-address" as the message body.

ACROBAT AND PDF

Adobe's Web site contains information about creating and using Adobe Acrobat, as well as general information abot Postscript. The latest versions of the reader software are available at the site, along with pricing information for the commerical versions.
URL: http://www.adobe.com

The newsgroup comp.lang.postscript covers issues relating to the PostScript language.
URL: news://comp.lang.postscript

FAQs covering Adobe Postscript
URL: http://www.cis.ohio-state.edu/hypertext/faq/usenet/postscript-faq/top.html

General information about the PDF format is available at
URL: http://www.ep.cs.nott.ac.uk/~pns/pdfcorner/pdf.html

GRAPHICS

News groups
news:comp.graphics.*
The FAQs
from the comp.graphics newsgroups can be found at
URL: http://www.primrnet.com/~grieggs/cg_faq.html

General graphics FAQs are at

URL: http://www.cis.ohio-state.edu/hypertext/faq/usenet/graphics/top.html

The FAQs on JPEG image compression, MPEG, multimedia compression, and Computer Graphics Resources are at

URL: http://www.cis.ohiostate.edu/hypertext/faq/bngusenet/comp/graphics/top.html

Index

in forms, see Form, text field

   legibility 172, 173

   strange behaviour 90

Text editors 82, 83–84

Text field (in form), see Form, text field

Timescale 38–41

Title (of HTML document—‹TITLE›) 86, 126

Tracking readers 45

Transparencies, see Images, transparent

Tree diagram 49–50, 54, 59, 70

Tristram Shandy 15

Typeface, see Fonts and typefaces

Typesetting 13, 19, 21–23, 28, 66, 279

Typewriter text (‹TT›) 98

U

"Ugly CEO Syndrome" 7

Underlined text (‹UL›) 98

Underscore 258

Universal Resource Locator, see URL

UNIX 17, 88, 154, 161, 265, 292

URL (Universal Resource Locator) 5, 26, 31,
       71, 102, 104, 117–121, 130, 153–155,
       162, 240, 244, 245, 250, 262,
       279–280, 287, 294, 296, 309

"URL not found" 74

Usenet 287

V

Value (of form button), see Form, VALUE

Video 9–10, 13, 16, 57, 64, 157–159, 189,
       239–241, 287, 289–90, 291, 293, 294

Virtual reality (VR) 296, 299–308, *337–349*

Virus 296

VRML (Virtual Reality Modelling Language)
      286, 301–303, *337–349*

W

W3 Consortium, the 166, 192, 265, 266, 276

Walk through of Web site 191

WAV file (.wav) 159

Web, see World Wide Web

Web authoring software, see Authoring tools

Web browsers, see Browsers

Web Force 292

Web page, see Page

Web production house 161

Web server, see Server

Web Space 302

Web surfing 29

WebMap 153

WebSTAR (see also MacHTTP) 161

White space 61, 66–68, 115, 231

Windows 83, 88, 158, 292, 306, 308

Windows 95 88, 292, 295

Windows NT 292, 295

Wittgenstein, Ludwig 27

WOOs (Web MOOs) 284–285

Word break (‹WBR›) 184

Word processor 83, 265

World Wide Web

   and commerce 11–13, 166, 287

   and computers 3, 13, 58, 282

   and other media 3–6, 8, 9–11, 13–15,
      19–20, 57, 60–61

   and publishing 8, 12–15, 309

   and social space 284–286

   as a medium 3–6, 7–13, 62, 242,
      289–290, 309

Becoming a Prentice Hall Author

Getting published with Prentice Hall

1. Can I do it?

It is easy to think of the publishing process as a series of hurdles designed to weed out would-be authors. That may be true of some publishing houses, but not Prentice Hall.

- ❏ We do all we can to encourage new talent.

- ❏ We welcome unsolicited manuscripts.

- ❏ We carefully examine every proposal we receive, and we always write back to let the authors know what we think of it.

Although many of our authors have professional or educational experience, we look first for a passion for computing. Some of our most successful books are written by first-time authors. If you have built up expertise in any computing-related topic, please get in touch. You'll be surprised how easy it is to get through.

2. Is Prentice Hall a successful company?

Prentice Hall is a highly respected brand in technical and scientific publishing, a status reflected in our relationships with the book trade and various professional bodies. Our reputation has been made with classic computing titles such as Kernighan and Ritchie's *The C Programming Language* (over two million copies sold) and Bertrand Meyer's ground-breaking *Object Oriented Software Construction*.

We're part of Simon & Schuster, a $2 billion dollar global publishing company. Simon & Schuster is host to Macmillan Computer Publishing, home of renowned computer imprints such as Sams, Que, Waite

Group Press, Ziff-Davis Publishing, Hayden and New Riders Press (NRP). Simon & Schuster is itself owned by Viacom Inc, one of the world's largest entertainment and publishing companies. Viacom owns film and tv studios (Paramount Pictures), world-wide cable networks (MTV, Nickelodeon) and retail outlets (Blockbuster Video).

3. What sort of books does Prentice Hall publish?

The computing revolution in the office and home has prompted a massive and diverse market for computer books. That diversity is reflected in our approach. We are happy to consider book proposals on absolutely any computing topic.

Essentially, Prentice Hall publishes books for anyone whose job or hobby connects them to a computer. We are already familiar with your intended readership, whether your book is written for professionals, students, enthusiasts or beginners. Our progressive editorial policy encourages new authors and gives us the flexibility required in a rapidly changing technological environment. However, we do have a 'books wanted' list – contact the editorial department for the latest copy.

4. What are the rewards of writing a book?

Prentice Hall royalty rates are among the most competitive in the industry, and many of our authors earn considerable sums through royalties. Payments are calculated along industry-standard guidelines, i.e., the author receives a percentage of the publisher's net sales revenue. We always offer preferential royalty rates for senior figures within the computing industry, or for books on hot topics written by experts. For the right book at the right time, the financial reward to the author can be extremely generous. This is especially true of books aimed at professional software developers.

If you are a computer professional or an academic, your livelihood depends upon your professional reputation. Successful Prentice Hall authors enjoy a constant stream of business and employment opportunities as a direct result of being published. A book works like a business card, advertising the author's talent across a vast network of potential contacts.

5. How do I know my ideas are good enough to publish?

In assessing the market-readiness of book proposals or finished manuscripts, Prentice Hall editors draw upon a huge database of technical advisors. All of our reviewers are senior figures in modern computing, and their role is to offer free advice to potential authors, highlighting both the strengths and weaknesses of proposals and manuscripts. The aim of the review process is to add value to your ideas, rather than just approving or rejecting them.

We understand that errors are inevitable when writing books, but as a Prentice Hall author you need not worry about the quality of your finished work. Many of our authors have not written a book before, so we are there to help – we scrutinise all our manuscripts for grammatical accuracy and style.

6. How much control would I have over my book?

We understand that a book is a highly personal statement from the author, so we invite your participation at all stages of the publishing process, from the cover design through to the final marketing plans. A Prentice Hall book is a co-operative venture between author and publisher.

7. Will I get any help with the technical aspects of book production?

Our highly professional staff will ensure that the book you envisaged is the book that makes it to the shelves. Once you hand over your manuscript to us, we will take care of all the technical details of printing and binding. Beyond the advice and guidance from your own editor, our 64-page *Author Guide* is there to help you shape your manuscript into a first-class book. Our large and efficient production department is among the quickest in the industry. We are experts at turning raw manuscripts into polished books, irrespective of the technical complexity of your work. Technical queries can be answered by your production contact, assigned, where relevant, to you at contract stage. Our production staff fully understand the individual requirements of every project, and will work with you to produce a manuscript format that best complements your skills – hard copy manuscripts, electronic files or camera-ready copy.

8. How quickly can you turn my manuscript into a book?
The production department at Prentice Hall is widely acknowledged
to be among the quickest in the industry. Our turnaround times vary
according to the nature of the manuscript supplied to us, but the
average is about four months for camera-ready copy, five for electronic
file manuscript. For time-sensitive topics, we can occasionally turn
out books in under twelve weeks!

9. Where would my book be sold?
Prentice Hall has one of the largest sales forces of any technical
publisher. Our highly experienced sales staff have developed firm
business partnerships with all the major retail bookstores in Europe,
America, Asia, the Middle East and South Africa, ensuring that your
book receives maximum retail exposure. Prentice Hall's marketing
department is responsible for ensuring the widest possible review
coverage in magazines and journals – vital to the sales of computing
books.

Our books are usually present at major trade shows and exhibitions,
either on our own stands or those belonging to major retail bookshops.
Our presence at trade shows ensures that your work can be inspected
by the most senior figures within any given field of computing. We
also have a very successful corporate and institutional sales team,
dedicated to selling our books into large companies, user groups, book
clubs, training seminars and professional bodies.

Local language translations can provide not only a significant boost
to an author's royalty income, but also will allow your re-
search/findings to reach a wider audience, thus furthering your
professional prospects. To maintain both the author's and Prentice
Hall's reputation, we license foreign-language deals only with publishing houses of the highest repute.

10. I don't have time to write a book!
To enjoy all the advantages of being a published author, it is not
always necessary for you to write an entire book. Prentice Hall
welcomes books written by multiple authors. If you feel that your
skills lie in a very specific area of computing, or that you do not have
the time to write an entire book, please get in touch regardless. Prentice
Hall may have a book in progress that would benefit from your ideas.

You may know individuals or teams in your field who could act as co-author(s). If not, Prentice Hall can probably put you in touch with the right people. Royalties for shared-author books are distributed according to respective participation.

11. Could my company benefit?
Many Prentice Hall authors use their book to lever their commercial interests, and we like to do all we can to help. If a well-written book is an excellent marketing tool for an author, then it can also be an excellent marketing tool for the author's company. A book is its own highly focused marketing channel, a respected medium that takes your company name to all the right people. Previous examples of marketing opportunities with our books include:

- ❑ free advertising in the back pages
- ❑ packaging in suitable corporate livery (book covers, flyers, etc.)
- ❑ mounting software demos in the back page on disk or CDROM.

Although Prentice Hall has to keep its publications free of undue corporate or institutional bias, in general the options for cross-marketing are varied and completely open to discussion.

12. I have an idea for a book. What next?
We invite you to submit a book proposal. We need proposals to be formatted in a specific way, so if you have not received our guidelines, please contact the Acquisition Editor at this address:

Jason Dunne
Professional and Consumer Computing
Prentice Hall
Campus 400, Maylands Avenue
Hemel Hempstead, Herts.
HP2 7EZ
England

Tel: +44 (0)1442 882246
Fax: +44 (0)1442 252544

e-mail: jason_dunne@prenhall.co.uk